- If we've all lived genuine past lives, why do so many people claim to be the same historical figures, such as King Tut or Napoleon?

- Isn't reincarnation contrary to the Judeo-Christian tradition?

- Reincarnation seems to say that we come into this life for a purpose. Do we choose this purpose, or is it chosen for us?

- If they're so close to the surface of my consciousness, why can't I remember my past lives right now?

Learn the answers to all these questions—and learn how the unconscious mind lives on after death, carrying the patterns from past living into future life.

The very life you're living now.

LIVING YOUR PAST LIVES:

The Psychology of Past Life Regression

Karl Schlotterbeck

BALLANTINE BOOKS • NEW YORK

Library of Congress Catalog Card Number: 86-91595

ISBN 0-345-34028-0

Manufactured in the United States of America

First Edition: March 1987
Fifth Printing: December 1988

DEDICATION

First of all to my clients, whose confidence and courage made all of this possible.

To Carl Jung who broke ground to make a space for the spirit in modern psychology.

To Morris Netherton who carried that spirit into practical realms and shared it with us.

To The Spirit of which this work is an outworking example of its process toward wholeness.

To The Mus(e)ic of Vollenweider who in so many ways is doing the same work.

To the Gift from the Temple, a reminder of things accomplished and inspiration for things to be done.

FOREWORD

My professional life as a mental health worker was once quite conventional. As a school psychologist, my responsibilities called for helping parents and children cope with immediate problems in this life. I had been rather scrupulous about staying within the traditional boundaries of therapeutic technique and avoiding any practice that might be considered controversial—a residue from my own past lives—even if it were effective. I avoided not only the practice but also the appearance of unconventionality.

Then I discovered some exciting breakthroughs based on unorthodox treatment, and this gave me pause to consider the cost of my caution. I had withheld using what I knew worked on the grounds that it would mark me as being in the occult or on the fringe. Therefore, when I began my private practice, I noncommittally coined the more objective term for past-life therapy: "regression imagery."

It took the power of my own regression experiences and the therapeutic effectiveness of the method with my own clients to give me the courage to say outright what I was doing: working with the memories of past lives. Each session gave increasing force to an inescapable momentum within me. I went public. Colleagues within the system where I worked gradually discovered my private interests and practice and reacted favorably. I established the Institute for Past-Life Therapy in Baltimore, and later the Atlantic Guild for Past-Life Awareness.

Then came radio and television programs, and requests

for lectures at libraries, fraternal organizations, holistic health groups, church groups, and esoteric societies. There was clearly not only a therapeutic need for such a service but also a significant public interest in past-life therapy.

My attempt to maintain my position in mainstream counseling and to only subtly bring-in the use of past-life therapy in my work ended. I began to firmly establish myself in the past-life field and worked to help both conventional therapists and lay people to understand the theoretical precepts and technical features of this therapeutic method.

In my pursuit of past-life therapy, I often waded into the muddled waters of all those on the fringe, associating with psychics, mystics, meditation groups, mystical and occult groups, witches, shamans, pagans, as well as ordinary folk. None of these individuals looked unusual or had more than one head. They were professional people, blue-collar workers, ministers, housewives, and business people.

Under that once muddy surface I found a firm and reliable foundation on which to stand. I was often pleasantly surprised by the positive interest of many orthodox practitioners. My waning concern about my reception and reputation was itself clear evidence that I could no longer honestly couch past-life experiences in conventional logic. I felt confronted with a truth I could not deny, explain away, or conceal from those who might find it threatening (shades of past lives). My belief became a conviction.

As I grasped the depth of the past-life experiences and observed the therapeutic techniques I found most useful, it became obvious that past-life therapy is not so different from other therapeutic modalities. Arguments, if they arose, would be over theory, dogma or belief. And although I had distinguished myself from my psychological colleagues, I had no wish to separate us, but to build bridges of the commonalities of our goals, and the desire to provide effective help for those who came to see us.

In this way, the client could be offered a means of change

and exploration that would not demand the adoption of an alien philosophy. My goal in past-life therapy has always been relief, not belief. In addition, by operating within the beliefs of the clients, we can allow them to make their desired change without getting bogged down in philosophy.

> Be parent, not possessor,
> Attendant, not master,
> Be concerned not with obedience but with benefit,
> And you are at the core of living. . . .

> If I keep from imposing on people, they become themselves.

—LAO-TZU

We need not impose on our clients the expectation that they believe as we do but, if we care for them, we can attend to their difficulties and experiences openly. It is far better to let them focus on their relief. As for myself, I believe:

We have lived before and memories of those lives are available to us now! Such images are too vivid, too consistent and sometimes too verifiable to call them the whisps of daydreams, fantasy, or mere symbolism.

Living Your Past Lives developed naturally from the experiences of my clients in past-life therapy. The accounts of the regressions presented here come from either tape recordings or detailed notes of client sessions. They have been edited only to clarify the presentation or to eliminate redundant or irrelevent comments. In the therapy, for example, I ask many questions, have the client repeat emotionally charged phrases, or make references to events in the client's present life. Such inclusions would be a distraction to the flow of these true past-life stories.

In most cases the descriptions and names of clients have been purposely altered in order to ensure the confidentiality of the material presented and to protect the privacy of those involved. Any resemblance to specific individuals is therefore coincidental. However, since many of the issues, events, and experiences presented here are very common, many readers will identify with them or think they know someone to whom they might apply.

This universal relevence is my motivation and goal here. Through this book I hope the reader may begin to see how present-day patterns of behavior, events, and emotional reactions are related to past-life experience. If the source of the problem lies four-hundred years ago in Italy, that is where we need to go in order to understand it and to help change our reaction to it most efficiently.

In addition, astute readers will begin to recognize patterns in their own lives and, with or without therapy, gain some solace, understanding, or insight into their inner world and their lives.

Finally, past-life therapy offers a unique means of change and exploration. Through its practice I hope that many people will come to realize the potential depth and vastness of our personal human experience and our connectedness with that undeniable force that inexorably moves us toward greater joy, competence in life, and wholeness.

ACKNOWLEDGMENTS

Help for this work came from many quarters:

Morris Netherton's teaching and sharing;

Psychic Sallee Riggler who became the first signpost on this journey;

My parents, who held my karma till I got here, and who show their love without having to fully understand their middle son;

Friends (especially Jerry, Carol, Cathy, Cissi, Muffin, Tara, and Bob) who have been my most consistent support through this and other trials, and who have acted on their own to take care of me where I have been neglectful;

Past wives and present daughters (Erin and Anneliese) who have been sources of love, learning, and motivation;

Rita Francomano who has provided space and encouragement for many of us to try our wings;

That Inner Spirit which has not tired in attempting to express itself through my work;

Marilyn Oatis for her editorial comments;

Arthur Orrmont's link in the chain of events that brought these thoughts into your hands;

Editor Cheryl Woodruff's encouragement and understanding;

Teachers, seen and unseen;

and the Others that remain unnamed.

TABLE OF CONTENTS

PART I

PAST LIVES
LIVE—THROUGH
PATTERNS

CHAPTER 1

THE PATTERNS IN
YOUR LIFE

Patterns, roles, feelings, and habits—how often have you felt that you've done the same thing before? Have you often seen someone attracted over and over to the same kind of person? Have you noticed attractions that defied all reason? Each of these is an example of a "pattern."

We're seldom aware of the patterns as they begin but can become painfully conscious of them in hindsight or when something goes wrong.

Within relationships there are patterns of:

domination	passivity
submission	approval-seeking
service	dependence
sacrifice	distance. . . .
responsibility	

Patterns may emerge in the habitual roles we play of:

protector	helper
victim	leader

exhibitionist   mother
teacher   lover
savior   obedient child. . . .

We may all too frequently feel:

helpless   nervous
trapped   angry
uncertain   vulnerable
insecure   alienated
driven   betrayed
burdened   fascinated. . . .

We may feel we have to prove our:

worth   strength
loyalty   innocence. . . .

We have *fears*. One of the most debilitating problems of humankind is anxiety. I firmly believe that fear is related to survival. Feeling trapped or fearful, we seek to escape or avoid something—or someone.

Fears are partial memories or the re-living of some trauma of the past. The way in which we experience fear is the first clue to the nature of the event from which it comes.

Anxiety comes in many varieties:

stomachaches   spasms
headaches   high blood pressure
throat constriction   fast heartbeat
vision problems   cold hands
breathing troubles   desire to run or escape
trapped feelings   blanking out
muscle tension   confusion. . . .

We can get into a situation and find—again in hindsight—that we:

   overreacted
   underrated
   misjudged . . .

even when hindsight tells us there was enough information there from the start to save us from our error.

   There is an answer to the questions:

   "Why do the same things keep happening?"
   "Why do I do the same thing over and over?"
   "What's in my emotions that makes me react this way?"
   "Why am I blocked?"

Who hasn't wondered at the power that seems to drive us to do what we would have chosen not to do—the clouds that obscure our perception and judgment of things and people?

   All of this—the power, the patterns, the fears, the conclusions, the reactions—come from events in our past lives. In fact, the more unreasonable, unexplainable, ingrained, intractable, persistent, chronic, or acute it is, the more likely it is to have come from before birth—from other incarnations, other times, other places. If you think about it, you could find some other situation, some other context, that would explain your feelings; some place, time, or situation in which your most secret or obvious trait would be perfectly appropriate.

   Feelings of murderous rage, crushing depression, helpless entrapment, immobilizing anxiety—all have settings in which they would not only be appropriate but expected.

   Your life is already full of the residue of past lives—and you remember much more than you think. Your memories are much closer to the surface than you imagine.

THE PATTERNS IN YOUR LIFE

Think of some of the people you know well. If I were to give you a description of one of them, you'd be able to tell which acquaintance I was referring to, wouldn't you? Of course you would. You'd recognize their combination of behavioral, character, physical, and emotional traits that make up the pattern that distinguishes that individual from any other.

After all, the only difference among faces is that pattern of the features.

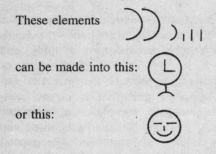

These elements

can be made into this:

or this:

Most of what we do is an expression of our personal pattern—habits, fears, ways of getting dressed, ways of approaching our jobs, kinds of physical problems, ability to relax, and preferences for food, colors, historical periods, careers, and people.

Actually, everything we do, from the selection of a car, to a mate, to our hobbies, is motivated by psychological forces, most of which are unconscious.

Patterns of behavior in the lower animal kingdom are well accepted and recognized: the way the moth lays her eggs, the way the caterpillar feeds, the way salmon swim upstream to the place of their spawning, the way baby chicks recognize their bird-of-prey enemies, the imprinting of the gosling on the first moving object it sees after hatching. All these are motivated by internal species-specific patterns and activities on which the survival of the species depends.

In regard to the existence of patterns, human beings are not so different. However, our ability to recognize that pattern allows us to be more than our animal brothers and sisters. That is to say, we have a type of consciousness that allows us to become aware of those patterns. In addition, our awareness of the transpersonal—psychic or soul-related—aspects of living gives us the ability to go beyond the predetermined patterns—or to live them out more effectively and joyously.

Childhood events and conditioning are often used to explain the elements of the pattern. However, the existence of the pattern cannot be so glibly explained. Nor do childhood events explain the constitutional differences with which we respond to, ignore, adapt to, rebel against, or comply with our past conditioning. The interplay of genetics and environment—the old "nature vs. nurture" conflict—is becoming increasingly accepted. This principle states that we have certain constitutional limitations and inclinations that determine the degree to which we respond with these inborn patterns or inclinations to environmental conditioning or triggers.

There are a couple of ways of looking at this whole question. One is that a child comes into the world as a fairly impressionable being and can be conditioned to behave, believe, and feel in whatever way the environment teaches. The extreme opposite suggests that we're born with our behavior already programmed within us and that the growth of life is simply the rolling out or unfolding of those sequences of behavior.

My position leans fairly strongly toward the internal point of view: that there are already inborn in each of us many predispositions and patterns of behavior, reaction, and attraction. Not only does the environment provide the triggers that set off these patterns—as when fear suddenly overwhelms us after an innocuous event—but the internal press to actualize the inner contents causes us to seek and construct outer events that will allow their release.

This is a way of creating one's own reality. We've all seen the angry person who seeks a fight in order to release his aggression. Yet, this is no stranger than the individual who desires to be an actor going where he can find such work. This allows him to release his repertoire of acting behaviors. Another example is the therapist who takes training in order to bring out his or her own abilities for therapeutic interaction. Practice and instruction naturally help improve and refine behavior.

Lest I be thought a fatalist, I do believe there are areas of "free space" in which absolutely new behavior may be learned or conditioned or adopted or "traumatized." This is the way that progress and evolution occur. However, it's my conviction that these free spaces are available only as the more potent predispositions allow.

Even if nothing at all could be done about the working out of each individual's pattern of living, it would still be valuable to become more conscious of it. By being more aware of where you're headed, and what you're really doing, you can take steps to do it more effectively or more efficiently or with less conflict than would be the case if you let the elements unfold by chance and with resistance at each step.

Resistance only causes conflict and subsequent self-defeating behavior. By analogy, if one is fated to make a certain journey, it's far better to make provisions to prepare and train for that journey than to be dragged into it resisting, objecting, and not knowing its purpose or destination. Energy that could be used creatively can be lost in railing against the Fates. Knowing your own patterns gives you a chance to make your predispositions useful to you. Resisting only makes you useful to the pattern.

Nowhere are these patterns more obvious than in the selection of love and marriage partners—and the way in which those relationships change over time. It's very clear that people seldom love the actual person as he or she really is. Rather, the attraction is to a certain type that matches the internal disposition. The infatuation allows us to be blinded to the discrepancies as nature strives to perpetuate the species.

For all of us there are kinds of behavior or inclinations in our partners that are repulsive to us and kinds that are attractive. When we're in conflict within ourselves, there may be a set of personality elements in our partner that at one time attract us and at another time repel.

And this is what we see in relationships where there's a great infatuation in the beginning. Over time, much of the same behavior that originally attracted us gradually begins to destroy that feeling as the competing set of needs begin to emerge and the relationship grows cold. The two people become more and more distant, until the relationship begins to feel like a trap to one of the partners.

In addition to relationships, patterns are evident in the kinds of colors one prefers, the music one enjoys, the kind of art liked or rejected. Psychologically, one could say that most of these preferences in some manner give us greater feelings of security, or excitement, or self-esteem, or control—or whatever needs predominate at the time.

There is the question, however, of exactly what it is that connects the need to that particular manifestation. If a woman's need is for security, why does she seek that security through a jealous husband? She has other options of seeking security through a career or through her family of origin, in philosophy or religion, in a cult or a convent, in public acclaim or in shunning all such recognition.

Saying that someone seeks such a restrictive relationship to feed his or her security needs is not sufficient to explain why the needs moved in that particular direction. Also, the realization of that need isn't sufficient to release one from that predisposition.

Early childhood events are not logically adequate to explain these conditions fully. Even if the woman in question did have a restrictive and tyrannical father—which conventional thought would tell us she sought in her husband to replicate her early situation—it doesn't explain why she was not repulsed by the situation. That is to say, the childhood situation doesn't tell us why that particular individual either accepted or rejected the impress from the environment. Even to attempt a genetic explanation leaves a gap between the behavior and the gene that is supposed to have caused it.

So we can see there's a significant gap in most of the explanations of why we do what we do and how much we accept or reject what we're presented. To a great degree, this gap can be filled by that elusive activity of the mind and brain that is now being studied under such guises as dreams, imagination, guided imagery, and right-hemisphere activity. These all have to do with the relatively spontaneous production of images in the brain, whose only known connection with external behavior is a similarity in patterns.

For example, the man who has been married several times may develop images of being a sultan with a harem. Now, the images of being a ruler with many simultaneous wives and having the power of life and death has little direct resemblance to the man in this life. He feels rather helpless in the face of his attractions, which turn out to be more punishing than rewarding.

The connection between past and present lives, between the inner and outer world is found in the pattern that emerges in exploring the feelings and images: the pattern of being responsible for many women and having everything depend on his activity. His associations around the sultan image even run counter to the expectations of cultures that favor the idea of one man with several women. Instead of the expected gratification, this man felt childish competition among the women for his favor which only left him with feelings of burden and responsibility.

From the perspective of past lives, having been a sultan in a previous life predisposed him to set himself up as the provider of happiness and security for women, and to expect too little in return. However, the recognition of that pattern—through the images of the sultan—led him to raise his expectations so that he might engage for the first time in an egalitarian relationship. When a woman would begin to rely on him unfairly, he was able to see it and stop it. In other words, he also stopped reinforcing dependent behavior in the women around him. Because of these inner images, he was able to see that he had helped to create the very dependence that was now draining him. The emergence of the images into his consciousness helped rescue him from that pattern.

It seems strange that hindsight allows us to see these patterns. We're oddly blinded when they're first revealed to us; we become awakened to their presence only after we've become embroiled. This very fact—poor foresight and excellent hindsight—reveals the presence of some mechanism related to the very issues with which we're concerned. Something operating in our own minds brings us the very things we fear or hate. However, in working through these blind spots therapeutically, we develop the foresight to recognize these patterns at their approach and to make the decisions necessary for more conscious acceptance, avoidance, or change.

Initially, such patterns of being, acting, and relating may bring gratification. But there's usually an increasing feeling of frustration when the needs being expressed in these particular patterns begin to overshadow other needs or create situations that are dangerous or intolerable.

For example, the submissive wife who marries someone abusive endangers her health through his acts of violence. This pattern may then overshadow what were initially the

positive aspects in their relationship. In fact, his volatility
may have been attractive to her at first. This pattern also
stunts the process of growth that would otherwise have
allowed them to grow closer over the years.

The difficulty comes when the wife recognizes that she
should not be treated this way, that he should not behave
this way, and that things they had mutually agreed to or
pledged to do are not being carried out. She finds herself
being cooperative when it's not appropriate to do so. Although she may think she's protecting him, his pride, or
herself, she's only protecting the pathology. Thus, she fails
to take the action necessary to save the relationship. That
is to say, she tries to adapt or cooperate with her husband
rather than seeking the kind of help necessary to salvage
the relationship. The threat of its loss may block any hope
for change.

The hurts pile up one after another until it's too late.
Thus, the pattern of submission, which was initially undertaken to assure the success of their relationship, and
which gratified some of her needs as well as his, eventually
serves to contribute to the destruction of the relationship
and to increase the frustration of one or both of the partners.

There are somewhat simpler and less obvious patterns of
self-sabotage, such as the individual who does not quite
complete what he undertakes—the executive who seems to
sabotage his own rise to the top, coming close but always
doing something to prevent final victory.

These are all patterns—just as surely as color and form
in cloth or the skyline of a city—and it's these very patterns
that are the manifestation and foundation of karma, our
connection to the past.

Briefly, karma is the manner in which we reap in the
present those seeds we have sown in past lives. Karma may
appear as a debt owed because of misdeeds, as benefits due
us as a result of right action, or as behavior patterns learned

in other lives, whether appropriate to the present life or not. A more complete explanation of karma, its workings, ramifications and ultimate purpose are found in Chapter 10.

The patterns themselves are memories, not of the sensory information, but of the impression of previous events. They are the first awareness most people have of their own past lives—even though they're seldom recognized as such.

But these patterns and impressions are only appetizers when we're looking for our past lives. We all wish for clearer memories in the form of sensory information. We want to be able to see, to hear, to feel the life that seems to be motivating us. The connections to be able to do just this are the images within the mind.

Before discussing the various forms of images in the mind, let's look at how the patterns I've been talking about relate to images that come from past lives. While hypnosis is the usual means of getting in touch with past lives—it's not the only way.

Hypnotic Induction Vs. Netherton Technique

In routine hypnotic induction, the client is led into an altered state of consciousness through relaxation or concentration. If relaxation is used, for example, the client will be instructed to lie back in the recliner, to close his eyes, and to observe his breathing. Then, after a deep, relaxing breath, he's told to let go of tension, beginning with the feet and going up the body. A relaxed state is induced by progressively calling attention to the parts of the body. This is also the beginning of the trance since the client's awareness has begun to detach itself from the things in the environment and to focus on a few inner sensations.

Having quieted and focused the mind in this manner, the next step is to prepare to receive the memory images. A bridging technique is often used here. For example:

See yourself going into a cave. See how dark it is. There's barely enough light to keep from stumbling. Feel yourself walking through the tunnels of that dark cave until you see light coming through an opening some distance ahead.

As you walk closer and closer to that lighted opening, you will be going back in time—back into a past life. The closer to the opening you get, the farther back in time you are.

When you come to the opening, you will step out into a past life important to you now. . . .

As the client responds to this imagery, he is being prepared to receive the impressions that await him at the end of the tunnel. Thus, a vehicle is prepared in the mind that allows for the bridging of the gap between the memories of this present life and the recollection of other lives.

As soon as the client steps out of the tunnel, he's asked to describe his surroundings, his appearance, and his concerns at that time. Having established this memory link to a specific past life, questions can then be asked about events in the past—or the future—of that life. Mentally, he's there. As you can see, the transition from present consciousness to past-life consciousness is ritually marked off with recognizable steps.

My particular past-life regression process, which I will explain in more detail later, is derived from the work of Morris Netherton, Ph.D. a Los Angeles psychologist who developed his own procedures.

Netherton's methods are much more subtle than traditional hypnosis. He discovered that simply by careful interviewing, the past-life experience can be brought closer and closer to the surface, until its presence becomes obvious to the trained observer. Let us look at how Netherton's procedures work in relation to past-life patterns.

JOHANN'S FRUSTRATION

Johann was sent by his father, who made the appointment for him. The father had come to this country from Europe and had industriously created a successful business. He complained to me of his son's lack of motivation. Johann had just been graduated from engineering school and was being rather passive about seeking employment. As could be expected, Johann was concerned about his own lack of motivation as well as annoyed at his father's pressure. As he said, "I don't like to be pushed, but maybe I ask for it."

Johann appeared to be a restless and active individual—at least in my office. As we talked, it also became evident that he was quite bright. Instinct told me he might be a good prospect for the Netherton Technique in order to access the past-life events responsible for his attitudes and current situation.

Thus, instead of using hypnotic induction on Johann, I interviewed him in such a way as to gradually focus his attention on his subjective and emotional reactions to his predicament. This allowed his emotions to surface. His patterns of behavior became obvious as he grew more and more absorbed in his inner, subjective experience.

For example, Johann was already aware of his pattern of waiting until the last minute to accomplish necessary tasks, such as college term papers or household chores. He attributed this to "having no motivation." He did recognize, however, that this wait-until-the-last-minute habit was also part of a pattern of working better under pressure.

As we talked, I guided him to be more and more descriptive and specific about his internal, subjective experiences. Rather than simply discussing specific events, such as what his father was asking him to do or what he was doing instead, I repeatedly queried Johann about how things made him feel, regardless of how irrational those feelings seemed to be.

Johann's comment that his father seemed rather "disdainful" of some of his interests, such as rock music, led to his admitting to feelings of guilt. In order to elicit even more subjective ideas from him, I asked the often revealing question, "What does that do to you?" He responded immediately, "It burns me up!"

Pursuing his feeling of guilt, I asked him again what it was like for him to feel guilty. He replied that it brought up the question of "Why is this happening to me? I don't like to give in." Further discussion indicated that he often felt like a non-person. My next question was, "What's it like to be a non-person?" Johann replied, "My brain just lies in my head. I just want to forget everything through drinking or losing myself in an activity." This was clearly a defensive measure against some internal experience, and we both needed to know what that was. So, I asked what it felt like when he couldn't lose himself. And he replied, "I feel like I'm going to explode any minute."

In this way, I directed the discussion from the external events of Johann's conflict with his father and his way of handling the demands of his environment, to the very subjective experiences of guilt and being a non-person, to the more intense feeling of the impending explosion.

When I asked him more about these emotional links in the chain of his associations, he described feeling exasperation, desperation, and "not knowing what to do." Naturally, the more we talked about them, the more these feelings gradually rose to the surface. He obviously began to feel them, for his physical restlessness diminished as the internal emotional intensity increased.

This whole process of internal movement induces a partial trance state by bringing to the surface the complex of ideas, emotions, and behavior that are themselves an already existing trance state. The trance that was alive within

Johann consisted, in part, of the emotions of exasperation and guilt, the feeling of being a non-person, and the self-judgment of being unacceptable.

I judged this moment in the interview—when he described his feelings of desperation—to be an appropriate time to begin the associations that would access the rest of his past-life experience.

I knew I was on target because of the way he quickly produced what might be called a metaphorical situation. Focusing on his feelings of desperation, I asked him to give me the first desperate situation that came to mind. He answered quickly, "I feel as if I'd done something wrong and was about to be punished—by guillotine—at any moment."

This statement was the bridge between his external life's pattern of delay and dissatisfaction and his internal experience of irritation and desperation. In the real world he had little to be desperate about since he was being well taken care of. It's just this sort of inconsistency that indicates the existence of a past-life pattern—Johann's internal experience of the situation didn't fit what would be expected given his external reality.

Using this bridge, I needed only to ask him to close his eyes and repeat his statement of having done something wrong. Then I asked him to describe the place in which he was feeling these emotions.

He immediately saw himself in "an impenetrable dungeon." It was dark and cold and empty, "Just me and the four walls." His feelings at the time were of loneliness, as if he'd been "shoved aside." He felt himself bent over, scratching and clawing at the walls, on the verge of insanity. There was no way out.

This then, was the real source of his feelings of desperation. So we went back in the memory of that life to the judgment that had led to his being in the dungeon. He heard a voice, "not overpowering, just disdainful," saying, "You're not worth anything." ("Disdainful" was the same word he had used to describe his father's attitude toward him.)

More details showed me that he was being detained because of his political or religious convictions—not for overt actions against the ruling powers.

Having gained this perspective of his past-life situation, we returned to his experience in the dungeon, which was our entrance point into that life. He described his gradual deterioration, the feeling that he had been spiritually killed and was now being physically drained. And yet he anticipated no relief if he were released from the dungeon—he knew his fate.

> His jailers' echoing footsteps announce their arrival as they come for him. He's beaten and then dragged outside to a courtyard. "They take me to the platform and shove me into place in the guillotine. Once there, they just let me wait, to prolong the agony. This wrings the last ounce of heart and courage from me. I really am a non-person."
> At the moment of death he makes himself feel nothing while his body experiences a "great last surge of energy and I just go limp . . . . The body is discarded like common trash."

There are many psychological interpretations that could be made regarding this rich set of images; but we're dealing with the experience as it is being felt by the unconscious mind—as a reality.

Further discussion revealed Johann's ambivalent feelings about the dungeon as both a place of exasperation and a "temporary haven. As cold and unforgiving as it may seem. . . . I knew that once you leave here, no one's going to try to help you."

Although a punishment in itself, the dungeon was also a haven from the final beheading.

Now, as often happens, we discovered that this one life-time wasn't the only one involved in the present pattern, and we immediately went on to access two related lives. One was an experience of living in a rather shallow society in which Johann eventually sought solitude as an escape from the lack of sincerity he felt around him. His dissat-isfaction with the shallowness of the mores in the society indicated to me that he must have had a contrasting expe-rience at some time.

Seeking this polarity, Johann remembered a life as an older man. Although this third life had not been a fun one, never-theless, through his fortitude and efforts he had been re-warded with the respect of others who now sought his vice.

By putting him in touch with this polarity, his hopeless and desperate psychological state was now softened. "I had some value," he said. "They respected me and what I was about. They gave me a chance—at least they took a second look."

As you can see, this regression did not have the usual formal hypnotic induction but relied on the already existing emotional complex that was giving rise to much of Jo-hann's experience in his current life. By listening to him carefully, I recognized his core experience of feeling pun-ished. Having Johann focus on his inner experience of feel-ing punished brought to consciousness those memory images originally giving rise to those feelings. The recog-nition and use of such trigger phrases and core emotional experiences are the hallmarks of the so-called non-hypnotic induction.

Finally, Johann's pattern of delay—described as "no motivation"— was analogous to his being in the dungeon, which, although not rewarding in itself, was preferable to the guillotine.

CHAPTER 2

THE IMAGES IN
YOUR HEAD

IT MAY SEEM THAT I HAVE COVERED ALMOST EVERY POS-
sible area of patterned life in my discussion of events, relationships, emotions, preferences, and roles. But there's
one area that's even more intimate and correspondingly
more powerful than those already mentioned—images.

Accompanying each of the significant patterns in our
lives are images that we carry within us. These images
usually remain fairly unconscious, but they rule us nonetheless by reinforcing the feelings that we have and by
inclining us to act in ways that may be against our conscious choices.

Yet, the images in our heads make themselves known
through patterns that we see. And so, while one may feel
"like a slave," one may seem to others "like a monarch."
One may feel desolate and alone—as though on a desert
island. One may feel cautious and vigilant, as though
"they're out to get me." One may have a stabbing pain. A
woman may gain five pounds and feel as though she were
pregnant. A man may constantly blame himself for all the
troubles that occur around him, as though he were responsible for everything. On the other hand, you may know

someone who blames everyone else for things for which he was responsible—as though he were a helpless victim.

All of these descriptions are experiences that many people have had. They are all metaphors and express metaphorical thinking. Some people view these metaphors as leaving the world of concrete reality and indulging in fantasy or figurative thinking—entertaining but of questionable use. However, it's my contention that this metaphorical left-brain thinking is closely related to the right-brain images that give us direction, habits of response, expectations, and attitudes. Whether these images are fantasies or actual memories is of secondary importance to the fact that *they are the ruling element in our behavior*.

The man who acts as though everyone were out to get him will actually provoke people to do so. The woman who acts overly submissive will induce males—and females as well—to dominate her. This principle is one more way in which we create our own reality.

Even though we may be unaware of these images in our own minds, they influence not only our behavior but also the behavior of those around us. Thus, the man whose internal images include those of a monarch with many wives—submissive, dependent, and unproductive—may eventually incline anyone with whom he becomes involved to be dependent on him. This can occur even though his conscious choice would be for an equal partner. Note the example of the sultan image that has already been discussed.

These images, emerging as metaphors, resemble what psychologists term ''primary process'' which is the unconscious urge to seek immediate discharge of sexual or aggressive impulses. This primary process is never itself conscious but we may be aware of its residue or expression through unreasonable urges, behaviors or fears. Since the metaphors are much like these primary processes, paying attention to them will take us closer to that which motivates us and molds our behavior.

Regular or repetitive behavior that isn't under our conscious direction or that confuses us, or behavior of whose roots we are not aware are fruitful for exploration. They all express and point to unconscious motivations, expectations, fears, desires, or attitudes. Attached to every one of these motivations, behaviors, or patterns is an image. We need only temporarily withdraw our attention from the things we're conditioned to think of as the cause of our predicament and turn inward.

When we withdraw from the things we see, hear, and feel, think and remember from this life at this very moment and turn our attention inward, it often has startling results, as many of these case histories show. If we haven't blocked our perception of such processes, as we turn inward we will find a world of color, form, events, and emotions that is oftentimes far richer than what we normally experience in everyday reality. These images, words, and series of events emerging from that inner world are coherent, often vivid, frequently surprising, and powerfully therapeutic.

THE NEXT STEP: INTO THE PAST

Thus far in my discussion of patterns, I've said little that can't be easily accepted or observed. Anyone with any kind of awareness has observed habitual patterns of response, of relationship, behavior, and thoughts—both in themselves and others. Brain research has verified the fact that the left half of the brain specializes in the kind of linear thinking that underlies language, and that the other hemisphere deals primarily with visions, images, gestalts, and patterns.

Some people have become aware of these images through repetitive dreams, frequent daydreams, or, for a few, even visions. I contend that the source of these images lies in our past—not only in the past we remember—or distort—from this life. Rather, the majority of such images come from previous lives, are carried by our subconscious mind, and seek expression in order to resolve something unfinished in the memory images or to help us to be whole.

This principle is similar to the Freudian idea that unresolved or traumatic material is suppressed or repressed and may emerge in neurotic behavior through such mechanisms as projection, conversion, and hysteria. In traditional analysis, the therapist encourages the inner exploration of these trains of association as well as projecting on to the therapist unresolved relationship pressures. These are then worked through and resolved in the analytic relationship.

I would assert that these images we carry in our minds have their basis in very real and concrete events that we do not consciously remember. Nevertheless, these events and patterns of feeling, thought, behavior, response, ideals, and relationship that issue from them are survival patterns. They are learned or conditioned ways of living that at some time in the past we have thought ensured our survival or self-worth. Some of these images become known spontaneously through dreams, fantasies, or even psychic readings. Parts of them also manifest spontaneously and apparently unbidden.

DREAMS

Dreams can reflect memory images and emotions from the past—the past of this life or other lives. Past-life dreams may be very vivid and accurate or may be subject to the usual distortions of dreaming. A repetitive, haunting, or disturbing dream indicates that something is seeking attention and resolution. In my practice, repetitive dreams have provided some of the most fruitful areas of past-life research for my clients. They often report having had an unusual dream just prior to the first therapy session. Such a dream is almost always significantly related to the problem at hand.

CAROLINE'S DREAM OF DEATH

Just as the repetition of events and patterns in our external life has a serious impact on us, so do those inner events known as repetitive dreams. These are dreams that we have over and over again. There is often something unsettling, incomplete, or even frightening about them. Here's an example from Caroline, a teenaged girl, who regularly had this dream:

> I see me dead. Kids are playing nearby, people are crying. I'm as though asleep but with a frown. It looks like me older—say in my twenties. I was in those baby-doll clothes with the puffy sleeves.

This dream naturally left Caroline feeling somewhat disturbed, especially since she took it to be an omen of her future—to die in her twenties. My past-life experience and orientation, however, led me in the opposite direction—into the past.

It was a ticklish situation. She had no belief in reincarnation, and various other circumstances prevented my approaching the subject directly. She was, however, willing to engage in an "experiment." I explained to her that we have images constantly going on inside our heads, like a continuous movie. We could begin with the images of the dream and let them unfold just to see what would come— what her own inner mind might present to her. It would be like dreaming while awake.

I led Caroline into a light state of relaxation and these images began to emerge:

> It's an old country, on a farm. I'm sweeping. I'm 23 and wearing a pastel dress, humming to myself. Things are happy, slow.
> (Moving back into childhood, she sees her large family sitting around a wooden table, "like a picnic table",

with wooden chairs. We come forward in time then, to when she has apparently moved out of the family home.) I'm arriving at the house with lots of suitcases. Nobody's there to help. I'm sad. I don't have anybody. Don't know where my family is. The house looks cold, dusty. I got there by buggy.

(Coming forward in time.) Still in my twenties—angry, throwing things around, breaking things, crying. She's been told (note the change into the third person) she's going to die. A doctor told her, "The test came back today; it's a rare disease; don't have long to live." She screams "No! Not me!" and runs into her house. In the bedroom she picks up a picture of some people and sits on the bed. She gets angry and throws the picture, saying, "I'm going to miss you; I don't want to go. Why me!"

(Moving a little forward in time) It's getting cold outside. There are no leaves. The wind's blowing hard. She walks into the house, puts a fire into the fireplace and one in the bedroom. She gets into her nightclothes and lies there looking at the fire, crying. She looks out the window. It's raining; there's wind. She stares out that window. After a while she gets out of bed and gets that picture and gets back in bed. She's weak, sad her parents aren't there.

Later, she can't move. She's wondering why she can't move her legs, and she's screaming, holding the picture tighter. Then she's floating. Her body's on the bed. She can see people coming into the house laughing. They open the door, see the body, and start to cry. (I asked her what she would like to have said to them and she replied.) "I'm O.K.; don't worry. I love you all." She watches over them.

(Coming forward to the time of the burial.) They have her dressed in the white dress with the puffy sleeves (of her dream). Flowers are around, pretty flowers—pink roses and white roses. (As she moves away . . .) People are crying and I'm saying (note the return here once more to the first person), "Don't lower me there; I don't like it underground." They're throwing flowers in. Then they all go. . . . I don't want to go.

(I ask her what holds her there.) My mother; she looks so sad. (She herself starts to cry.) She doesn't look too

good. She's been crying a lot—about me. I don't like it
when she cries. I try to say, "Don't cry. It will be O.K.
I'll be there when you come." She's getting into her
car and drives away. I'm getting peaceful. It feels warm
and I'm smiling.

The years pass and I see people enjoying themselves.
I see Mom laughing and it makes me happy. She talks
to me in her prayers. I sit up and watch her—help her
through tough times.

As you can see, Caroline's experimental dreaming
brought emotions of anger, sorrow, separation, and sensations of cold and rain, which turned spontaneously without suggestion into peacefulness, warmth, and communion.

The dream never returned. It was not necessary to make
suggestions. Caroline didn't need to adopt any belief system. The only requirement was to follow her own inner
images to their own conclusion.

FANTASY AND DAYDREAMS

Caroline's dream was fairly clear and coherent. Many
repetitive dreams, however, are not so sensible. They are,
as most people have found, full of such images as drown-
ing, being chased, feeling trapped, or awakening with fear.
They may have the usual distortions of the traditional
Freudian dream process.

Rest assured that underneath these confusing images lies
the repetitive experience that you recognize—perhaps
mainly through your feelings. One step beneath the surface
are the inner, more coherent images from the past life.

This doesn't mean, as Freud thought, that the dream
distorts in order to hide some reality from us. I take the
more Jungian viewpoint that these dream experiences are
attempts at communication from the unconscious. The unconscious mind is trying to present to us some piece of

information, experience, or memory but is sometimes constrained by the need to translate the original scene into something with which we're now more familiar. Thus, a chariot from a past life could be turned into a car, or an attacking enemy into someone familiar to us.

To further confuse things, two separate but real experiences may be combined, one on top of the other like a photographic double exposure. And so a birth experience could be mixed up with some past-life event, such as being trapped or feeling pressure. This doesn't happen because our unconscious is playing tricks on us but because it knows that our conscious mind will more easily recognize a modern representation of the event.

I have also found that consistent daydreams may also have a great deal of past-life material in them. By consistent daydreams, I mean those that maintained a fairly regular scenario, not those that change every time we think of them. Although such daydreams are often gratifying and part of our wishful thinking, they may be as much memory of the past as they are hope for the future. For example, daydreams of sexual gratification may actually be a partial memory of an event or situation in a past life—as a harem member or possessor, or as a member of the opposite sex, or any number of other possibilities.

In this instance we may be replaying in our minds some pleasant part of that memory. A thirty-year-old client of mine daydreamed about receiving a great deal of sensual attention in his regression from several females as part of a religious rite. However, after he enjoyed these pleasures he was sacrificed.

The fantasy of the more pleasant parts of the memory emerged in his adolescence, as do many of our fantasies, but it was not until he underwent the regression that we recognized the consistent, almost rigid and ritualized nature of his fantasy.

Dr. John Money of the Psychohormonal Research Unit

of the Johns Hopkins Hospital reports that every one of us carries around what he refers to as a "love map." This love map is the pattern or combination of interpersonal attractions and sexual behavior that we carry throughout our lives. According to his research and thinking, this map—what I usually call a "script"—is pretty well set by the age of seven or eight and does not change, although it may unfold or evolve.

The Freudian idea of the imprint of the parent of the opposite sex on our attractions may hold true for more obvious and socially accepted encounters and behavior. However, the kinds of fantasies we secretly entertain, and actions we perform covertly, must bear the stamp of some other model. Witness the example of the young teacher who had fantasies of exhibitionistic sexual activities with many partners but whose real life parental model as well as her own behavior were publicly quite conventional and modest.

The test of whether the fantasy or daydream is just fantasy or an actual memory—or memory derivative—is its consistency. If you can easily change many aspects of the fantasy, or its core events, it's less likely to be a true memory than one that remains pretty much the same. If you can change it but it seems to change back to its original structure or images, this indicates that the fantasy is carrying on a life of its own, independent of your volitional imagining. That is to say, it's not just a construct of our fantasy-making consciousness but derives from something more real—a memory.

ERUPTIONS

If you just observe many of the things people do, much of their behavior doesn't seem to belong in the present moment. Sometimes it's very obvious that what was just said or done doesn't fit the present time but might fit another context. There may be too much anger, or fear that's out of proportion, or they may be adhering to a standard of behavior that seems out of date. Just the awareness that these eruptions may actually be past-life material slipping into the present does much to reduce the confusion that would otherwise occur.

MARIANNE'S LOSS

Marianne, visiting from North Carolina, had obtained my name from a past-life therapist in Chicago. She called me in order to explore an experience that had occurred the previous year.

She told me that she'd been riding in a car with a couple who were deeply involved in a relationship. There was discord between them at the time. As the pair were arguing, out of Marianne's mouth came the phrases: "You won't get another chance," and "Listen to her; I'm her mother." Needless to say, this surprised them all. This was obviously one of those situations in which the response seemed to have nothing to do with what was going on. However, Marianne recognized the probability that she might be providing some response from another reality. During the subsequent year she pondered what it might mean, especially in connection with some dreams that she'd had seven years before. "Coincidentally," she found the piece of paper on which she'd written these dreams just two days before she came for the regression session.

The regression itself involved a life in which her mother died when she was very young. Marianne became pregnant, and her lover was sent away. Later, she was told that he'd been killed; then their baby was taken from her through the machinations of her father and stepmother. Finally, she was confined to an abbey for six years until her family came for her.

The emotional residue of the memory of these losses was

triggered in this life by hearing the discord between her friends. That is to say, these past-life experiences resulted in her sensitivity to the discord, her feeling of protection toward her former child and now friend, and her sense that "there was only one chance." This insight helped to quiet the nagging discomfort that was brought about by the eruption of those original phrases, "You won't get another chance. . . . Listen to her; I'm her mother."

There are documented accounts of people who have experienced complete spontaneous memory flashes that may include the whole of the life with its details and feelings. Researchers such as Frederick Lenz, author of *Lifetimes*, Ian Stevenson, M.D., who wrote *Twenty Cases Suggestive of Reincarnation*, and H.N. Banerjee, who wrote *Lives Unlimited*, have amassed considerable numbers of accounts of such spontaneous memories. Many of them have been investigated and verified.

DÉJÀ VU

Déjà vu is thought to be a vague recognition that one has previously been through something that one is just now encountering. The movie *Patton* contains a scene in which the general recognizes a terrain and knows intuitively that an ancient city had once lain nearby. Diverting his jeeps to that ancient battlefield, he told his compatriots of the Roman legions' attack on the Carthaginians ". . . 2000 years ago— I was here." This memory, at least as presented in the movie, revealed Patton's perception of himself as a soldier whose spirit was firmly entrenched in centuries of warfare.

GLEN'S FLASHBACK

Glen, musician, actor and entrepreneur, had a similarly clear experience while traveling in England. It was so vivid that he didn't realize it was a memory until after it was over.

He was visiting Westminster Abbey, which he'd done six times before—but not this particular chapel. It was dark and musty. Over the doorway was the inscription, "Elizabeth." He stooped through the doorway and saw a sarcophagus with an effigy on it. He said to himself, "It looks just like her—I know it!" And there the conversation began. "We talked about her health as though I were a close and trusted friend—but the conversation was interrupted."

Prepared for the regression, Glen was taken back to the last time he saw Elizabeth I, queen of England. It was when she was young:

> She's dressed in an ornate gown with a high collar and lots of pearls. [Even in this informal occasion with an intimate] you couldn't forget she was the queen. She was an achiever. You couldn't forget she was the monarch. When the others came in she had to put on her other self. Otherwise we could relax and there was a mental give and take. . . . I was involved in keeping her Protestant—in getting the Roman missal out and the Protestant prayer book in. I'm dressed in black slippers and a cassock with the buttons stretched tight.

I asked Glen what was important to him in that life and he replied:

> Power. I wanted to be powerful—but in the church rather than political. We [Elizabeth and I] were friends. We used each other but with respect and admiration.
> She was concerned about my health. . . . She fussed about my huffing and puffing. My color was bad. I was probably about to have a heart attack. The room was spinning. I was so fat. We had something important to discuss but someone else came in. It was someone young and thin, and I didn't like him at all. There was a blazing sun overhead in the garden.
> [Here he felt the sun so strongly that he opened his

eyes to see if his discomfort was being caused by the
small light in the office.] I have two big rings on my fat
stubby fingers. I'm a pompous old fart. I was always
fat; always a priest, too.

Glen recounted part of his youth in that life. He'd been
rejected by the other kids who used to throw apples at him.
According to him, what set him apart was the fact that he
was brighter than the others. His older brother was to get
the estate. He, on the other hand, was being educated for
the church:

> We were Catholic. Then my father was messed up
> with Henry somehow and we came out on the Protestant
> side. I was a priest by then and went on the Protestant
> side—for political reasons. To hell with the religion.
> Mary came back awhile [Elizabeth's older sister and
> a staunch Catholic]—what would I do then? If I made a
> stink before, I would have been in [trouble]. I kept my
> mouth shut. I went away, I want to say to Ireland, but
> it was Roman [Catholic]. I was just leaning to the Prot-
> estant side. . . . I just stayed away.
> I hadn't made up my mind yet. I really wanted to get
> away from it. My father had come out on the side of
> Henry and the Protestants. I came back when Elizabeth
> came in. I wasn't close to her then; I wasn't important
> enough.

I asked him what made the change to bring him to her
attention, and he went on:

> . . . the prayer book. I helped pushing that with her.
> She made or wanted revisions. I was afraid of her in the
> beginning, but I was important too. I was an arch-
> bishop—of Canterbury. I was the head of the Church of
> England with the monarch. [The spiritual charge was]
> as chief pastor, to name bishops, appoint priests. When
> Henry dissolved the monasteries, he threw out the re-
> mains of Thomas à Becket. I wanted the shrine of
> Thomas à Becket back.

I should have been positive, shepherding my people. But I was negative—against the Roman Church. Why didn't I help her with Mary? The prayer book helped her be queen because it helped sway people. . . . It was a statement, a symbol of their independence.

Taking him forward to the last conversation he had with her, he said:

I was fat and gray. My nails had gotten thick, yellow, and cracked. I didn't feel as bad as I looked. It felt good to be with her again. And then that someone I didn't like came in and interrupted. I think I knew I was dying or would be awfully sick awhile. I came to say good-bye, as well as to discuss other things. She was in the center of the garden. As I turned to resume the conversation [apparently after the dizzy spell], this skinny young man came in. It was the end of our conversation.

At the time of his death, not long after this conversation, he assumed he was having a stroke and was angry that "the ninnies were just standing there. They don't know what to do. I can't breathe right."

Glen's description of the events immediately following his physical death is both amusing and instructive. He had read Elizabeth Kübler-Ross's accounts of near-death experiences. The fact that his images coincided with the ones he'd read about gave him doubts about the validity of his experience. However, if he were simply suggestible, one would expect that his objection to the images would have changed them into something more acceptable. Here is his account as he goes through this death:

The two people standing there are not doing a damn thing—if I could get up I'd kick their . . .
I'm trying hard to see what happens. There's a bright light. It's like Kübler-Ross talks about. I doubt this. It's too pat. They didn't even loosen my collar. It was cold. I died when it was cold and I was not home.

Kübler-Ross must be right. It's like a sunrise . . . a
little light that just gets brighter. I can't stay in that body
after it dies. I'm afraid as I float out that my cassock will
flutter. I don't want to see the angels with my cassock
floating up around my rear end. Oh, this is too much of
a cliché! I keep floating higher. Oh, that's tacky.

Thus, against his own conscious wishes, he produced
the very images he thought were too pat, too clichéd. Glen
also described a phenomenon that often occurs immediately
after death: a confusion of the physical and nonphysical
worlds. His soul, of course, wasn't wearing a cassock, but
his habits of thought didn't immediately disappear.

When these past-life memories were brought close to the
surface, Glen spontaneously relived that interrupted conversation. It's often the case that something incomplete or
unresolved erupts most strongly. In everyday life these
eruptions may only come to us partially, as unexplainable
feelings, unexpected thoughts, or coincidences.

In the debate to separate fact from fiction, reality from
speculation, two things are clear:

- We as human beings carry out patterns of thought,
  feeling, and behavior.
- Focusing on any of these patterns produces images of
  other times and other places and situations.

The debate centers around the origin of those images. Are
they really an unconscious memory of past lives? Or are
they fantasy, wishful thinking, or a defense against reality?

CHAPTER 3

BUT IS IT TRUE: WHERE'S THE PROOF?

ONE OF THE MOST FREQUENTLY RAISED QUESTIONS IS about the validity of past-life experiences. People are intrigued by the whole concept—moved by the possibility that some of their inner inklings might be true. But they want proof that they've lived before. Where is it? How can we prove something so immaterial?

THE NATURE OF PROOF

Let me state at the outset that there's really no absolute proof of reincarnation—or anything else, for that matter. For example, if I were to ask you to prove to me that you were alive even yesterday, how would you do it? What would you rely on? Documents—driver's license, newspaper articles, birth certificates—could be forgeries. At best, they were written by someone else—they're hearsay. To make the question even more difficult, if I were to ask you to prove to me that you'd had a childhood, how would you do it without circumstantial evidence?

The most basic proof of your existence actually rests in

your memory—and your ability to provide evidence that
the things in your memory are matched by external facts,
or that your memory is supported by the memories of other
people. The external facts that help prove you had a childhood could be toys or photographs or report cards. Childhood friends would also be able to provide memories of
events you'd shared.

Thus, proof of any past event must rely on two elements.
One is circumstantial evidence, such as documents or objects that suggest something or someone has existed. The
other element is nothing more than memory—hopefully,
the memories of a number of people. When these memories
overlap and tend to agree, we say that something is true,
that its existence is proven. This is a consensus of memories, or what is known as "consensual validation."

My own personal odyssey on this question of the validation of reincarnation began with considerable uncertainty. I found reincarnation to be an attractive and
fascinating idea. It explained so many of the questions that
I shared with others about child prodigies, personal inclinations, preferences in friends, "love at first sight," and
good or bad luck. Nevertheless, when I began my practice
in past-life therapy, I called it "regression imagery."

The events I describe here are only a few of those that
convinced me the soul does indeed return after death to
pick up anew—often where it left off before. Reincarnation
explained to me why some people married the same type
of person again and again (and again). Past lives made
more understandable and easier to handle some of the mis-
fortunes we go through in this life.

As a psychotherapist, it gave me a sense of hope as well
as the responsibility to explore the human personality in
new ways and to minister to its problems.

During regression sessions, clients have all sorts of experiences. Images pour forth—images of all manner and
kind. These images tell of various experiences—some vis-

ual, some auditory, some physical—many people have them all. Some images reveal fears, anger, desires, and peace. Many of them are so meaningful they bring clients to tears.

I found—as did Netherton—that these images were close to the surface of the mind—closer than anyone would have thought. They could be provoked either with or without hypnosis. In fact, our very fears and compulsions and behavior patterns turn out to be part of the memory itself. I rediscovered that these images had healing powers. When clients relive them, many anxieties and unwanted behaviors are either eliminated or reduced.

Thus, even though there's no actual way to prove reincarnation to a determined skeptic, there's easily enough evidence to make such a belief very reasonable, if not compelling.

CIRCUMSTANTIAL EVIDENCE

The first hints I had that there was something significant in all of these images came in somewhat subtle ways. Being trained as a behavioral observer, I watched as clients entered these states of regression. I watched how people behaved, how they talked, and how they moved, and I listened to the tone of their voices.

One of my earlier regressions was with Ian. He was normally a talkative man until he described his life as an American Indian. The regression itself turned out to be hard work for me because of the way he responded to my questions: He gave one-word answers. Ian talked of travel by horseback and related the passage of time to the motion of the sun across the sky.

Another client, Barbara, was nearly through the regression when she experienced a surge of anger. As she did so, she opened her eyes, looked straight at me, and said, "I want to smite thee." We both burst into laughter as she realized how incongruous she sounded. There's normally only the slightest hint of her Texas drawl, and nowhere in her past had she been exposed to such a phrase. They just don't talk about "smiting thee" in Texas.

In another instance, a man in regression became agitated because I kept asking him, "Who is this Louis?"—a name he kept repeating. He was fully convinced that I should have known who Louis was, and that there must be something wrong with me that I didn't. "Louis," he said finally, "is the king of France."

These little personality changes, changes in inflection, and subtle implications—such as, everyone should know who Louis is—show departures from habitual patterns of behavior and expression. These changes show pockets of cultural attitudes and knowledge outside the ones with which the clients are familiar. These phenomena reveal at least the possibility of a reality other than the usual conscious one.

CONSENSUAL VALIDATION

The kind of evidence that is accepted in most courts is that of consensual validation. This simply says that the more people who agree (for the most part) with what another has reported, the more likely it is to be true. So we have these accounts in past-life therapy of people who independently report similar descriptions of the same event.

STEPHANIE'S DREAM AND TIM'S FANTASY

Stephanie, for example, wanted to be regressed to find the source of her relationship with her husband. During her session she described herself as being dressed in sandals and kimono, standing at the water's edge on one of the Japanese islands:

> It was in the 1800's. A boat was anchored offshore, sporting the Union Jack. She knew these Englishmen were after pearls for which she and some of the other women would dive. There was a steep, winding path to her house on the cliff overlooking the sea. She shared this house with her husband. "We built it," she says, "to look out over the sea." Her family was not originally from that village but lived in the mountains.
>
> She had met her husband when he came to her mountain village as a delegate accompanying some provincial prince. Their marriage was seen as diplomatically beneficial for both villages. Her husband taught her about the sea, about navigation, and some portion of his Samurai knowledge. He died in a boating accident, and she passed away many years later.

Stephanie was very excited over gaining this information but was curious to see what her husband Tim might produce in a similar regression. She didn't tell him what she experienced but encouraged him to come for a session of his own. Tim shrugged off the suggestion. However, when she returned for another visit about a month later, she told me of this uncanny "coincidence."

One morning, she described a dream about boating to her husband. In Stephanie's regression account he had died in a boating accident. Her dream triggered Tim to say to her, "You know what I think we were? I have a hunch we were Japanese. I was a Samurai warrior. We lived in a small house by the ocean in my village. You were a 'mermaid' and dived for pearls. We met when you were ice skating in the mountains before coming to my village. We built a small house overlooking the sea."

Now, it's not unusual for regressions to turn up similar information. But what makes this particular account remarkable is that one part of the story came from a regression experience and the other from a hunch. It's also not unusual for married people to incarnate together—although not always as husband and wife.

This form of consensual validation is partly what Ian Stevenson used in his book, *Twenty Cases Suggestive of Reincarnation*, to show how children could describe in detail events and facts from a previous life—facts that could be verified by the still-living members of the previous family.

HISTORICAL VALIDATION

I would next like to present one of the most dramatic accounts in my practice. To me, it's clear evidence of a verifiable reincarnation experience.

TED'S LIFE ON THE MISSISSIPPI

Ted came to my office for a regression motivated primarily by curiosity. Briefly, the life he described was of being born in the latter part of the 1700's. He did some traveling and trading before returning to his hometown. There, he established what was to become a very lucrative lumber business. He made a marriage of convenience that never warmed up. His wife was apparently a religious fanatic and very critical of his disinterest in religious matters, as well as his visits to some of the less reputable parts of town. His only emotional gratification in the marriage was provided by their three children. The wife was only interested in entertaining traveling preachers.

The regression began with Ted's entry into the life as an old man sitting in front of a brick house in which he had lived. "I'm not sure it's mine, but I live there. . . . [with] my daughter and a son and other people. My wife is dead . . . She died of pneumonia." Ted went on to describe the house in detail—the rooms, even the books lining the shelves, with some of the household accounts of horses and slaves.

Then I regressed him to an earlier age in that lifetime. Ted found himself working at the lumber mill, providing lumber for a foreign country at war. His contribution to the war weighed on his conscience—a weight that was eased by the profitability of the action.

After his day's work was over, he didn't always go home: "I go to the inn sometimes. They serve wine and drinks and you can go upstairs if you want to. . . . I don't like my wife. . . . I go to the inn a couple times a week. . . . I do like to go home because I love home. I love the children. But my wife—when I think about her I feel cold, confused."

I next regressed him to the stage in that life where he first met his wife. She was with her parents on their way to church, near the river. The town was named something like "Nazarod or Nazarie, I'm not sure." I asked him what it was near, and his immediate reply was, "The Mississippi River."

Ted didn't have a good feeling about marrying but didn't give me the reason why he was doing it. It was almost like a social obligation he owed to her parents. His parents were not at the wedding ceremony, and he had no friends he felt close to except for one: "Andrew Bark. . . . We've done things together. Andrew rides the boat, a paddle boat. He might be a gambler."

Ted went on to say that he and his wife had three children. She was a very religious person whose primary interest was extending hospitality to traveling preachers and their wives. Despite its formal nature, the marriage lasted until her death at an advanced age. His death followed his wife's a few years later.

Ted was rather surprised by the clarity and vividness of what he'd related. He wanted to know if it had made sense. His surprise had turned to incredulous excitement by the next day when I received a telephone call from him. He had set out to research his experience and had found a book in the local library that told an incredibly similar tale to the one he had related to me. The book was called *Natchez on the Mississippi* by Harnett T. Kane. Using the clues of the Mississippi River and the town whose name began with an *N*, he set out to research the past and was rewarded with a piece of local history.

I could imagine his excitement as he read the account of "Eliza, the Early Bride." This chapter told of a young man named Peter Little, who other people were sure would make a name for himself. It told the story of how Peter started out as the first lumberman along the river. His first encounter with his wife-to-be took place when she was with her parents on their way to church to hear a traveling evangelist. Eliza's family invited Peter to go along with them. He declined, figuring religion was all right for those who wanted it, but he could take it or leave it. Actually, he would leave it and Eliza would take it. Years later when Eliza's father passed away and her mother was taken seriously ill, Peter was entreated to look after Eliza and to be the administrator of her estate. Soon after, "for reasons of property and to protect Eliza in her dealings, they had thought it best" to marry. It was not a love relationship, but one of convenience. Eliza was sent away to school immediately after the wedding.

Peter built a red-brick house, matching the account given by Ted. The three children were not born of this marriage but were adopted. Near where Peter worked was an inn, which no doubt added fuel to his wife's religious fire. In that part of town "riots broke out by the hour. Gambling dens, dance halls, bar-rooms, rooming houses, race tracks, bordellos, peep shows—it was everything and anything."

Much to Peter's dismay, Eliza's religion became her sanctuary. He found a solution to the steady stream of visiting ministers by constructing a separate building called

"The Parsonage." Here, his wife could entertain as she chose.

Peter Little had one close friend. His name was Andrew Brown. In the Natchez account, Andrew became Peter's partner and eventually took over the ownership of the lumber mill from Peter. The gambling Ted had referred to was clarified in the story: Andrew took more chances than the average conservative townsman when it came to business—but his risks paid off. The lumber business did quite well as the Mississippi River provided easy access to New Orleans and its business advantages. Eliza died in 1853 and Peter followed her three years later.

Here, we have two versions of apparently the same series of events. One comes from the unconscious mind of a subject undergoing a past-life regression, the other from a history book. Could it be coincidence? ESP? Had Ted once been Peter Little? The main points of what he'd related to me—Peter's business, his meeting with his wife, the nature of their relationship, their three children, the scenes in the house, the inn, the one friend named Andrew—were all substantiated in the book. Having never been to Natchez (nor heard of it), nor having seen this book before, what was the source for these facts?

Fact after fact validated the idea that he had made contact with a specific past life. Interestingly enough, Ted had not correctly identified many of the people's names. Except for Andrew, and then only the first name, and the Mississippi River, the names he reported didn't match up with those in the book. This phenomenon is a frequent stumbling block for research and a major point of criticism from the skeptics. Yet, the similarities of the regression account to the history are undeniable. There are just too many correspondences to discount the whole thing. But the discrepancies are as interesting to me as the correspondences. We all wonder, in this process, what it is that provides such a tantalizing series of similarities but is so inaccurate in pro-

viding correct names. An analysis of the situation reveals
that the differences are those of labels.

I can offer six possibilities that may account for such
discrepancies. Some refer to cosmic or karmic issues, others are quite mundane:

- First of all, there's the level of trance in which the
  regression took place: Working in light trances for
  therapeutic effectiveness can allow the nonemotional
  material to be contaminated with ideas from the conscious or unconscious minds.
- Memory improves with use. Many of the questions
  I'm exploring here might have been cleared up by
  further exploration in the trance—had we wished to
  take that time.
- Most of us are better at remembering experiences than
  dates and details. Thus, it's not at all unusual for
  memory to become distorted or to abandon us in such
  an instance.
- There's always the possibility of errors in historical
  documents, which in the final analysis also rely on
  someone else's memory.
- There's the strong possibility of "bleed-through."
  Since the relationship between Peter and Eliza—as
  with most of the significant ones—existed prior to the
  lifetime we examined in the regression. These other
  names could have come from lifetimes before Peter's
  and Eliza's. That being the case, the discrepant names
  may have been a message from the unconscious that
  there's more to be explored between Peter and Eliza.
  Indeed, at the close of the regression, a "guide"
  spoke of a karmic debt owed to the wife that was paid
  through Peter's forbearance and care.
- Finally, names are important to us only because we,
  as conscious egos, identify with them. To the unconscious mind, these names are external, superficial,
  and temporary as the soul travels through its various
  incarnations. Names are like the clothes we put on
  and take off from day to day. It's therefore less common to be attached to the name than to be able to
  recall the pictorial images.

For example, the person who is now known as Karl

Schlotterbeck has had a different name in each past life. However, his karmic pattern—the repetitive experiences—would be more consistent and therefore more easily recalled. It's much like a dream: we may recall only the feeling or the tone—details will be unclear; people may be confusing, seeming to be more than one person.

There may, of course, be other possibilities. However, these are some of the most likely factors. They warn us to never be too complacent or credulous regarding the products of either the conscious or unconscious minds. It's not that they present us with untruths, but that we may miss where the significant truth lies in what we're presented. Always remember that the inner mind lives in that world in which time and space interpenetrate. Yet during regressions, client after client has related experiences of which they had no previous knowledge—experiences later validated by documents, other people's accounts, and by the changes in their lives.

Over a period of ten years, Morris Netherton has heard accounts from eighteen different people who witnessed the same execution—none of whom knew any of the others. He has also had five descriptions of the crucifixion of Jesus, all of which included an event not reported anywhere else. In each instance, Netherton's clients made reference to a man who was knocked down and slashed across the head with a spear as he ran toward the cross after pushing his way through the crowd.

THERAPEUTIC VALIDATION

There's another class of validation that could be more important than any of the others. I call this "therapeutic validation." I say this may be the most important one only because my main purpose is to relieve suffering—and that's

what happens. Many times, clients have come to my office
with fears, pain, anxieties, or behavior patterns that were
out of control, and they've left feeling peaceful and contented. Over and over again I've discovered how therapeutic it frequently is for most people to relive these
experiences. There are numerous accounts of such healing
effects throughout this and other books. I'll only mention
a few examples here.

BARBARA'S ANXIETY

Barbara was an anxiety-ridden young woman who had
been involved with psychiatric therapy and an entire year
of hypnotherapy, yet, elevators and other enclosed spaces
still terrified her. After about three regression sessions, including prenatal experiences and memories of being bur-
ried alive at another time, and being attacked by rats, she
was able to ride on one of the more anxiety-provoking
means of transportation—a small commuter airplane.

NAOMI'S YEARNING

Naomi came to see me because she was unhappy about
the ending of a relationship. It was several months after
the end of the affair, yet she still hoped that he would call.
During her regression, she spoke of being an Indian maid
and of being raised by her parents. Her father was the chief
of the tribe. He often traveled to distant tribes to hold peace
talks.

One afternoon, she was at play when she heard her father
had left the village to cross the mountains and meet with
other chiefs. She was overcome with sadness at not being
able to say good-bye. She left the security of her village
and started out after her father in treacherous weather. She
followed his tracks as long as she could, but the cold set
in. She was found days later, frozen in the ice.

Naomi had been emotionally stuck in this psychological

position of sadness and regret at not having had a chance to say good-bye to her father. We reviewed a time in that life when she had been involved with her father—a time when "he said he loved me." By going through the regression experience, Naomi was able to both consciously and unconsciously recognize that, although her father was physically leaving the village, he was not abandoning her emotionally.

When Naomi returned for another session she told me she no longer felt that need to cling to her old relationship. For her, it was finally over. She was relieved to be able to go on to new experiences in her present life.

Many other kinds of problems have been helped by regressions. For example: a woman who let herself be used by men; a young woman with knee problems; a boy with migraine headaches; a man unable to study. I could go on and on.

THE VOICE OF THE CRITICS

These colorful bits of evidence, which can be woven into a very attractive tapestry suggesting the existence of reincarnation, do not by any means convince everyone. Indeed, there are some fairly standard criticisms of these past-life experiences. Here are some of these criticisms and the shaky ground on which they rest:

"Subjects are simply responding to the wishes of the therapist"

One of the most frequent attempts to discredit the reincarnation phenomenon is the claim that the client is merely responding to the therapist's wishes. I've already recounted the incident of the client who became agitated because I didn't not know who Louis was. I certainly had no wish for him to regard me as a dunce. In fact, he resisted my wish as well as my repeated requests to tell me who this Louis was.

Clients never mindlessly take the suggestions of the therapist. Anyone with extensive experience with hypnotic and other regressive phenomena knows this to be true. For example, at the beginning of Ted's regression, I asked him to tell me what he was standing on. The doctrine of the client's responding to the therapist's expectations or suggestions would have required him to describe himself as standing and then to give some set of related ideas. Apparently, however, Ted hadn't heard that he was supposed to do this. He snapped back at me, "I'm not standing. I'm sitting down."

Many times I've been fooled or surprised by a client's account that turned out to be quite divergent from what I'd expected. In addition, clients are definitely not carrying out the wishes of the therapist when "resistance" raises its frustrating head.

"Cryptomnesia"

It's a recognized hypnotic phenomenon that a person in a fairly deep trance will be able to recount in detail long-forgotten memories. It is not necessary that there be a deep trance—it's just that this is what's usually expected. However, critics often use this phenomenon to discount all regression accounts. Cryptomnesia suggests that someone who claims to recall from a past life, for example, a chariot race may be only recalling forgotten memories of having seen a movie such as Ben Hur. Although such an incident could happen this way, the fact that it does so doesn't disprove a thing. Such erroneous accounts are easily avoided by well-trained therapists. Even if memories of the movie Ben Hur were to be accessed during a regression, it would be the responsibility of the therapist to move the client further back in time in order to determine why those particular scenes from that movie were of such significance out of all scenes in all the movies he or she had ever seen. Thus, the critic's claim that the regressed person is only repeating something experienced in this life is inadequate to explain either the importance or the meaningfulness of that forgotten memory.

In my own case, someone who had partial knowledge of an execution in which we were both involved in a past life failed to recount the memory as I had reported it to her some time before. Rather, she erroneously described a different method of the death—as she had thought it occurred. The reason she didn't know the correct ending of the tragedy was that she'd had her eyes closed at the crucial moments in that life. Thus, even though she had consciously been given the correct information, during the regression she returned to her inaccurate account—having to guess because her eyes had been closed.

It may be somewhat begging the question to assert that the truth is made irrelevant by the importance of the thematic material—the series of events or thoughts or feelings that symbolically represent some issue with which the client is dealing in this life. If people plagiarize from books or movies in their regressions, it would only be because that story was significant to their lives; the real past-life event may be threatening; or there may be a block presented by the conscious mind against gaining past-life knowledge.

The story would have contained some germ of truth about their present life or it wouldn't have been retained in the memory and then revealed at the time of the regression. For example, someone who is concerned about being persecuted may have seen war movies, but the movie itself would not be the basis of his psychological state. Again, a competent past-life therapist should be able to detect such fabrications and move the client back into the real regression experience.

"Fantasy and wishful thinking"

Some skeptics claim that the client is "making it all up." This is one of the most superficial of the criticisms. Anyone who has actually undergone a regression, or more especially a series of them, has had firsthand experience of the difference between fantasy and past-life memories. Anyone in an ordinary daydream or fantasy knows that the fantasy can be changed at any time. It can be turned into whatever we desire. This is, after all, the essence of fantasy. But past-life material tends to be concrete, down to earth, very real—and very consistent.

For the most part, the people who come to see me do so because they're curious, troubled, anxious, or cannot cope with a present-day situation. The regressions seldom provide an outlet for wishful thinking. Rather, they very frequently take the client through traumatic or surprising events. Afterward, they often say to me, "I certainly didn't expect that!" or "Where did that come from?" They wouldn't have wished to undergo the kind of difficulties that emerged. Here, their subconscious mind rules and provides these images from past-life memories—regardless of where their wishful thinking would have taken them.

Too many times the clients' expectations are not met— no matter how strong those expectations. One woman came to me convinced that she'd been her own grandfather. He had died before she was born. But she held such feeling for him and had amassed over a hundred coincidences in their lives. She had found correlations of names, initials, and preferences that had convinced her of the identity. The only reason she came to me was to verify that they were, in fact, one and the same person and to find the answers to some questions she had about his life.

Despite her conviction, expectations, and wishful thinking, she was to be quite surprised by what the regression revealed. If her wishful thinking had come true, she would have seen herself in the regression as her grandfather. However, she discovered that she had not been her grandfather but her aunt, the grandfather's child. The instinctive knowledge and closeness she felt toward the grandfather was not from having been him but was a result of the closeness and care she had felt from being one of his daughters—her own aunt.

CRITICISM VS. CONSENSUS

Under close investigation, these criticisms from the skeptics turn out to be superficial excuses for not really investigating all of the phenomena and implications involved.

There have been poorly designed experiments claiming to show that regression experiences are imaginary. These experiments, reported in the April 1983 issue of *Psychology Today*, were seriously tainted by the experimental methods used. For example, messages were clearly given to the subjects that it was not acceptable to have or attribute the images to past lives. Thus, the subjects were given a double message by the experimenter to first produce past-life memories but then to discount them. This message to look for a present-life source of the past-life images would naturally cause the compliant subjects to obey. This is not evidence that past-life images are produced by present memories but is proof of the subject's obedience to the demands of the authority/experimenter. Although the instances were fewer in number, many people had the images nevertheless.

As we have seen, the real evidence for anything comes to little more than consensus. We agree to the fact that we are here now and that we had a childhood. Your consciousness tells you that you are now here, reading this book, and your memory tells you that you have existed in the past. Lapses of memory about things in your past do not mean that you didn't exist then, only that those memories are simply momentarily out of reach. It's the same with past-life memory.

It's quite possible to find evidence of past lives and to find other people who can verify your past-life images from their own memories.

My clients have validated the existence of past lives for me. It's up to you to do so for yourself.

THE NAPOLEON PHENOMENON

Another favorite argument of the skeptics is, if all this is true, why are there so many people claiming to be the same famous historical figures, such as King Tut or Napoleon? People do sometimes make errors of identification under hypnosis. This comes from the wording of the hypnotist's or therapist's instructions to the subject, and it's easily prevented.

This kind of phenomenon occurs when someone close to or admiring of these figures identifies with the important, awe-inspiring leader. It happens in almost any group where there is great love, great fear, or another strong emotion directed toward the leader. The citizens and followers identify themselves and their plights with the leader. Thus, every follower who has an emotional investment in another person—leader or lover—is open to this identification and the resulting unity and suggestibility that occurs. We literally feel the other's feelings under these conditions. Such leaders can inspire crimes or heroism. The emotion may be positive, such as the woman who thought she was her grandfather, or negative, as in the psychological phenomenon of "identification with the aggressor."

Because of this strong emotional identification with another, a regression may tap into the feelings of identification with the leader rather than the person's truer identification with his own life. When the president of the United States is attacked, most of the country feels attacked and vulnerable. This mis-identification is most likely to occur when the client is given a suggestion to observe the events in the regression from a "higher level" or from the "spirit level." It can also often happen in group regressions.

Let me give you an example of what happened in Sophie's regression in a group and then individually. She had come originally to a workshop during which the participants were regressed as a group. She had the impression of seeing herself as a Nazi officer who was disenchanted with the Führer; he was using his officer's sword to slice and cut a picture of Hitler.

Things turned out differently in her individual regression. Rather than being the officer, she was watching him from across the room—but was united with him and his action by their common feeling. As we moved her into the physical position from which her consciousness was observing this event, we found her to be the unborn baby of the officer's wife.

Obviously, the first thing we see in a regression, as anywhere, is not always ourselves but rather whatever our eyes are looking at.

We might expect that in a few decades regressionists will turn up a number of people claiming to have been John F. Kennedy or Martin Luther King because of the way in which they aroused such devotion and sympathy in their followers and, of course, the dramatic and emotionally charged nature of their tragic deaths.

Skeptics are also fond of pointing out that people being regressed tend not to speak in the language of that past life. When a client begins to speak in a foreign language, I instruct him or her to tell me the meaning of what was transpiring. It is, after all, the meaning of the events to the life of the individual that is crucial.

CHAPTER 4

WOMB FOR IMPROVEMENT: A NEW CONCEPTION OF PRENATAL LIFE

WHEN YOU MENTION PAST LIVES MOST PEOPLE IMMEdiately think of faraway places and times and exotic events. To be sure, these are part of our past-life memory banks. However, there is an area that is much more intimate, recent, and possibly more influential than anything in our previous lives. I'm referring here to the prenatal period of life—the nine months or so that our physical being develops in intimate contact with, within the environment of, and subject to the experiences and chemical changes of our mother.

This intrauterine period of time, plus our genetic makeup, marks the material bridge between our karma and our physical being. Prenatal development is, after all, not totally genetic but is subject to many influences. That is to say, within a genetic and karmic structure, life in the womb begins the development and expression of both the past karma as well as the potential for either a resolution or continuation of that karma.

The newborn comes to us with a history that includes past lives, experiences in the womb, predispositions to act in certain ways, a level or restlessness or passivity, and a significant ability to provoke its caretakers to everything from love to angry rejections, depending in part on the behavior of the child. According to an August 1983 *Psychology Today* article titled "Baby Face," the newborn child even has a repertoire of facial expressions.

Let's now look at this whole area in more detail, as well as some examples of the very powerful prenatal experiences shown by regression.

THE OLD WIVES MAY HAVE BEEN RIGHT

The period of life between conception and birth has been, with few exceptions, generally neglected in terms of significant psychological interest. However, because old wives have shown an interest in this period, the thought that the unborn fetus has any sentience or impressionability is often criticized as an old wives' tale such as a pregnant woman listening to music in order to give her unborn child similarly refined tastes.

In contrast, considerable medical interest has been shown regarding the physiological development of the fetus. There is fair medical evidence that various chemical agents can significantly affect the growth and development of the fetus. Such things as the effects of smoking, alcohol, LSD, marijuana, and other drugs have been studied in relation to the process of fetal development.

There has been much less interest shown in determining if—or how much—chemical factors influence the psyche of the unborn human. It seems ludicrous to me to think that such agents could affect our whole process of development, the ability of the nervous system to do its work, our rate of growth, and our intelligence and not have some psychological impact. Even organisms without the massive potential for consciousness that we as human beings possess respond to positive and negative environments. The lowly

worm can be taught to avoid what it has learned is a negative situation. The simplest of organic life tends to avoid
conditions of inhospitality and to seek to live and reproduce
in more beneficial and life-supporting environments. Who
could suggest that human beings are less wise?

This avoidance of pain and gravitation toward pleasure
seems to be the basis of the nature of life itself. My hypnosis instructor was fond of saying, "Everything necessary
for the preservation of life the Creator made pleasurable."

Alongside the old wives' tradition of the impressionability of the fetus is the tradition that prenatal life is equiv-
alent to floating in a sea of bliss, that the fetus is protected
from the environment by immersion in the amniotic fluid
in the womb itself, which is further enclosed by the mother's body. What has been forgotten here is the fact that the
amniotic fluid is also a chemical environment; that the fetus
is connected physiologically to the mother by means of a
channel (the umbilicus); that the limitation of what crosses
over, and in what direction, between mother and fetus is
not fully known; that the mother's body is itself an environment that radiates its own sound and sensations of
movement—and that all of these depend on the mother's
thoughts, moods, and activities, whether conscious or not.

Traditional scientific research has discovered that the fetus not only carries on apparently innate reflexive behavior
patterns as thumb sucking but also responds to loud noises.
Most mothers have noted that there are times when their
unborn babies are most active—often when they are most
quiet.

Of the two traditions of prenatal impressionability and
insensitivity, both hypnotic and past-life investigation, as
well as a growing body of other scientific evidence, suggest
that the truth lies on the side of the old wives.

We can look first at some external observations of fetal
differences and then at some of the inner experiences and
memories people have reported.

Most mothers can attest to the fact that many of their infants are different from their siblings right from birth. These differences have been generally regarded as genetic or congenital in nature. There is evidence, however, that some of these differences are correlated with events that occurred in the environment of the mother. In addition, such psychological factors as the child's activity level, sense of security, pain threshold, and irritability will be major influences on his development, moods, and personality. Obviously an irritable, fussy, and restless infant creates an entirely different environment for himself through the reactions he provokes in others than does a baby who is cooing, making eye contact, smiling, and accepting affection. This is another way in which we create our own reality.

As medical workers have expanded their view from the examination of organs to the interaction of the whole being—both within the human and between the person and the environment—there have been more frequent correlations in the recognition that the mother and her environment influence the fetus. Both research and common sense show clearly that the more stressed the mother is during her pregnancy, the more likely the child is to have some physical, emotional, or behavioral difficulty.

Let me assert here—before mothers and mothers-to-be indulge in guilt and hopelessness—that the fetus will absorb only what it is predisposed to accept from previous incarnations. In addition, as knowledge expands, we will also discover how it happens that some people do well under stress, and, what is more, ways that preventive or protective measures might be undertaken in even the worst situations.

The real question is not whether there are such prenatal influences, but how they influence us and how much.

LOOKING AT BIRTH FROM THE OUTSIDE

One early psychoanalyst, Otto Rank, asserted the importance of the ''birth trauma'' on later psychological development and reaction to stress.

Birth experiences have generally been looked at from the outside. Parents and medical personnel ''observe'' the newborn. The baby's weight, length, and Apgar scores are used as a measure of fetal health. Until recent years, however, there's been little interest in looking at the birth experience from the inside—from the subjective perspective of the newborn.

Part of the problem, of course, is that babies cannot talk to us in our language. These experiences come to the child before it has language; and language is our main tool in communicating conscious recollection. It's usually easier to retrieve language-encoded experiences than it is to recall those that rely on images or feelings. The things that happen to us before the acquisition of language tend to be relegated to the unconscious or to be overwhelmed by more recent events.

Without language, the storage units of memory must be in the form of sensory data—colors, sounds, emotions—which are organized into the compex combination that we recognize as an ''experience.'' The question of whether there are clear and accurate memories to be recalled from the time of birth must be answered in the affirmative. But there are really two questions here: first, are these memories encoded; and second, are these memories retrievable? In other words, do they exist and can we get to them? Research using hypnosis has given clear evidence that such memories are both present and accessible—and are detailed enough to be verified as accurate.

Evidence for birth influences comes from diverse areas. Of course the most obvious influence is the actual physical trauma. At a more subtle level is the effect of oxygen deprivation, which may result in learning disabilities or behavior difficulties. The next more subtle area of influence has been documented as significant—the act of making birth as pleasant as possible for the newborn. Of special interest here are the "Leboyer babies." These are children born according to the methods developed in France by Frederick Leboyer, M.D., who advocates hushed voices in the delivery room, dim lights, a warm room, and a warm water bath. Children born under these conditions developed substantially higher psychomotor functioning and were reported to be especially alert, adroit, inventive, and ambidextrous. These children also experienced fewer toilet-training difficulties, feeding problems, and digestive and sleeping disorders.

Thus, some of the early psychoanalytic theorists have been at least partially vindicated in their emphasis on the importance of the birth experience.

LSD RESEARCH

Support for the importance of birth experiences comes from yet another area of research. Stanislav Grof, M.D., is a Czech-born researcher who has used LSD as a psychotherapeutic and research tool. Birth memories have been so abundant when unconscious memories are brought to the surface, he's been able to classify four typical stages of the infant's experience of the birth process.

STAGES	EXPERIENCE
I. Primal union with the mother.	Symbiotic unity.
II. Antagonism to the mother.	Entrapment, claustrophobia.
III. Synergism with the mother.	Struggle of both to finish and be free of the mutual discomfort.

IV. Separation from the   Tension followed by relief.
     mother.

Past-life work has produced some very similar data.
There is the unity with the mother—although it's not always blissful—in which both share a common world. Then
my clients relive the physical sensations of contractions,
pressure on the skin, pressure on the head, and the reality
of what is seen in symptoms of claustrophobia—feeling
"the walls closing in", trouble breathing, feeling trapped,
anxiety, and the desire to escape. Compare how close these
experiences are to common symptoms of anxiety—birth
may be their source.

Indeed, the infant's survival now depends on getting out.
Feelings of separation are sometimes felt well before the
completion of birth when the mother has been drugged.
The mother's loss of consciousness and subsequent non-
participation in the birth are often felt by the fetus as
"abandonment." Otherwise, clients recall, sometimes
acutely, their expulsion into a cold, bright, noisy world
where large beings often ignore their cries, put a cold substance into their eyes, and generally treat them as if they
were not people. Fortunately, newborns are gradually gaining the status of human beings as a result of the treatment
advocated by Leboyer and others.

PSYCHIATRIC RESEARCH

Thomas Verney, M.D., is a psychiatrist who has recognized the influence of prenatal and birth experience in
his own work. He has also reported on the research of other
investigators in his book, *The Secret Life of the Unborn
Child*. His conclusions are that, "the fetus can see, hear,
experience, taste and, on a primitive level, even learn *in*

utero. . . . Most importantly, he can *feel*—not with an adult's sophistication, but feel nonetheless (p.12)."

We learn from Dr. Verney that the fetus not only feels but also responds to the mother's thoughts, to her feelings, and to music. Part of the mother–baby connection is apparently the neurohormonal link between the mother and fetus. That is to say, when the mother has a feeling, it causes a chemical change in her body. That change further affects her own feelings. The change in her body also changes the environment of the fetus. What's more, the chemical change involves the substance of emotion—and the unborn child responds. It has been known since the 1920s that blood from a terrified animal will cause fear reactions when it's injected into another animal.

The mother's emotional and physical world constitute the environment of the fetus. Science has a long way to go, however, to find just how the fetus responds to the mother's thoughts. As Verney reported: "An unborn child grows emotionally agitated (as measured by the quickening of his heartbeat) each time his mother thinks of having a cigarette. (p. 20)." The unborn also has differential responses to music. In one experiment, music by Vivaldi and Mozart quieted the unborn. Brahms, Beethoven, and rock provoked violent kicking (p. 39).

Psychosomatic factors have also been discovered. The mother's emotional states of ambivalence, acceptance of responsibility, or anxiety apparently influenced the health of the fetus and the newborn.

Naturally, some children are exceptions and do not respond as expected. This is due, at least in part, to the fact that thousands of years of past-life experience also have their effect.

Verney has also found that prenatal influences are not limited to the time they occur but become part of the memory bank. For example, problems with the umbilical cord being wrapped around the neck at birth have been associated with later throat problems. He's also found unconscious birth memories being revealed in the content of dreams.

He even postulates why we may not consciously remember birth. Oxytocin, one of the physiological chemicals present at birth, promotes amnesia. On the other hand, the chemical known as ACTH enhances memory. This substance is released into the system in response to stress. Thus, the degree of memory or amnesia may simply be a question of which of these two substances predominated at the time.

Verney portrays the unborn child, especially in the last couple months of the pregnancy, as a feeling, responding, learning, remembering individual who already has a well-established relationship with its mother by the time of birth. I'm reminded here of Carl Jung's statement that the child lives in the unconscious of the parent.

HYPNOSIS AND PAST-LIFE THERAPY

It has been left to hypnosis and past-life therapy to provide sufficiently clear information that can be checked with hospital records and mothers' secret memories. Birth memories have been repeatedly shown to be more than fabrications, hallucinations, or the promptings of the therapist. David Cheek, a physician and hypnotherapist, and psychologist David Chamberlain have shown verifiably accurate accounts of such specifics as the mother's hair style, the obstetrical instruments used, conversations in the delivery room, the behavior of doctors and nurses, the mothers' emotional state, and similar factors.

The question is no longer whether there's any substance to these claims but how long various members of the research and therapeutic communities can continue to ignore them.

Past-life therapists using the Netherton Technique have also produced information that has been verified, such as attempts at abortion, parental discord, and birth difficulties.

PRENATAL PROGRAMMING AND EXPERIENCE

Prenatal and birth experiences leave each of us open to programming on two counts. First of all, the conscious ego has not yet formed sufficiently to provide adequate discrimination and judgment. In addition, the vulnerability of the fetus and newborn leaves them subject to any number of stresses, which adds a second degree of openness to programming and what goes on in these times of stress. Thus, such programming inclines us to accept or internalize behaviors, attitudes or beliefs from other people which we might not have consciously adopted if we had been more aware.

Birth is the gateway through which we all emerge into new individual life. Similarly, the prenatal and birth times are the gateway for the preparation of the body that is to receive the incoming entity. It is during that time that the two aspects of being—body and soul—experience the process of becoming united. When we consider karma, we must realize that its expression depends on appropriate physical and social factors. As will be more fully explained in Part III, the fetus, as a potential entity, must identify with some aspect of the life of its parents, which will be carried out psychologically in its own life.

JOANNE'S GUILT

One of my first clear encounters with prenatal memories came in the case of Joanne, a young woman who came to therapy because she was feeling guilty and ''responsible for everything"—including her parents' poor relationship and poor mental health. The full account of her regression experiences appear in Chapter 7, "The Unspeakable Thought."

We used the Netherton Technique to place her in the environment where she first felt that things were "all my fault." Joanne described herself as being in a "room" with soft walls that became smaller and smaller. When she described the feelings of pressure on her head, moving down from her crown to her forehead, which would have marked the beginning of the birth process, I moved her back in time to the source of the feeling that things were all her fault.

When asked about the phrase she had produced—"It's all your fault"—Joanne immediately heard the words being spoken in her father's voice. As she focused on that voice, the situation became clear. "It's my father," she said, "He's talking to my mother and it's about me. He's blaming her for the pregnancy, telling her 'It's all your fault.' "

The pregnancy was a stressful one for them all. Her mother used it to avoid marital relations with the father, which only worsened his antagonism toward the mother and consequently toward the unborn child. It was stressful for Joanne because she was aware of the conflict over her very existence and her alleged responsibility for their difficulty.

Anyone who deals with families in conflict knows that a child blaming itself for the difficulties of the parents is not an unusual event. It's not at all uncommon for children of divorcing or fighting parents to assume that it's their own fault. This is especially true when the child was conceived and carried with the hope of cementing, improving, saving, or compensating for an insecure marital bond.

In a manner of speaking, Joanne's existence was responsible for a great deal of difficulty. However, these difficulties did not begin with her. The parental problems had been going on long before her conception. She was a newcomer to an already problematic situation. Now, she had taken the first step toward releasing what had seemed to be an exaggerated sense of responsibility as she realized the way in which her father's accusations toward her mother acted as unconscious hypnotic programming while she was in the womb. The guilt, if there were any, belonged to her mother.

This case clearly demonstrates the effect of environmental discord and the manner in which ideas—because of predispositions set up in previous lives—are accepted by the unconscious of the fetus and carried around psychologically throughout life. How many programs are you carrying around right now that stem directly from the womb?

In this way the mechanism of carrying over past-life material is translated from the encoded previous context into the present linguistic, social, and cultural context. Things from other times and places are re-clothed in a more recognizable and up-to-date form.

Although one may view the fetus as the helpless victim in this drama, it must be remembered that the parents and their marital situation already existed prior to the entrance of the soul entity. That is to say, this soul personality apparently chose the situation and an environment that allowed her to play out and, we hope, resolve her issue with responsibility.

It's not really surprising that children come into this world filled with their parents' scripts and expectations. After all, people conceive and give birth to children for all manner of overt as well as secret motivations and intentions. Generally speaking, the situation in itself represents one of feeling incomplete. And so the remedy becomes the child who is born carrying these expectations and unrealized hopes.

On the one hand, children are conceived and born out of a set of needs of the parents. On the other hand, souls come into these bodies for needs of their own. Thus, if victimization does occur, it could be said to be happening on both sides. Each party uses the other to play out reciprocal or mutual needs—much like a dance between two partners.

This in no way reduces the responsibility of those who seek to intervene in cases of abuse, nor does it reduce the need for compassion for all suffering creatures—even if the suffering is of their own making.

The secret expectations of what the parent wants the child's life to be are transmitted initially in utero. What is often felt as a "cosmic purpose" may simply be the covertly transmitted expectations of the parent. On the other hand, the parentally conveyed message may be the preparation for such a cosmic purpose. The situation requires close examination to determine if the felt purpose of life is a worthy one or really meant to be transcended and left behind. A great deal of past-life work involves the process of discriminating between what is really ours and what has been imposed upon us from the outside.

MOTHER'S NEED FOR JUDY

Judy, a thirty-six-year-old woman, relived her prenatal and birth experience and could feel not only her father's rejection but also her mother's desire to not let go of the pregnancy. The pregnancy represented a safe refuge for the mother in her difficult relationship with her husband. When it came time for the birth, the mother's desire to not let go and the doctor's instruction to "Hold it," not to push down with her abdominal muscles until the cervix was sufficiently dilated, combined in a way that was not evident until Judy's next session, when the situation was relieved.

When she returned for a second regression, she reported that the constipation that had plagued her for some twenty years had suddenly disappeared. Apparently because of some internal predisposition, her mother's desire to not let go acted in conjunction with the doctor's suggestions to make Judy "hold it." Women who have been through conscious childbirth will recognize the similarity between some of the feelings of delivery and those of bowel functions. Judy's life-long tendency to hold herself back now had a context.

Not only was her constipation relieved, but she became aware of her unconscious program of self-rejection that had begun in the womb. This rejection was, again, of the father toward her mother, a situation in which Judy seemed to be an innocent bystander—although she was aware of having chosen to come into that pregnancy. Judy's unnecessary identification with her mother was released and her self-image began to improve as this block to receiving love was removed.

It's interesting to note how the unconscious mind can hear a command from the outside—the doctor's saying, "Hold it."—and have that, through her mother's experience of birth, become focused on Judy's bowels. It's this kind of identification and transfer that marks the potent elements of prenatal life and perinatal experience.

What follows are examples of the dramatic ways in which the prenatal experience influences us in sometimes surprising ways.

TERRY'S REDEMPTION OF MOTHER'S GUILT

Another example of a prenatal program was revealed in the case of a very bright research scientist. Terry was consciously aware of his feelings of "never being good enough" for his father, or so he thought; and he felt his mother was "intrusive." His current-life predicament was that of rebelliously failing to apply himself to his job. Our discussion aroused memories of his childhood feelings of wanting to rebel against the duties imposed upon him by his mother.

The regression found Terry in a prenatal period, reexperiencing his mother's fears and worries about her fetus's health and potential ability. "It's not my fault if it's not all right," she defensively thought to herself. Her ruminations about my client's normal development arose from two sources. Most immediately, she already felt herself to be a failure as a mother since her previous child had been born with a birth defect that resulted in death shortly after birth. Reassurances had done nothing to reduce the mother's worries or guilt.

The second source of her anxiety was an example of something that often occurs in pregnant women: the mother-to-be begins to recall, consciously or not, her own prenatal and birth experiences. In this particular instance, my client's mother had herself been an only child. Her birth was followed by miscarriages and an eventual hysterectomy. Thus, pregnancy-related anxieties had been transmitted from the grandmother to the mother. This anxiety was then reinforced by the birth of the defective child, which set up the combination of anxiety, approval needs, and self-doubt that was thrust upon the new fetus (my client) to somehow resolve.

The job that was assigned to Terry by his mother, and which he accepted by his entrance into that particular womb, was revealed in this part of his prenatal memory: "Mother goes to the doctor with her parents. She's afraid they won't love her if I'm not perfect." Thus, Terry was to redeem his mother's guilt. She felt guilty for being a disappointment to her own parents as well as for being a failure as a mother. Through Terry's perfection she would prove herself worthy of her parent's love and be absolved as a mother.

In this manner, the mother's self-doubts leading to her need to produce a perfect product was imposed in the womb upon this man who was still behaving as if his mother's worth depended on his job performance. Terry resented and resisted the imposition. Even his achievements belonged to his mother, not him.

The conscious realization of this imposed script and its relationship to his job prepared the way for Terry to reown the credit for his achievements. He no longer needed to resist the demands of the job as an act of rebellion against his mother's desperate expectations. His achievements could now be his, if he wished to have them. Terry would now be able to take the first steps toward releasing this program of unrealistic perfection that is self-defeating in anyone.

CASE STUDY: THE WEIGHT OF SHAME

Sarah had "lost and found the same twenty pounds" many times. When heavy, she felt discouraged and disgusted with herself, and concerned about her appearance. She wanted to promote spiritual living but was worried that her appearance might detract from her message. As she was an attractive woman her fears seemed rather unrealistic. Inquiry about her feelings regarding the extra weight revealed an uncomfortable self-consciousness. Without the weight Sarah felt free, full of energy, sexy, and happier with herself. However, when we focused on the discomfort and the heaviness, underlying feelings of shame emerged.

Knowing her history from our initial interview, I suggested that she go back to the time in her mother's womb when there were these feelings of shame, weight, and "wanting to run and hide." She had already described her mother to me as a "prude," although she knew that she'd been born before her parents were married. Her mother had always been very skinny, fashionable, and attractive.

She [my mother] was very fat at that time—very bloated. She was really concerned about the way she looked and couldn't wait to get rid of the baby. . . . I was very aware of the fact that my mother felt disgusted. . . . I was feeling her unhappiness at being unwieldy and uncomfortable.

Sarah's father had not been supportive, and her mother felt "she had to go it alone. I felt that way, too. I'm really alone." The things that her mother had planned for herself now had to be put off. She was embarrassed—"Now everybody's going to know." She knows she's "going to show and be too big." She tried to hide it at first but eventually planned to go away for a while. The early pain of shame later gave way to a tougher attitude as she decided to go on with her life in spite of the pregnancy. Psychologically, the pregnancy made Sarah's mother face her own dependency on her public image.

In the regression, we followed her experience through birth and into early childhood when she rediscovered the way her mother and grandmother played her against each other. We also rediscovered her own childhood feeling that her mother was too busy for Sarah to interrupt her. That is, Sarah carried the inhibition formed at the time when her mother felt the pregnancy was an interruption to her fashionable way of life.

So we see in Sarah's case how the mother's shame at "showing" her weight gain was imprinted on the unconscious fetal memory of my client. This imprint sought resolution by finding expression in Sarah's weight gains, which in turn allowed the surfacing of the imprinted shame. The release and resolution came in the recognition that the shame belonged to her mother and not to herself, and that the rejection she felt from her mother's wishing to "get rid of the baby" referred really to the pregnancy—the carried weight—and not to the baby.

It should be noted here once more that my client was predisposed to accept this program of weight gain and rejection. She might also have reacted with rebellion, negativity, or some other behavior pattern.

Only time will tell now if this realization will be sufficient to allow her to release the extra weight or if there are other past-life programs with admonitions against her being "free, full of energy, sexy, and happier."

CASE STUDY: THE PSYCHOLOGICAL BIRTH

A dramatic example of the profound effect of a prenatal experience and its related memories was provided by Bonnie. Intelligent, sensitive, and already prepared for the accessing of internal images by her previous work in "Guided Imagery and Music," she was able to turn her attention quickly and fully to the meaning of events as they transpired. It was in fact her Guided Imagery and Music coach who recognized recurring words in their work together. Her coach had worked with me before, and she suggested to Bonnie that past-life exploration might be helpful.

In the introductory discussion Bonnie talked of feeling that she had a "special mission" and that she often found herself "in service to a man, with a mission to him" that would prove her "mettle and strength in defending some cause of good." She said she tended to give over to men a lot of her own personal power in these "missions."

Bonnie's first regressive experience began with a situation in which she is set apart from others in a past life and given a special charge to carry out a particular responsibility of honor. She is given a small chest that is part of her charge. In that life she was to always "remember who you are . . . and what I expect of you." Bonnie says, "I'm his son and I'm part of a line of warriors who accomplish great things and who lead other people."

But the son enjoyed more worldly pleasures—especially eating. His stomach "stuck out like a stuffed ball" (or, I might add, like a pregnancy). He apparently failed in his quest.

This regression experience recalled to her mind a time in this life when, as a child, she was sent away to camp. She felt her attachment to her mother made her different from the other children there. There was also a parallel charge from her father who said he knew she could stay successfully at camp. But she herself felt there was something she had to watch over at home.

It will be more obvious that the charge to watch over something came both from that past life as well as the prenatal period. The job of "watching over" was left unfinished and unresolved from the previous failure.

The scene then changed into that of another life. Again as a male, my client is confronting a "steel-coated warrior" who has him backed against a wall and is gloating over his helplessness. But he lunges at his protagonist and kills him. In the discussion at the end of the session, a conflict was revealed between her own inner feelings of violence and of the struggle for her own independent life. Once more, regardless of the historical validity of the past-life experience, it is dynamic in the way it allows the inner psychodynamics of the person to emerge in a dramatic way.

Bonnie's second session, two weeks later, began with a discussion about her eighteen-month separation from her husband of fifteen years. In her ambivalence about whether to go back to him or to go on, she was plagued by thoughts of having babies. Talking about being away from her husband brought on a sadness that was not related to him but to her mother. "If I had a mother," she said, "I'd be all right." Bonnie ached for nurturance and gentleness, feeling that her mother had never hurt her feelings and had provided safety "before the world came in."

I began to move her into the regression by focusing on the impact of that attachment to her mother and her husband—and the loss of the attachment to her husband. She reported feeling frightened, starved, bereft, left empty and dying. As we moved into the imagery of the session by focusing on her statements and the emotional content, she could feel a sob rising in her chest that she tried to suppress.

She'd begun to be aware of her mother's ambivalence and oppression. The words that came to her were, "Let me out of here . . . out of your stomach. . . . I'm a prisoner here!" She described being in a crouched position and afraid to move. Her descriptive image was of "horrible huge fingers, pressing my body to try to squash it. Pressing on my shoulders, trying to crumple me up. Pressing me all around." This image graphically expressed not only her birth but also her mother's attitude toward her, as we shall see.

Bonnie's mother had her own feelings of being separate from others—she'd thought no one understood her. During her pregnancy, she envied other women and their graceful movement. Bonnie's mother's thoughts were "There is something different inside of me." This same set of thoughts occurred to Bonnie when she was left at camp.

Bonnie's earlier sense of mission became evident in her mother's thoughts at the discovery of the pregnancy. This baby was to be a remedy for the mother's feelings of isolation and sadness: "I'm going to have a baby that's going to love me and understand me. . . . That baby will save me."

At only a few weeks of age in the womb, Bonnie is already charged with saving her mother by repairing her unhappy life. Bonnie is rewarded by the happiness her mother already feels in expectation. Her mother's expectation was that "a baby is coming to be just like me and not like the others." When Bonnie's mother tells Bonnie's father of the pregnancy, "He expands his chest, pounds on it, and lets out a roar, saying, 'I hope it's a little boy.' But Bonnie's mother says to herself, 'No, it'll be a girl. This is my baby; you won't understand about this baby.' '' The mother is programming the situation and Bonnie to believe that no one will understand her.

This now-conscious experience brings up a realization for Bonnie. Figuratively, she describes her mother as ''. . . clutching at me in the womb. I feel her fingers enclosing me in her own spirit . . . I fear I'm not going to get out to my father. I'm a secret weapon and he doesn't realize it.'' The mother's secret thoughts are: ''None of the others are going to understand. . . . We'll keep each other alive. [Recall the child's need to return home from camp to watch over something.] We won't need anybody else at all.''

Coming up to the end of the pregnancy, labor brought increased physical pressure, which the fetus experienced as the mother hurting her. This experience is not necessary at birth, but was set up by the mind set of the two of them protecting each other. Now the mother seems to be abandoning the pact. The pressure at birth mobilized Bonnie's previously unconscious anger at the invasion of her own individuality by her mother's expectations.

Labor was also accompanied by the mother's screaming and rage, which was subsequently transferred to the fetus through her experience of: ''Lights, hands are rough, men who make noises. . . . Mother and I hurt, and there are men who are not paying attention. They don't care at all.''

A review of the birth brought to light the mother's experience of delivery as she's told to push because ''they say so. . . . They make all the rules. . . . They have all the power.'' Not wanting to be released from the safety of the mother's womb but finding it impossible to remain there, Bonnie feels unready, but: ''I have to. . . . She pushes at me and they're pulling at me. . . . I have to go out of control and surrender. . . . The next thing I know is, I'm out.'' Although she feared the invasion from her mother into her personality, the danger of the men who ''make all the rules . . . have all the power'' frightened her more.

And so this newborn's birth, rather than being an experience of release and new life, was imprinted with her mother's own feelings of helplessness. It represented a loss of control rather than the gaining of new freedom—a sense of having to surrender to the control of men who seem to be indifferent.

Her entrance into this world was also marked with feelings of exposure, which reflected back to the prenatal sharing of her mother's having felt guilty about the sexuality that resulted in the pregnancy. The pregnancy for the mother meant being exposed as indulgent. It was the mother's parents who'd induced that feeling of shame. Bonnie's grandfather was a fundamentalist minister.

The psychological dynamic here was for Bonnie to use her husband to replace the lost attachment to her mother, which had not really been given up unconsciously.

By the third session, more of the current-life dynamics emerged with the realization that her husband had always felt more like a mother to her. This explained her negative reaction to natural sexuality with the husband. There was a feeling of ''invasion'' about it—undoubtedly a reexperiencing of her mother's feelings about her father's sexuality, the physical invasion Bonnie had felt while in the womb, and, most important, her mother's invasion into her own destiny. Actually, this was a way to help her destiny emerge.

In the prenatal regression we traced the formation of Bonnie's feeling of invasion back to her mother's experience of being very, very pregnant and yet having the father's desires forced upon her. The mother didn't want anyone to touch her—she was trying to ''protect'' the unborn baby. She felt vulnerable. Her protectiveness also increased her assertion of, ''This is mine. . . . I'm going to try to keep it safe from you so you don't hurt it.''

This helped set the script for Bonnie to be fragile and to belong to her mother. The message that Bonnie received from it was, "You need me to take care of you." The mother's feeling was, "He shouldn't be there. He should wait until it's over—until delivery." This feeling about premature sexual activity carried right on through into Bonnie's marriage. She, too, had the attitude of, "having to put up with it; having no choice." In other words, the mother's helplessness was imprinted on the child, who was predisposed to receive it because of past-life experiences. Again, the scripting in prenatal life is as significant as that arising out of the past lives.

Bonnie's therapeutic separation from her mother began with the in-session realization that, "She only took care of me afterward when it was easy for her. . . . If she couldn't say no [to her father], I had to pay the price." Also with this double-consciousness review, Bonnie was able to realize the falsehood of her mother's "I'll take care of you" promise. It really was a plea: "You take care of me." Bonnie was thereby able to mobilize her own recognition of her separateness. Her new dynamic became, "You don't have the guts to stand up to him, to put me first; therefore I want to show you what should be done. . . . I will be the strength." Naturally, as she becomes the strength, men will no longer be a threat to her.

With this prenatal programming released, we were free to move back in time to the previous life, which had also contributed to the entire scenario. Bonnie found herself a woman inside the gates of a small wooden fortress that was being attacked by barbarians. She died there, feeling powerless and guilty since she was unable to take care of and protect her own children. She had feelings of sympathy toward the children as "poor little innocent things . . . nobody to protect them . . . innocent . . . left alone. . . . I couldn't do enough for them." In this life, she had taken their place in experience if not in equal intensity. This particular past-life event had clearly helped set the form for. how her scripting would be carried out in this life—a woman's helplessness in the face of male aggression and indifference, and an inability to protect the child.

We went back further in time to the "karmic event," which was the series of events and attitudes that had made it necessary for her to experience this helplessness. In that earliest of lives she was a "great smasher." She described herself as a **very** muscular man who was able to "smash" others in the head with just his fist "so they wouldn't come into my territory"—another invasion theme. She saw her/himself as very primitive. "You protect what you have. My home and wife and family got protected. I did my job well, and I died happy."

Thus, over the course of three regressions, she experienced the extremes of powerlessness and vulnerability versus tremendous personal power. When asked for the words that would release all of this unnecessary scripting, the spontaneous offering from her unconscious mind was, "I want to let it go . . . be balanced. I am strong. I can protect myself and those who are dear to myself. I am strong enough to not allow invasion. I can say 'No.' I have great power and can use **it** when I want to. It's all right that I have power. It's good power, clean power."

And so Bonnie **was** able to arrive at that position of choice where she was free from both the fear of others' exercise of power as well as of the previous guilt over its excessive use. She was now free to find her own balance, to be neither obsessively helpless nor compulsively aggressive.

This description of the regression more or less as it occurred in my office, shows a nonlinear process that appears disorganized because of the way we jumped back and forth in time from one life to another. Actually, however, the material is highly organized by the emotional and scripting content, which is recognized by advanced therapists as more important than chronological ordering.

It's the making of these trans-life connections that releases the trapped energy that has been experienced as fear, compulsion, or behavioral habits. This manner of operating also helps uncover conflicting or parallel programs that might otherwise be missed by a logical, linear approach.

In Bonnie's case, there existed side by side the dual and self-contradictory programs of protection by the mother as well as vulnerability to her invasiveness. This contradiction resulted in her turning in this life toward a man for protection and mothering, while also feeling that men were dangerous, and best when served.

In a chronological review, we first see the primitive karmic event of excessive power that led to the necessity to experience its opposite. We then see the formative events—the way power and powerlessness would become manifest—in the situation of being invaded. And we see the way in which she chose to resolve these issues by her choice of a mother who would recreate both conditions in a new life. In embracing it all with full consciousness, Bonnie was able to heal the split between her power and vulnerability.

"For the first time," she said, "I feel separate from my mother." Bonnie is an excellent example of how we may undergo a physical birth and physical separation from our mother, but not accomplish the same separation psychologically until many years later.

EXISTENCE VS. EXTENT

A word is due here to the skeptic who simply cannot believe that all these things could occur or that we could be conscious of them before birth. It's very true that most of the evidence for past lives is anecdotal. However, one verifiable connection will indicate that these things are possible and that they exist. Although, there are many such instances, it only takes one to establish a reality—the number of occurrences after that establishes the extent. Therefore, the only reasonable debate would be the degree to which such events occur in the general population.

True scientists will no doubt be interested in investigating the phenomenon. However, they may—as they often do—get lost in the degree of importance they're willing to attach to the phenomenon. That is to say, if their research shows that only five percent of all subjects display verifiable or useful memories, the tendency of science is to say that the phenomena is not "reliable" or is not "significant." Research findings often require a confidence level of 95 to 98 percent to show significance. I leave such questions to those who are more interested in debate and research than in the use of what obviously does exist.

For me, as I state many times, the overriding validity is a therapeutic one. These prenatal sessions tend to be some of the most powerful experiences in the life of the individual. One may debate about the reality of the prenatal period of consciousness, but there's no question about its impact.

PRENATAL LIFE AND KARMA

The basic structure that allows for the working out or expression of the karmic pattern for this life is laid down prenatally, as this is the time for the formation of the physical vehicle that must carry the karma. The prenatal time is a crystallization of the karmic pattern that will become manifest in the current life. The family is the psychological and social foundation for the expression of that part of the karmic pattern.

The recognition of the life and consciousness during the prenatal period is another step toward the recognition that life is a continuum. This recognition of the prenatal time helps to fill in one of the gaps that has deluded us into thinking that our lives are somehow separate.

AARON'S REJECTION

Aaron's case demonstrates the manner in which prenatal material may present itself unexpectedly. "Things just haven't come together for me," he said as I spoke with him on the phone. He elaborated this theme in my office in terms of both finances and relationships: As soon as something comes together, something comes to tear it apart. Not that life had really been all that bad for him. As he said, "I always knew what I wanted but never set goals. What I wanted would come anyway—but less than I had hoped."

Although things tended to work out for him, at least partially, he never considered himself ready to handle his good fortune—until now.

In this present life, he was born out of wedlock and reared by his grandmother. This undoubtedly contributed to his nagging feeling of having no roots. In relationships he described himself as a giver. "I give all of me—and attract takers." Yet when people tried to give to him, he was strangely disinterested. In a relationship there "has to be a challenge" he said, "or it's just too easy." But once he's in the relationship, restlessness sets in and he feels a need to get out. "It seems I've got to be working at getting what I want rather than enjoying what I have. After all, life is nothing but a challenge and a risk."

In order to induce his receptivity to the past-life images, I had him close his eyes as I reviewed his description of the kinds of feelings he had—of good fortune, restlessness, of life's being a challenge. In response, he said he now felt insecure, there was a feeling of anxiety in the pit of his stomach. He said his body felt "bound up, incarcerated, restricted.'' Moving in deeper, he felt himself wanting to run away. "I want to get away—but I can't."

He found himself in a past life bound to a chair, with bindings across his chest, legs, and mouth. The chair was cold and hard and he was at this point alone. They had left him there saying, "We'll teach him," but he couldn't figure out what he'd done to deserve this treatment. "I'm petrified. I just want to leave."

Having elicited the past-life location of his present emotional condition, I began to expand the context in order to see what was going on. I asked him to go back further in memory to the first time he had come under "their" control. He began shaking in my office chair and tears ran down his cheeks as he said, "I don't know why they chose me. I didn't do anything. They just walk up and say 'we'll take him.' "

When they came, he was sitting, daydreaming on a porch on a hot, muggy day. These men who came were foul-smelling and ugly. "They're white and I'm black." He sees anger in their eyes, but says, "I've done nothing to them." They take him away with everyone simply watching, which suggests to him that nobody cares for him at all. He is terrified.

They threaten him some more with the ominous "We'll teach him." To him it's all incomprehensible. "I don't understand it. I don't cry. I have fear but no tears. I'm just a boy. I don't understand why they're taking me. And I don't understand why no one comes forth."

Aaron is petrified beyond tears as they walk him into an old barn and close the door. All the time they're tying him to the chair and threatening him, he's consumed with the question, Why? "I don't know why. I can't understand why. Why me? What did I do?" It all becomes too much for him and he decides not to be there. "I'll show them. I won't be here."

I didn't understand what Aaron meant or how he was

going to suddenly "not be there" when the men returned. He explained: "I leave, not physically. I see myself sitting in the chair but I'm not there." It seems he's been literally frightened to death and died in the chair. "I'm above everything when they come back. They see I'm dead and they're angry. They take the chair and body and toss them around. I've defeated them. I'm stronger than they are. I feel good."

At this point the regression took an unexpected but profitable turn when I asked for more of what that life was like. I meant to have him review the past life he'd just recounted. Aaron's unconscious mind, however, took this to mean his current life, and he began to review his feelings of worthlessness and anger, experiences of contention in his family, his lack of friends and feelings of rejection. Other children taunted him for being different—"You don't know who your daddy is. You don't know who you are." Aaron began to cry once more because, as he said, "Nobody cares. I just want to feel accepted like everybody else." He made the decision then to try to be like the other kids; but inside, he said, "I don't feel like I belong to anybody, anything."

Still thinking we were reliving a past life, I instructed him to move into the womb to find out what his mother was like when she was carrying him. He described her as "rebellious" and doing things her mother tells her not to do—one of which was sexual activity.

We went through some events and descriptions that led us eventually to the death of his grandmother. The date was clearly in this life; I could no longer mistake his accounting to be anything other than the present life.

Aaron's mother also did not feel good about herself. She shared his feelings of rejection and feared ridicule at being discovered to be pregnant. She bound her stomach in order to hide the pregnancy, which of course Aaron inside felt as even more confining than normally occurs in utero.

Nevertheless, the pregnancy became evident, but still she denied it. "I can't believe it," he says. "She doesn't want me. Maybe I should go back."

There are always those core feelings we share with our mothers on a very instinctual level. For Aaron, this was the combination of feeling rejected and the desire to be loved. His mother obviously didn't want the pregnancy but was confused about what she did want. As he said, "Because she's confused, I'm confused." When we reached into his perception of her deeper mind, he found, in spite of his anger at her, that what she wanted most of all was love. What she received instead was rejection.

His mother's love making was both an act of defiance against her parents and an attempt to reach out for love in the only way she knew how.

In the womb, Aaron was faced with a similar situation of being bound and desperately wanting freedom in the face of the restrictions on him and her rejection of him. In the womb he was tense, unable to relax, and desirous of freedom.

Birth for him was intensely frightening. He was aware of the anxiety of those around him about how they were going to feed another mouth. Sniffling, Aaron says again, "Nobody wants me—maybe I should just go back." But since he cannot go back he makes a decision: "I'll show them; I'll be better." Of course, this determination to regain a sense of self-worth by "being better" was a substitute for what he really wanted—"to be accepted and loved." Once more he choked up.

His grandmother who took care of him "always encouraged me. She told me I was different, that I could do better than the others. My grandmother was the most important one in my life, and I've always wanted to give her what she deserved [she died nearly a decade ago]."

Once again we see the major themes emerging in the

prenatal and past-life accounts. When faced with a restrictive situation, Aaron's instinct—actually conditioning from these limited-option past-life events—was to seek escape. Hence, freedom became the major value of survival as well as validation of his self-worth. And yet this drive for freedom has not allowed for adequate intimacy. His resolution, reinforced by his grandmother's admonition that he was different, that he could be better, was always to strive for more, never to rest with what he had.

Being different was clearly a double-edged sword; an attempt to regain lost esteem that also kept him apart from others. For him, victory and power came through the act of leaving—even if that meant death.

Aaron had planned to return for further past-life work since he already felt some relief of his poor self-image. Work demands, however, took him to another part of the country. He called to say how much he appreciated the session in making the first step toward realizing that he need not remain on an endless treadmill of unsuccessful achievement but could begin receiving the acceptance and love available to him.

Aaron's case demonstrates how past-life events, and prenatal and birth situations reinforce one another. These connections are what tie past-life events to the present.

It seems ironic that the love that Aaron's mother didn't feel from her mother was to be later bestowed on the product of her act of defiance—her expression of the need for love. What his mother was never given, Aaron elicited from the grandmother.

TWO KINDS OF MEMORY—TWO SETS OF PARENTS

In the work done by Netherton and others, one can explore the moments from conception through birth in the fetal state. Some traditions, however, insist that the soul does not enter the body until much later, or during the birth, or even shortly afterward. One client, for reasons unknown even to himself, insisted that he entered at five month's gestation. Yet he too had memories that went back beyond that time.

This has led me to postulate that there are two sets or processes or repositories of memories. One is the soul's memories with which people become familiar when dealing with metaphysical subjects. The other might be called "cellular memory" in that it resides in the cells of the body. In that sense, the body remembers even if the soul has not arrived yet. Through the ensuing process of identification with the body, the soul-entity takes on the memories of the body that it has essentially formed in its image. That is, the soul takes on the body's memories.

Adopted children are those entities who, for their own particular karmic needs, require the genetic and prenatal experiences of one set of parents or circumstances, as well as the family environment and influence of another set. The child may psychologically focus on either the rejection by the biological mother or the acceptance by the adoptive parents. Karma and past-life experience will tip the scales toward one or the other.

CHAPTER 5

THE PHYSICAL BODY: MIRROR TO THE SOUL

AMONG THE PATTERNS IN OUR LIVES ARE THOSE OF THE structure and function of our physical bodies. We recognize other people through patterns of speech, expression, facial and postural configurations. We refer to that composite of various patterns as the identity of the person.

In everyday life we recognize certain correlations between emotions or attitudes and their physical expression. Facial expressions are the most obvious example. Anger, for instance, causes muscular and structural reactions that act as signals to other people that the person is angry. The same thing happens with happiness or joy or other feelings. A sad person clearly doesn't look the same as someone who's feeling on top of the world. Unless we're looking for a fight, we tend to use such signals to avoid people in unpleasant moods and to seek out those who buoy us up.

Facial expressions are so familiar, they're taken for granted. A somewhat more subtle level is that known as "body language." Body language acts in similar ways as facial expressions to show feelings, emotions, or attitudes. Dance and movement therapists specialize in the knowledge, interpretation, and treatment of a person's movement and use of space around the body. We all recognize, simply by observing someone's posture, whether that person is feeling dejected, proud, relaxed, or anxious.

Persistent physical or behavioral attitudes cause the body to take on the characteristic configuration of that attitude. And so people develop their own particular tight spots in their muscles and even certain skeletal deformities. This is a clear example of "mind over matter."

Interestingly, this can work in the reverse. A person who consciously assumes a dejected posture will generally have some sense of the emotion of dejection that goes along with it. Or someone who wants to put on an air of confidence and optimism can assume the movements and postures of those emotions and have some real, if temporary, sense of what it would be like to feel that way. This simple fact is what makes the great array of physical activities—exercise, sports, massage, body work—therapeutic. They all give us feelings of vigor, vitality, and mastery. They may not lead to a deep-level change of the psychodynamics that led to the original need, but they may give sufficient confidence and new experiences to counterbalance that need.

Most of the patients seen by physicians are suffering from what are known as psychosomatic disorders. Such problems include ulcers, headaches, muscle tightness, high blood pressure, vision problems, poor circulation, and reduced immunity to disease—all of which are recognized as stress related. Each of these disorders is part of a maladaptive response to internal or external stress.

The complex interplay among the emotions, glands, and hormones, and all of their effects, can lead to surprising manifestations. It has been shown that the menstrual cycles of women in dormitories tend to synchronize. A man's testosterone level tends to peak about seven days after his partner ovulates. In psychosocial dwarfism, children under a great deal of stress will fail to grow. However, when they're removed from the stressful situation and placed in foster homes, they resume normal physical and (sometimes) intellectual growth.

This mind–body connection is especially evident in past-life therapy. Most physiological events are shown to have not only a biological history but also a psychological history whose roots may extend well into the past. Their manifestation may be direct or indirect.

In the following examples of direct manifestation, the correlation between the past-life events and current physical problems happened to be recognized only after the regression. That is to say, the individuals came for a particular problem or out of curiosity and then discovered the parallel between an event in the regression and the area of life mentioned.

DARLENE'S TREMBLING, REJECTION, AND SEIZURES

This story comes from one of a number of sessions with Darlene. This particular session was to deal with parental criticism that seemed unfair and judgmental because she was held responsible for deeds done by her siblings. She had telephoned me the night before this session. She was very upset, crying and saying that she was shaking uncontrollably.

The emerging images of the regression showed that she'd been accused of malevolent actions in a past life because of her "evil look." As the session deepened, Darlene found herself at times shaking and unable to control her limbs. She was trembling visibly in the recliner.

As it turned out, she'd been an epileptic in that past life and the townsfolk thought she was possessed by demons. When other children were kidnapped by bandits and held for ransom, the fact that she was left behind was taken by the villagers as evidence that she was responsible for the tragedy. What they failed to realize, of course, was that she'd been rejected by the bandits for the same reason she was being shunned by her own clan. She was eventually executed as "a she-devil, daughter of demons."

At the end of the session Darlene reported that, as a teenager, she would become so upset at her father's accusations of wrongdoing that she would begin shaking and black out. After a number of these incidents, she was sent away to school. The blackouts subsided, but the shaking response to parent-induced stress continued—until this session.

The way she'd been treated in her past life had set her up to be sensitive to unjustified criticism, and when conditions were strong, to recreate the shaking and loss of consciousness in this present life.

Darlene's parents' anger was a perfect trigger for her unconscious memory of epileptic rejection since she often felt unjustly criticized by them. Because of its unconscious connection with this complex, the memory led to the expression of the seizure—the shaking and blackouts. Indeed, we see how she was rejected and sent away to school in this life.

Such patterns often arise in an unfortunate incident in a past life where, because of their traumatic nature or some unfinished aspect, they carry over into the present. Then, like Darlene, we become subject to unexplained reactions that seem strange in the context of the present. On identification and reflection, however, the reactions not only become understandable by virtue of the past-life context, but also are often freed from the necessity to intrude into the present.

TO BECOME A MAN

Jacob had undergone a previous regression in which, as a ruler, his people had believed him to be immortal because of his legendary prowess. He had felt overrated but constrained to maintain the image of proud invincibility. He brought to this session his concern about his compulsive desire to smoke. Discussion showed the smoking to be tied up with ideas of defying death. He cited the following past-life experience:

He is born the son of an embittered and disabled Indian warrior. This once-great warrior is both honored for his past and pitied for his infirmity. The father's bitter negativity and criticism arouse the young Indian's own doubt and fear of not being worthy. [In this past life Jacob is underrated.] Others, like the chief named White Hawk, encourage him and provide an increasing sense of self-worth. He constantly feels the need to do his best.

In his desire to be a warrior, the final test is assigned to him: to overcome his own fear of death. He goes off alone to prepare for the test in meditative prayer. This is to help him concentrate his attention and energy. He is afraid, of course, but not to endure means disgrace [as well as giving in to his father's negative opinion of him].

His test is to enter a cave from which not everyone in the past has returned. He enters the cave with a torch. The cave eventually opens up into a large room after he crawls through a narrow passageway with his torch. He then has to climb down a cliff. About to lose his grip, he lets the torch fall, which leaves him suspended in total darkness on the face of the subterranean cliff. He tries to keep going but slips and falls, losing consciousness. When he regains consciousness he can feel the skeletons of those who have been there before him.

He makes many attempts to climb out. Finally, mustering his strength and concentration, he scales the wall. It's not until he's made it completely out of the cave that he realizes he's actually survived.

Meanwhile, the ceremony to honor those who've passed the tests has already been held. Therefore, he's later allowed to sit in a circle of men where he is named "Brown-Bear-Claws," for clawing his way up the cliff. The sacred pipe, smoked as he says, "by men and true warriors who've proven themselves in battle and who are worthy to protect this tribe," is handed to him by

White Hawk. After puffing on the pipe, the symbol of passing the test, he at last realizes that indeed he is no longer afraid. He let's out a yell indicating his realization that, "I am a man!"

Through this experience—in addition to the sacred meaning of smoke for many Native Americans—the particular timing of Jacob's realization, that he had not only survived but has attained the status of manhood, brought the strong association or imprinting in his mind of the connection between tobacco and manhood, competence, and overcoming the threat and fear of death.

Jacob's desire to smoke was not relieved by this regression. Other sessions indicated that additional factors were involved, such as a conflict between emotion and intellect, and an inner doubt about whether he deserved to be successful. However, a change in Jacob's circumstances (divorce and new partnership) brought about the support which did, indeed, help him to quit smoking. Still later, he became part of a small group engaging in occasional Native American pipe ceremonies and viewed this to be the return of smoking to its proper place in his life.

SHOULDERING THE WEIGHT OF RESPONSIBILITY

Marcia's first regression found her as a male. He was a child who was being given the mantle of rulership after his father died. Deprived then of play, fun, and affectionate touch, he was acutely aware of the literal weight of responsibility as a purple toga was placed on him with the words: "You have no choice—this is your destiny."

His basic conflict arose from being a figurehead who had control over others' lives but not over his own. His robe weighed heavily on his left shoulder. Only much later in that life did he gain the courage and determination to take charge of his authority and challenge the power of the advisors who had long ruled him.

A second regression, undertaken to seek the source of other concerns, revealed a situation in which Marcia, as a female this time, was part of a harem. Trying to escape, she was forcibly restrained. In the process, her arm was wrenched, bringing an incapacitating pain to her left shoulder. Her shoulder, she later informed me, was sore for two days after the regression.

The memories of the first regression represented a life reflecting not only the exercise of power but also a great deal of emptiness in terms of personal expression because of social limitations. This is an example of a situation where power is so structured that the individual personality wielding that power feels helpless to express its own individuality without upsetting, if not disastrous, social consequences.

In these lives, the emphasis placed on the left shoulder revealed its symbolic importance in expressing Marcia's reaction to unsought weight and restriction from responsibility in the first regression, and the incapacitation of being caught in the harem's restrictive social structure in the second.

These meanings were expressed physically in this life through the polio she suffered at age nine—affecting her left shoulder. Through these regressions, she gained insight into the past-life cause of some of her present-day concerns.

CASE STUDY: THE COLLAPSE OF A RELATIONSHIP

Angelina is a young woman who came to me because of relationship difficulties. Her regression was not typical. Past-life information for her came in rather disjointed phrases. However, an examination of these pieces of information revealed the following scenario:

Angelina was also a woman in her regression. She was involved in an important relationship that had reached a crisis. The man with whom she was involved had been given false information about Angelina. He was enraged at what he'd been told, and she was hurt that he could believe that she'd had anything to do with whatever it was.

Apparently, he was being falsely accused with information that had been erroneously attributed to Angelina. The accusation against him was as false as his against her. In the ensuing argument, she was stabbed in the right side. Her hope, care, and protection of her "friend" collapsed into disillusionment and death.

The pattern of dangerous and unstable relationships is obvious. But the influence of this past-life experience had dramatic physical effects in this present life. Her relationship difficulties were about to culminate in the finalization of her divorce. On the day she was to sign the papers, her right lung unexplainably collapsed.

A QUESTION OF CAUSALITY

One could hypothesize that Angelina's or Marcia's current-life difficulties and attitudes, by a process of association of ideas, produced the images they experienced as memories. That is to say, one might argue that the current situation might have caused the thematically related "fantasy." Such an explanation, however, is grossly deficient in its inability to explain among other things how the production of such fantasies resulted in a change in their emotional or physical condition. Even though alternative explanations for the effectiveness of the technique are possible (see Part III, "Technically Speaking"), they're rather weak, amounting to suggestibility as well as an imaginary inner world that is peopled with what we also see outside of us. More questions are raised by such an explanation than are answered.

The above examples show how past-life events had results that were in some way identifiably related to the current life. The cases related epilepsy with shaking; a stabbing with a collapsed lung; a shoulder injury and restriction with polio.

There is, however, another class of manifestations that are more indirect. Their relationship with the past lives is less obvious. Indirect manifestations connect not with the obvious form from the previous lives but rather with its overall life impact. For example, although we would expect a back problem to be related to a back injury in a previous life, the actual physical condition may not be as important as its *effect*. This case of a young woman may be instructive.

Theresa's current–life concerns about her back were eventually overshadowed by what the back problem had created, or what she had created using the problem: reduced social mobility, self-consciousness, and underlying them all, the question of whether she deserved to have happiness or relief. Her slipped disk was getting progressively worse and she was having to curtail some of her previous activities such as camping and jogging. She was also forced to face painful psychological realities such as having to depend on other people more, and anxiety over being less acceptible to others if she were less active or wore her back brace.

The regressions certainly didn't change the defective physiological structure that had caused Theresa's physical difficulty. However, they did shed light on her feelings that surrounded what she was doing with that problem and how she was using it to bring to light questions about her general self-worth.

Because of the back problem, she'd had to consider such issues as: suffering through it—out of virtue; trying to correct it herself as a display of self-reliance; placing herself in the hands of someone else for medical treatment as a display of trust; or simply accepting her limitations and turning her mind to other pursuits. These were the concerns that brought Theresa to me.

PAIN AS PROOF OF EXISTENCE AND SELF-WORTH

Although the structural defect had always been there, it did not present itself as a real difficulty or interfere with Theresa's activity until she had relationship difficulties. Thoughtful and intellectual, she had already spent useful time recognizing that her problem required her to face the myths she believed about herself concerning the limits of self-reliance and her need for a certain social image. "Until my back is free," she said, "I'm in a cage." She had tried many self-help remedies, a back brace, and other therapies. Now, she was running out of options but fearful of going under the surgeon's knife. She could move neither forward nor back.

Theresa's fairly long series of eleven sessions are summarized here to show the main themes that emerged:

The first seven sessions brought to light Theresa's belief that suffering was proof of her virtue and respectability. Attached to this belief was the fear of expressing anger. To her, anger meant the loss of love and safety. Aggression was therefore to be avoided at all costs [including the aggressive invasion of the surgeon's knife.]

As her self-acceptance increased over the sessions, Theresa was able to envision a worthwhile existence that didn't have to depend on pain and struggle. She could find worth and virtue through other means. In addition, anger became less frightening to her.

The eighth session brought to light a new issue. Theresa recognized in herself a desire for freedom. Pain had now become a restriction rather than a badge of courage and virtue.

A prenatal regression in session nine revealed the source of much of her feelings of vulnerability. The pregnancy was "too soon." Her parents were not yet

ready for children. Theresa sensed herself pleading in
the womb, "Let me live—I'll be good. Please let me
stay. I'll be good."

Another lifetime accessed during that session was one
of a half-breed in early America. She was a male then
and his very birth as a "half-breed" was shameful to
both races. That lifetime of shame and rejection again
raised the question of her self-worth and whether or not
she deserved to be well.

When Theresa returned for her eleventh session, she
said she'd had feelings during the week of being deserving, as well as feeling open and vulnerable. "I'm
not ready to feel that good," she said. Once more we
were faced with the question of how good she deserved
to feel.

In her last regression she relived a life in which she
was involved in a relationship with a man. She was
unjustly accused of and blamed for taking his love away
from his wife. The social mores of the time could only
see her as wrong and evil. People failed to appreciate
what she was doing for the man.

His love for his wife had been lost long before he'd
met Theresa because of the way they'd treated each
other. The failings of the wife were ignored and only
the "affair" was considered important.

Theresa had a son as the result of their liaison. In the
end, he had to reject her and the child he desired. Theresa and their son lived an ostracized, condemned life.

When Theresa reviewed the incidents in the regression, she was able to see more objectively:

1) The suffering of the others had existed before her
   involvement;
2) The additional suffering that came of her actions;
3) The injustice of their actions against her;
4) That she had "paid enough" for what she had done;
5) That she'd taught the others an important lesson of
   love, sacrifice, and giving.

Theresa looked at me tearfully and said at last, "I deserve that love." Her previously poor self-regard, combined with the unconscious idea that pain was a sign of

virtue and courage, placed Theresa in a situation in which she would suffer through unnecessary pain. By shouldering the responsibility herself, she avoided the treatment that might have brought relief.

Eventually, she sought that treatment and began a new way of living, which allowed greater focus on the pleasures of life, as well as her deserving the love and care of others.

CASE STUDY: YOU DON'T BELONG HERE: SALLY'S REJECTION

"It's like I'm not supposed to have health—I'm not supposed to exist," Sally complained, referring to her allergies and addictions. "I spent my first 30 years not really here," she said. And yet she talked of a fear of "not existing," and that if she didn't drink coffee in great quantities she wouldn't "be awake, ever."

Sally felt that her problems were telling her, "You're not supposed to be here." I recognized this as a programmed belief and script that was helping to create her difficulties. Using that phrase as a focal point, she regressed to a Native American lifetime. Part of the life she had accessed before while doing guided imagery, but the events revealed by the regression explained what made it so important:

Her name was Laughing Rock. She was a young Indian girl who was in preparation for a rite of passage for womanhood. She had already spent some time alone in the woods and was now in a tent being dressed by some of the women. She described some of the designs on the tent. They were primarily circular, some blue, some reddish, but mostly earth tones.

Suddenly the sounds of horses' hooves and screaming tore through the air. She ran out of the tent and saw cavalry soldiers coming to drive them out. [A message of, "You don't belong here."]

She was attacked by two soldiers on horseback. One

hit her in the back of the head with a rifle. They spun
her between the horses. She died filled with her anger.
When I asked what kept this traumatic event alive for
her, she replied, "I'm too angry to leave."

In addition, as sometimes happens to people who die
suddenly or unexpectedly, she didn't realize that she no
longer belonged to this physical world. Laughing Rock's
disorientation and her attachment to her rage attracted
her to the last places where she had experienced life.
Her spirit wandered in the vicinity of what remained of
the Indian camp and the place in the woods where she
had been preparing for her new status.

By returning in this way she had inadvertently become a haunting ghost. The surviving tribespeople were
disturbed by her ghostly presence and undertook to send
her on. She realized then that even her own people didn't
want her there.

They formed a circle around her belongings and
burned something. They chanted and moved their hands,
repeating over and over, "You don't belong here. You
don't belong here." They called for someone else from
the other side to come and get her.

Sally's life as a Native American was full of incomple-
tions, including the aborted recognition of womanhood, the
rejection of her tribe's right to be in their encampment by
the cavalry, the rejection of her humanity by the soldiers,
and the final rejection by her tribesmen when they sent her
on. Of course, it was also her predisposition to perceive
these events as rejections rather than looking at them as a
release.

This pattern of self-rejection and not belonging continued into this life. And it manifested indirectly in her addictions and the self-rejection that is inherent in allergies.
The connection between the events in the previous life and
her symptomatic behavior in this life was through the impact of the sense of not belonging. Thus, her allergies re-
created her feelings of not belonging to this world.

Sally's addictive behavior was reduced from cocaine to

coffee after the regression. Although this gave her some relief, it was still a symptom substitution, which indicated to me that at least part of the basic issue had not been totally resolved. However, she didn't continue her sessions through the resolution of the residual coffee habit or the allergies. Therefore, the long-term effect of her regression cannot be assessed.

CAST STUDY: COUGHING UP GUILT AND ANGER

Beth was a young-looking forty-seven-year-old woman. She complained of a chronic cough that had been diagnosed as post-nasal drip. She constantly felt as though she were going to choke. By focusing on the sensations in her throat and the emerging emotion that came, she felt her face become increasingly hot. The emotion that came was anger. Eventually she felt numb but still hot. These sensations released to her conscious mind the memory of sitting in front of a fire that was about to go out of control.

"I can't get away from it," she said, as she felt the air become hot and dry. "My arms are hot, but my legs don't seem to have any feeling. When I try to breathe, the air is so hot. . . . It's so hot I can't even scream."

Moving further back in time to the earlier parts of that life, Beth found herself in the prenatal period of a previous life about to be born to a woman who had long awaited the event. Her mother, never healthy, died during the birth. Beth absorbed the grief felt by the others in the form of guilt.

This newborn, separated now from the mother with whom she had established the usual prenatal relationship, fell to the care of other members of the family. She grew up feeling herself to be a burden—a feeling fueled by her grandmother's comments and intensified by her own guilt. She felt they only took minimal care of her because they had to.

Her anger was squelched by the "oppressive air" in

her environment. "I was so angry I couldn't say anything. I wanted to run away. But they had loved my
mother, and they were sad she died."

The situation was intensified by a fall that left her
crippled. This further increased her sense of being a
burden and made the expression of her own grief and
anger even more difficult.

So she ends up alone, facing a fire out of control—
and unable to move away. "I feel the heat, but I don't
get burned. I just can't breathe. . . . I gasp for breath
and it feels like choking at first. . . . I'm afraid. But it
doesn't last very long." Her body gets heavier feeling
and then, "I feel like flying, light."

The therapeutic work came in the deeper examination of
Beth's regression experience, which showed the guilt—self-
blame—for her mother's death to be unwarranted. The grief
of the others, which she had internalized, could be let go.
She felt lighter.

The completion was effected by the additional realization
that in the pregnancy she had already brought her mother
the happiness she wished for. "I made her happy at that
point. I was loved." The incomplete elements in that life
had been the desire to have someone really care for her
and to feel that she had made someone happy. She unconsciously tried to do both during that life by being a "good
girl"—trying to please—and by becoming crippled—forc-
ing someone to care for her. But it had been the maternal
feelings that she'd needed—and finally received in the regression session.

The regression had more than psychological or symbolic
significance. Beth's coughing was immediately reduced by
80 to 85 percent she reported to me later. Others also noticed the absence of the coughing. The unresolved issues
and suppressed emotion became focused in her throat when
she suffocated by the fire. That is to say, Beth's past-life
disappointment, anger, and rejection were, quite literally,
caught in her throat. This emotional complex then became

associated with coughing when the suffocating air burned her throat as she died. Her coughing in the present was her unconscious trying to ''cough up'' and thereby release the guilt, anger, and rejection.

In addition, by reviewing that lifetime, Beth was able to transcend the negative program of rejection that she absorbed from her caretakers and realize the love that she received in the womb from her mother.

We see in this regression account, that it isn't always negative scripts and programs that are lost in the unconscious mind. In Beth's case, it was the love from her mother that also needed to be accessed.

THE PHYSICAL SYMPTOM

The physical symptom has the function of a dream image. Something from another world or time, or from the unconscious, is represented by what is more immediately available. The emerging symbol both points to as well as distracts from otherwise unconscious material.

We have the choice of looking at the symbol alone, or examining what it's pointing to, or both.

Through these examples we can see how past lives live through us—sometimes using our very bodies to attempt to express and resolve some dilemma, conflict, or incomplete action.

CHAPTER 6

RELATIONSHIP PATTERNS

Relationships are some of the most rewarding and most trying tasks we have in life. Sometimes it's the hardest work we do. And as we relate to various people, we find ourselves behaving in unpredictable and unexpected ways. Many times we have reactions to others that seem to come "out of the blue." Or we accept unpleasantness we don't deserve. There are times when we may recognize a similarity between an acquaintance and a parent, for example, that provokes those inner feelings we thought we'd forgotten and left behind in childhood. However, there's a very logical reason why those seemingly inappropriate feelings are there in the first place. There's a reason why our parents brought out those particular feelings in us.

Patterns in relationships may take shape through repeated situations. Haven't you found yourself in the same situation over and over again? It may be an attraction or fascination for someone; or you may be repelled by someone for no real reason. There may be an interest in being around people who have certain physical features such as dark eyes or a strong body. Note in Chapter 12,

"Freedom Through Work" how the Southern Baptist Maria was attracted to dark-haired, dark-eyed men, to Jewish friends; how she was uncomfortable with the blond-haired, blue-eyed Aryan ideal that she herself typified.

The pattern becomes clear when you maintain the same interaction or stay attracted to the same people. Research by psychologist Helen Wambach, shows that 87% of her responsive subjects reported having known people now who were also known to them in past lives. Thus, we find those peculiar partnerships in which one acts more like a mother than a lover or spouse. Or when it's "love at first sight." Or that feeling of meeting someone for the first time and "knowing all about them"—knowing just what they're going to say—a sort of déjà vu in relationships.

These patterns also color our roles within relationships. There's the woman who tends to mother everyone; the man who fathers or protects or takes responsibility for everyone; or the individual who always seems so young and childlike; or the executive who seems to think he should have absolute power; or the woman who thinks every other woman is out to get her man.

There are times, of course, when each of these roles might fit perfectly well. When someone is after your man it's not necessarily the time to simply consider it a "pattern." It may be time to act—and then wonder why it happened to you. These, and indeed all, roles can be taken off and put on as needed. The problems arise when we're stuck in some role even though it might be more rewarding or effective to adopt another one. It's like having one set of clothes to wear for all situations—from gardening to washing the car, to a formal dinner, to a job interview.

Take a look at your feelings and ways of looking at people. How many roles do you play? How many don't really fit the situation? Which ones do you carry on even though they don't get you what you want?

CHRISTINE'S IDEAL

Christine had separated from her husband the year before she came to me for help. It was a marriage marred by discord: her husband was occasionally physically abusive, he used drugs, and was unfaithful. Yet, when the marriage ended, Christine felt the "loss of an ideal." Even though the real outer conditions were unpleasant for her, she still felt inside that some pure and idealistic something had been lost. She was also concerned about "not feeling," or about being unresponsive. Someone could say something to her or address an emotional issue with her and she would simply not respond—she would almost go blank or change the subject.

Christine also found herself wanting to contact a man she'd not seen since her teenage years even though she was falling in love with someone else. In a regression that she undertook to address other issues, the source of the attachment to this old relationship was also discovered. As we focused on all of these feelings she found herself in a place . . .

. . . underground. I can see cells, barred-off areas and straw on the floor. There is a tunnel that's dark. We can see only by torchlight. It's all carved stone, like the bottom of a castle. There's someone on the stairs below the torch to my right. His dress is mesh—a fabric. It's what you'd wear under armor. . . . He's hooded like a guard.

There's a man with me, pulling me to embrace me, and not wanting to let me go. The embrace feels almost like a protection, and he's saying, "Let me keep you safe. . . . Stay with me." I reply, "I can't. I want to go." But he says, "It's dangerous out there." He loves me and wants me with him but I can't stay. I won't stay. My love is for another. I tell him I don't love him, I love another.

He waves his arm, gesturing to the other man under the torch as if to say "away with you." He didn't like him hearing what was going on. My suitor says he'll protect me and keep me safe. "Don't be a fool by going out there to him. He's only a jouster while I'm a knight. I will have prestige and you can be a lady of recognition rather than a simple worker around the castle."

Christine resists this knight's advances. Later, she goes on to join the ladies at a festive occasion.

My hair is long, wavy, and light brown or dirty blonde. I like the clothes, the feel. They're fitted to the waist and then are very full. It feels good to walk, like being carried by the clothes. There's a flow to walking.

The ladies stand and watch these tournaments outside on the lawn. They wear very long, sort of see-through scarves. The women are rather giggly and silly [Christine herself laughs].

Suddenly everything I was looking at stopped. It was frozen. There was a jousting accident. I didn't know it until it was over. He was already dead. I didn't even know it had happened because it wasn't scheduled. The knight has killed my love—legally, I guess. He did it by running him through with a lance. It was supposed to be a practice, but it wasn't scheduled. It wasn't supposed to happen. The knight made it look like a lark, a casual challenge; but it wasn't.

And there was my love lying on the ground—no words, no good-bye. There won't be any spring. [I asked, "How does that event change her life?"] I just wanted the smiles and the laughter and the light. [Christine began to cry.] The night is dark and there's nothing between that and being an old woman.

The knight is standing there, holding his headpiece under his arm saying it was an accident, they were just practicing. But if they were just practicing I knew there should have been precautions. They didn't practice with the same lance they would use to fight. They didn't look much different except for the tip. The knight's had been stuck in the ground and broken so you couldn't see the end. He didn't use the practice lance, and no one else will know.

I didn't have any reason to suspect that my love was

in danger. If I'd known I could have said something. It
might not have happened [She continues to cry]. There's
nowhere to go with the truth; nowhere to go with the
love either. No one would believe a woman's word
against a knight's.

This preceding part of the regression was obviously related to the feelings of sadness and the loss of the ideal
that we had originally begun to explore. As we amplified
these experiences, we went back in time in order to obtain
more background, especially since there had been no release from the sadness. In addition, we knew nothing about
her love. Christine described the better, earlier times in that
life:

Love was secret and innocent and I want to say casual—walking and talking. A lover was not a "lover"
[it wasn't a sexual relationship]. It was romantic. It was
romantic in the way of his telling me romantic things.
Just very, very light, like spring and flowers—like flowers blooming. It was sweet.
We meet in the garden a lot and walk. He holds my
hands and he says, "You are my lady," and I just feel
very happy. I enjoy it all. It's very free—fun and so
light.

Then came the recognition that brought to light the source
of the attraction in this life that had been plaguing her.

I know who it is! It's him! I can see the smile. He
laughs and smiles all the same! It's so distinct. His eyes
are bright. He's cute. It's the manner and the lightness,
like a kid. He should have been a jester, not a jouster.
He's just so light and fun. Life is easy, not complicated.

Thus, in this regression we inadvertently discovered the
source of the teenage romance that still held an attraction
for her some fifteen years later.
We were also fortunate enough to discover the source of

the other pattern that had been bothering Christine. She had come to realize how hard it was for her to express affection verbally. Her discovery emerged with reference to her dilemma about whether or not to say that she knew the death of her love was really not an accident.

> The knights have their own rule system. They don't recognize women. Women are supposed to hold in their feelings—to talk about needlepoint, stitches, children, and games—especially games. They don't even talk about love. You feel it, but you don't say it. In courting you don't say anything. You are just judged by the [nonverbal] response—or lack of response, acting as if you enjoyed it.
>
> My speaking out [in resisting the knight] killed my lover [by making the attachment known]. And by not speaking—if I had told him of the knight's advances he might have had a warning. . . .

And so we see how this initially idealized, romantic relationship ended in a murder that could not even be accused as such. It brought it all to a sad end with "no words . . . no good-bye." It was, her hindsight tells us, those very qualities of laughter, play, and lightness that had originally attracted her to her teenage love.

The regression revealed the life in which she was set up for the "lost ideal," which was experienced in Christine's present life as the failed marriage, as well as the premature ending to the teenage romance. This old, old pattern had lived on until the regression gave her the knowledge, understanding, and ability to change it.

Subsequent to these sessions, Christine was better able to face a difficult relationship. Eventually she left it. In addition, the haunting attraction to her teenage love lost its power, and when she fortuitously saw him later, he was perceived clearly as he is in the present. Thus, for Christine, unlike the next story of Hale and Rachel, an attraction that belonged in the past was left there, freeing her to attend to the present and its challenges and pleasures.

CASE STUDY: COMPLICATIONS AND GROUP KARMA: THE TEMPLE GROUP

The following case is an example of the power of past-life momentum as well as the way in which the karma and programs of other people are reactivated when one of the members of the earlier group begins to relive something. It's also an example of one of those times when the activation of a past-life program grips someone with such force that there seems no escape but to go through it. This may especially be the case when several people are involved with interlocking karma, conscious expectations, and motivations from unconscious memories. It's as though the collective karma is so strong it impels people to act out of character.

In this example we have a cast of six main characters. They are three married couples in this life and all are involved in a group pursuing common objectives and studies. The couples are Hale and his wife Mary Jane; Jane and her husband John; and Rachel and her husband Ron. These six, along with some others, have been together in a number of times and situations. They have been involved in powerful energies and important learning.

Our story in this life begins at a gathering of this group of individuals in which there develops an evident attraction between Hale and Rachel. Nothing is done about the attraction one way or the other, and neither of them have intention of carrying it beyond the safe and conventional social limits.

However, Hale's wife Mary Jane finds herself acting out of character by encouraging the relationship between her husband and Rachel. She suggests that Hale and Rachel get together and ''get it over with.'' Ron was similarly encouraging to Rachel, his own wife. However, this wasn't out of character for him as he's always advocated relatively free and open relationships.

Rachel and Hale then found themselves at the mercy of their own strong attraction, both spouses' encouragement, and the emerging unconscious program to complete an unfinished pattern from centuries before. At the beginning of this sanctioned liaison, everyone seemed to be ecstatic; they were getting many needs met. Hale had more energy and affection for both his wife and Rachel than he had had for Mary Jane before. He was "in love with two women."

Not only are such situations not publicly approved of in our culture, they're also extremely difficult to manage for any length of time. And so there arose various stresses. Although Mary Jane initially encouraged the whole thing, she soon became threatened by the intensity of the relationship between Hale and Rachel. Hale clearly felt the burden of responsibility of arranging things so that no one would be hurt and everyone's needs would be met—an impossible task with one partner, let alone two.

There was even talk of Hale and Rachel having a baby.

People around the two couples took various stances, most of them disapproving or antagonistic. Stress increased.

There developed a psychic unity among the three lovers. Many times, when one became upset, it would be felt by the other two. It was as though the trio were one unit. A disturbance in any part would be felt in the others. There were also psychic events in which each would know when the other two were together. Despite the strain, Mary Jane declined Hale's offers to break off his relationship with Rachel. However, that is what happened, but only temporarily. An irresistible force pulled them together again.

Now we must ask ourselves what would make four intelligent, rational, well-established, professionally respected, normally predictable adults go through such an atypical, stressful, socially questionable, and self-defeating sequence of interactions? Except for Ron, whose philosophy was already quite free, most of the events were out of character—especially with regard to the idea of the two lovers possibly having a baby. Why indeed would Mary Jane encourage her husband in a relationship that was very threatening to her—and even decline his offers to terminate it? Why would Hale assume the responsibility of trying to please both women?

To be sure, one could postulate unresolved needs or unconscious motivations, or guilt from this life that would allow one to be placed in a compromising situation. Such explanations, however, are inadequate and vague generalities. They really add nothing. While they may give us an idea of some of the motivations, they fail to tell us why the events took this particular form. Past-life events contain actual events—models, if you will—not just abstract needs or motivations.

What was really going on here? What was the question? What was seeking expression? What was trying to be resolved in this complex interaction? It was up to Hale's regression to tell us the real purpose of the attraction, the encouragement, the guilt—all the actions.

More of Hale's regression account of these ancient Egyptian experiences is given in Chapter 31, "The Teachings of the Temple." This section explains only the social relationships. As Hale tells us:

> This [huge white temple] is where I received train-ing—and where I was executed. I'm young, in my early twenties and in training for life. There are a number of things people of position should know. . . . Religious training covers all aspects of the soul—not just the ethe-real but the physical and secular. It integrates the soul and the mind with the body. . . .
>
> I've already been training in military tactics . . . weapons, command, strategy. The spiritual community is the next area of learning. . . .

With some of my fellow scholars I come into the temple. . . . The higher people address us. They are the council whose responsibility it is to oversee and coordinate the instruction. It's a group of six or eight. With them are the instructors, all dressed in white robes. They appear very learned and serious. I recognize some. I recognize Rachel. I'm immediately attracted to Rachel. It has quite an impact. I feel a stirring of emotions, a physical attraction. She appears to be the most beautiful woman I've ever seen. I've lived a sheltered life up to that point. She seems to be almost a goddess.

She's standing next to Ron. He looks very scholarly, very serious. Next to him is Mary Jane, who's also looking very serious but not quite so locked in you might say. Next to Mary Jane is Jane, and next to Jane is John. They're all looking at me, and I'm standing there—the three of us. On my right is Richard who's also a student like me. I don't know who it is in the middle of us.

The council is telling us what our course of study is to be: Rachel is to instruct us in aspects of love—physical, mental, spiritual—to experience it from all levels, beginning with the physical then transcending, being able to project into a higher plane. She's very reserved. She doesn't show a lot of emotion. The council admonishes us. We're anxious. This [the training in love] is spoken often about in the military and makes us fight hard. We have to graduate to be able to come to this training. We are admonished that this is serious business.

There is only one rule: that we do not fall in love. That's the rule Rachel must live by. It keeps the learning in proper perspective. It would otherwise be misperceived by others as more like a brothel than understanding a powerful part of life. Yet we all barely hear—she's so desirable, and we're so eager. She's gone through this with many such groups and knows how to deal with this. She's been very successful.

[Here Hale talks about the teachings of the various other specialties, which are included in Chapter 31.]

All of the teachers were so detached. They personally exhibited little emotion. They were kind and considerate of others' feelings but were detached, as if they were on another plane that one could not relate to at that moment.

[I move him to the point in time of his personal introduction to Rachel.] When it's my turn for instruction, she would begin to tell me of this [Hale sighs very heavily] introduction to love and everything from the physical mechanics to mental/spiritual elevation of love. Realizing my eagerness [as with most] and yet having that detachment, her job was not to "give a good time" but to show how things worked. It was very clinical. There were several sessions.

But something happened. I began to sense that she was struggling with the emotions. . . . She was not so detached as the sessions continued. And finally she began to realize that she was getting involved. I found that delightful. I was already involved. As soon as we acknowledged it, we had to hide it. We were breaking the one law governing that training.

We would procede with the scheduled lesson, but we would meet after hours outside the temple and just be with each other. It got to be difficult to hide what we were feeling to the others because they were so intuitive. I sensed that they were beginning to realize that something was amiss.

Rachel realized she was pregnant. This was something that brought about a feeling of impending doom. The penalty could be death. There was no way to hide it. By this time the council had been discussing it privately.

They called Rachel before them and demanded the truth, and she told them. Then they summoned me and I told them we were in love. They understood but couldn't allow themselves to feel it. Because they established the law, they had to stay detached and do their duty.

Ron [Rachel's husband in this life] who would have been the deciding vote was visibly troubled. Rachel told me she was betrothed to him in a marriage of convenience. The council took a vote. All voted for execution but John. Shortly after that the execution was arranged in the temple.

The council was on an upper level. The sword was brought forward. The executioner was one of the guards assigned to the temple. He had a pleated leather skirt and leather bracelets and breastplate and a helmet. There were other people around, including the other two students.

Ron announced the sentence. The executioner took the sword and thrust it in Rachel's stomach, and I [once more he sighs very heavily] held her awhile. She was dying quickly, and I felt a rage at the inhumanity of what was the crime: the irony that love was held in such high esteem but was punishable by death. I screamed as loud as I could. It echoed. I stood there. He stabbed me and I died.

The council was troubled because they knew I was right. The law was established to make sure one did not lose sight of the purpose. They wanted a powerful deterrent, but it had never been tested before. Many people that day were distraught by the brutality of the sentence.

Ron was too wrapped up in the man-oriented structure. Mary Jane found comfort in the security of that structure. Jane believed in rigid structure. The things she taught were rigid. John could see the [greater picture]. . . . His focus was on the frailties and the beauty. He alone understood the frailty of the law. He thought, as did the others, that it would not be tested. He understood the human tendency to not allow a breach of credibility. He saw the failing, yet he could not change it.

The people outside the temple were distraught. This attempt to keep credibility resulted in the loss of the credibility. They had to suspend operation. The prefect, ruler of that quadrant, heard about it and ordered it closed. Later it was one of several areas overrun by warring armies. The council was killed or taken prisoner.

There it is: the brutal sentencing as the result of expressing love. The execution was held in order to preserve the stability and authority of the council, and yet it ran contrary to the goals of the organization. Hale's personality had, to this life, carried the results of these events—to be really open about his affection meant death.

Mary Jane's encouragement of the relationship between Hale and Rachel in this life was from both her guilt and karmic debt. It was also a repetition of the older pattern in which she did indeed, in her official capacity as part of the council, condone the relationship. The council itself initially condoned the sexual relationship—until the ensuing pregnancy and personal attachments became evident. She was in the grip of ancient patterns of behavior and karmic debts that became activated by that core event of the recognition of the forbidden involvement or attraction.

For Hale and Rachel, their attraction in this life was the resumption of what had been so violently interrupted centuries before—including the pregnancy. And so we see the carry-over of the unfinished business of the past into this life.

What can we learn from those events of the distant and yet near past? Of course, we could moralistically claim that the outcome of their attraction, which resulted in the end of the school, showed that the one rule—to not fall in love—was justified and necessary. We might also question the purpose of trying to incorporate the sexual and the secular with the spiritual.

However, I believe these to be short-sighted positions. If we look at the broader picture, there is also the interpretation that this group, wise though it was, did not go far enough. They taught their pupils how to handle the aspects of love but outlawed its real experience. In the end, it was the council who failed.

As Hale went on to observe:

> It showed the council that they were not above the frailties of mankind—how they violated their own teachings. They were compelled, in order to maintain their authority, to hold to rigid compliance with their laws.

It also seems likely to me, because of the degree and compelling nature of the attraction between Hale and Rachel in that prior life, and the way it violated all of the then-current rules and training, that the attraction was itself something from a previous time. Their meeting in this way had provoked an even older pattern that they could not break. Past-life therapists, it seems, were even more scarce in those days than they are today.

Of course, few relationships are as complicated and dramatic as this one. But who has not felt at one time or another a strange inner stirring, a fascination with a particular person, or a desire for a certain kind of relationship that seems out of character. Indeed, it may be out of character for this life, but it may well have been perfectly natural in another.

For Hale and Rachel, the regression information did not reduce their attraction nor did they want it to. It did, however, show why Hale eventually left the untenable relationship with Mary Jane to form a new alliance with Rachel.

This was Hale's regression, and although other members of the group were involved in that other life, they lacked the emotional investment and distress that Hale was experiencing. Hale was later to say that the regression information "saved my life." An attraction beyond all reason now had a context. He realized that he would eventually have left the relationship with Mary Jane. The regression, he said, saved the time and agony of what was an eventuality. Prior to this attraction, he had acted according to a rigid code of responsibility, discrimination, and tradition. "At last," he said, "my action in the world was in sync with my emotions."

The regression experience became an historical part of their attraction that had continued into the present.

CHAPTER 7

A CASE STUDY: JOANNE'S UNSPEAKABLE THOUGHT

I AM PRESENTING THIS CASE AS IT HAPPENED. JOANNE was a young woman not long out of college and working in her first major job. She had recently been married. She came for a series of three regressions, each about a month apart. She was very bright and had done considerable writing in her high school years. But her abilities, her job, and her marriage did not erase the shadow on her mind. As she said:

> I feel I'm responsible for everything. My mother would sometimes hide under the porch and we would find her there. My father and stepfather rejected me. I just can't get out of my mind that it is all my fault.

As we began the regression, she found herself in a place that was stuffy, dark, and hot—in a corridor with no one to help her. The odd thing about the room was that it kept getting smaller and smaller. As the walls gradually closed in on her, I inquired about their texture and how they felt. They were, she said, soft but strong. They became tighter, squeezing her. When the pressure on her head began, I was then sure that she was experiencing what often happens in a regression of this kind. She had regressed to a time in her own mother's womb before birth.

Experience also tells the therapist that something must have been going on in the life of her mother that had made an impression on both mother and child. I instructed Joanne to go to the time and event that was the source of those feelings of responsibility. I asked for the words from her unconscious mind indicating that things were all her fault.

> They would be saying, "It's all your fault. It's all your fault." I can hear it clearly now. It's my father's voice. He's drunk and he's yelling at my mother. He's yelling it's all her fault for being pregnant. She should have done something to prevent it.
>
> I'm afraid they might kill me. I feel safe in here. I want to stay and be alone here forever. I don't want to hear what they say about me. There was no sex between them when my mother was pregnant. She used the pregnancy as an excuse. It's all her fault he runs around.

Here we see the beginnings of Joanne's feelings of responsibility being imprinted in this life by the blaming and assumption of fault attributed to her frigid mother by her drunken father. Without the ego boundaries that begin to develop after birth, the unborn child internalized the whole experience as though it were all directed toward her. The reasons that she was predisposed to accept such a program will become evident as the sessions go on.

The feared birth occurs and:

> . . . eventually she holds me. She's tense, afraid she'll drop me. I like the attention I get—especially when I get older. I cried a lot as a baby. I didn't want to be held. I would rather have been alone. [In the womb she'd learned to feel safer alone.] My crying made them leave me alone. . . .
>
> Later my mother felt guilty for not taking better care

of me. I wasn't such a pain to her when I could take care of myself. I could also get away from them and get a little attention. Mother will always take the attention away from me. Anything nice they say about me belongs to her. . . . If I got a compliment she'd take the credit.

I fought back by not eating. [This was about age five.] I remember being afraid all the time. I was afraid of the poison. . . .

"Mother's poison" was the rejection she unconsciously remembered from within the womb. The danger to Joanne that she'd experienced in the womb remained alive in her subconscious memory, only to emerge in her fear of being poisoned by her mother.

Life began to improve when she entered school and was able to get away from her mother. Realizing her intellectual abilities, she gained much attention for her academic success.

Joanne returned a month later complaining of "violent thoughts," of feeling that things were unreal and that there was no one to help. She was somewhat vague about these violent thoughts but was afraid she'd give herself away at work by inadvertently writing something threatening. As a result she checked and rechecked each piece of paper that she touched. Standard clinical thought would label this an "obsessive-compulsive" mechanism for the control of hostility in her case. These violent thoughts were quite foreign to her. She had no real desire to harm anyone and had lived a rather passive life in regard to aggression. Nevertheless these thoughts plagued her.

The regression in this second session took Joanne to a life as a seven-year-old girl in a European country. People in her little town had begun to look worried and talk in hushed tones. Men came in gray uniforms. She ran away into the woods, thinking of it more as a game. The game, however, ended when she was kicked awake after falling asleep in the woods.

She was put into a pit and left to die. Her mind was consumed with the thoughts:

> If I die there'll be nobody to talk about it—like it never happened. It's meaningless. It all seems so unreal. Nobody ever hurt me before.
>
> But why be the only one to tell? Maybe it's better that they [the outside world] think that we all died a more noble way. Besides, they may hate me for being the only one to live.

Again we see the repeated themes of the enclosed space, in both the womb and the pit, which brought both danger and safety, as well as Joanne's worries about her responsibility to the outside society if she should live. The threatened destruction in her current life in the womb had been a reality in a previous lifetime.

This second regression, however, still didn't really get to the heart of the matter because of Joanne's hesitance in divulging what was really bothering her. But she finally did—during the next session.

By session three the feelings of unreality had abated, but Joanne was still left with the "violent thoughts." She admitted not telling me the whole story before. "I can actually picture the words," she said. These words were: "I want to kill the president."

She was afraid for anyone to find out. This was what she was afraid of writing on papers at work. She harbored no such thoughts, feelings, intentions, or desires in this life—but the thoughts came in a fixed manner, she could see them written in her mind's eye—hence her worry about what might appear on the papers she handled. "I was always looking backward," she said.

Having admitted her unspeakable thought, I explored its origin in this life first. The thoughts had begun about two

and a half years before our session, after she'd participated
in an antiabortion march in Washington, D.C. At the time
of the march, Joanne had sent one of the movement's prepared cards and a rose to a congressman, which asserted
her position against abortion. After sending the card she
was unexplainably gripped with the fear of having written
the words ''I want to kill the president.'' By the time she
came to me, although a new president had been elected,
the thoughts continued.

Two different lifetimes emerged from Joanne's regression session, each having a bearing on the situation. The
first lifetime of the evening took her once more to a prenatal experience—but one related to another lifetime:

> It was like having a baby but something was wrong.
> I want it to be over. I'm struggling to get out like an
> energy wanting to be released. There are two men there
> holding down my mother, saying, ''It'll be worse if she
> moves. She'll hurt if she moves. Hold her down. Some-
> thing is going wrong.''

Having identified with the mother's thoughts, she found
them to be self-recriminating. As the session progressed
the story became clear. The mother had made a mistake in
marrying this man. She was ashamed of having married
him, ashamed of being pregnant by him, and feeling that
there was no one to care for her.

The mother's shame is increased when the drunken husband once more forces himself on her. She's afraid to move
lest she be hurt worse. The child she carries traps her—the
unborn child (my client) binds her to the man she loathes.
She was in conflict: losing the baby would give her a chance
for freedom from this man; however, she wouldn't think
of doing anything to herself. She felt guilty even having
the thoughts.

She resolves the conflict in her conscious mind by resigning herself to her husband's advances in disgust. But that's only the beginning of the uncertainty and struggle. She was, it seems, about to lose the baby. Because she had previously wished for it's loss, she felt guilty.

Further exploration in the session revealed the source of the mother's uncertainty and guilt—it all lay in her sexual activity while pregnant. She'd been told by her own mother that orgasm during pregnancy was dangerous. Thus, when she miscarried two days after her husband's attack upon her, she felt that if she'd only prevented the orgasm she wouldn't have had the resulting miscarriage. The influence of her mother's superstitious and misguided belief that orgasm causes miscarriage combined with her own wish to be free, making her feel as though she had allowed the "abortion." It was, she thought, her punishment for being pregnant, for being sexual.

This mother's uncertainty, guilt, trapped feelings, helplessness, and self-recrimination were imprinted on the vulnerable mind of my client. After the miscarriage:

> There's nothing I can do to stop this. Then it's over.
> It's as if someone is pulling and I'm falling . . .

This regression explained to me how the antiabortion march had served as a trigger to bring this experience to the surface—or perhaps the surfacing memories in her unconscious mind had moved her to express her antiabortion sentiments. However, it still wasn't clearly connected to the source of Joanne's violent thoughts, nor their relationship to a presidential figure.

I decided to focus on the words themselves—precisely as they had come to her out of her unconscious mind—and the past. The key was the fact that the words were always exactly the same—and that she could see them. I began by having her clear her mind of all the worries and inhibitions

about having such thoughts. This done, I asked her to focus
on the words and exactly what she saw:

> The words are there. "I want to kill the president."
> It's a feminine script—neater and prettier than I write.
> They are black letters on a creamy white paper.

I had her gradually expand her vision—both literally and
figuratively—and amplify what was coming to her:

> I see a woman's hand; she's right-handed. It's a pretty
> hand with nice jewelry. She's a nice-looking woman
> although middle-aged. She has money, nice clothes. The
> pen is an old type of pen. The writing is part of a letter.
> I'm getting it now. It's the [American] South during
> the war between the states. The war is Lincoln's fault.
> She's infuriated. She wants to kill President Lincoln.
> He's ruining our way of life. He has no right. I'm
> writing a friend in Europe. There's no one to work—
> the men are at war. I can't do it myself. I'm only used
> to supervising others. Our whole way of life is falling
> apart. We're not doing anything wrong. We feel genu-
> ine righteous indignation. I'm writing how things are
> different now. I'm the one who has to keep it all to-
> gether. It's all fallen to me. I'm afraid of the slaves
> now. I sleep with the door locked and a pistol by the
> bed.

This woman's name is Martha and she lives in Georgia.
She's in her fifties and struggling to keep the plantation
together in the absence of her husband and the other men
who would normally have been there to take care of things.
Once more Joanne is in a situation—this time as an adult—
of having no one there to care for her—and having to live
in danger:

> It becomes simplest to tell the slaves to go and to hire
> people to work. My husband finally comes home but
> he's ruined. He lost a leg. He's no longer himself. He

can't and won't protect me. It's still me running it all, and him arguing and not helping.

Another lady tells me the president was shot. It serves him right. I wish it had been me. I could have done it. He destroyed our men, our farms, our whole way of life. . . .

It should have been me, but I'm glad it was done. I hope he rots in hell.

This tormented woman's life was eventually to end in suicide and disgrace after she killed her husband who, in his deranged post-war state, prompted a hired hand to rape her. Leaving that life, Joanne said, was "not all that bad."

As we review this series of regressions we can see the progression of the themes as they evolved, beginning with the earliest and working toward the present. There was the initial frustrated rage at President Lincoln for ruining her husband and their way of life, and causing her vulnerability. The responsibility she wanted was denied her—killing Lincoln. The responsibility she wished to be free of was forced upon her—managing the land.

The question of Joanne's guilt began with the miscarriage she experienced through the guilt and uncertainty of her would-be mother. By this life, her feelings of vulnerability resulted in her wanting to stay in the womb where it was safe. Her assumption of responsibility was also reinforced there. She was once again blamed for the entrapment of her mother. When she should have been taken care of, she was given inappropriate guilt, responsibility, and danger. She was blamed instead of loved.

The question might be asked whether all these scenes were genuine unconscious memories or the product of a fertile mind already laden with the themes we've examined. Perhaps it cannot really be absolutely known.

However, the results of the sessions were clear and valid. The violent thoughts disappeared. When she called me some six months later to make an appointment for her husband, there'd been no recurrence. Joanne had been relieved of two and a half years of symptoms in a few hours of past-life therapy. I doubt that she would be concerned about the historical accuracy of what she reported.

PART II

THE TIES THAT BIND: KARMA, COMPLEXES, AND COMPLETION

CHAPTER 8

PSYCHOLOGICAL MECHANISMS

KARMA IS LIKE THE WEATHER: EVERYONE TALKS ABOUT it but no one does anything about it—except, perhaps, past-life therapists. Perhaps it's not even the karma that past-life therapists deal with directly but rather the results of karma no longer needed, or helping with the understanding and acceptance of the karma that remains. At best they may help release the behavior patterns that either result from or give rise to karma.

My purpose here is to make some tentative connections between the metaphysical concepts of karma and reincarnation and the kind of psychology we live in day after day in the material world.

But why bother with something so dry as theory? Is it not enough to entertain ourselves with the drama of many lives?

Any field of useful scientific or therapeutic endeavor relies on a combination of observation and a particular kind of speculation that is called "theory." Theories reflect how we think about the world: They are models of the outer world that we internalize. Theories, as models of the universe, help us to think about, order, and direct efforts at change. In our minds we build mental models of the way things seem to work from our observations, which are often clouded by earlier incorrect models. These models help us give order to the many pieces of data coming our way.

Reincarnation and past-life therapy are at a peculiar juncture in this process. In terms of public thought, past-life therapy has been a godsend for some; to others it seems like the raving of a fringe of opportunists; to still others it's unacceptable for religious reasons. But for some, it's a phenomenon to be investigated. Many people haven't even heard of it; others find it the noblest expression of a compassionate deity.

On the one hand, we already have a body of ancient dogmas from cultures and traditions that believe in reincarnation. On the other hand, there is also an increasing mass of data that calls into question some of these early theories or beliefs. Such events as spontaneous memories of previous lives, the ability to access past-life memories without hypnosis, the removal of what appears to be a karmic pattern in therapy, as well as the general ease with which past-life memories can be obtained all call for an adjustment in how we think about the influence of past lives as well as the nature of the conscious and unconscious minds.

In order to combine what I believe to be the highest principles of traditional thought with the implications of the new research, I'm offering what I hope is a fairly comprehensive model of the workings of karma and reincarnation in general. This is in no way meant to be the final word on these subjects. It simply happens to be the way my observations have organized themselves to make it easier for me to order and explain to others thousands of observations and experiences. "The finger pointing at the moon is not the moon."

Naturally, I expect to revise or at least augment this model as new data comes to my attention. I welcome my readers' comments.

In Chapter 1 I gave examples of the kinds of emotional, behavioral, and relationship patterns that are observable in each of us. Let's now take a brief and simplified look at the psychological mechanisms that give these patterns form and then maintain them—sometimes in spite of new learning and seemingly impotent yet endless attempts at change.

It may sound complicated to those not acquainted with psychological principles, but most of these mechanisms can be put under the categories of "programming" and "complexes."

PROGRAMMING

Hypnotists are familiar with programming—and most people connect human programming to hypnotic trance. But advertisers and others have found that we're all susceptible to being influenced by means that do not involve trance at all. Hypnosis has also shown that we absorb suggestions from the environment at other times. There are at least seven types of situations in which we're vulnerable to being programmed.

Before I list these vulnerable times, let me define what I mean by "programming." Simply put, programming occurs when something is incorporated into our mind or behavior that inclines us to act in a particular way—and does so without our having made a clear conscious decision to do so. Our parents do it. Religions do it. Friends and spouses do it—everyone who wants something from us tries to influence us.

Some of these programs are easy to change—we need only make the decision to do so. Others are strong and resistant to change. There may be unconscious needs or fears involved. Anyone who thinks we need only make that decision has never been on a diet.

I believe that most of our behavior is programmed—even

when we think we've made the decision. Just look once
more at the patterns in your life.

First Impressions

One example of the normal, everyday vulnerability to
programming is first impressions. It's well known that "first
impressions are lasting impressions." The strength of these
first impressions reflects the fact that, by virtue of it being
a new situation, there are open questions about the nature
of both the other person and the interaction.

These open questions make many of us uncomfortable;
we want the questions answered as quickly as possible. We
want to fit this new encounter into our mental world—into
our model. This helps us to make sense of meeting this
new person, seeing where he or she fits in with our own
values. The other person becomes integrated into our personal reality in this process.

The first impression is strong because of that open moment—but not only because of that open moment. With the
open moment often comes the desire to close it again. If
this desire for closure is very strong, we make make premature judgments.

Of course, people vary greatly in their willingness or
comfort in having these open moments. We don't all shift
perspective or "reframe" our ideas equally well. The inability to do so leaves us rigid and unable to see what does
not fit into our model or reality.

Emotional Upset

This is another time when we're suggestible. It too is an
open moment, for something has turned out not as we expected. In order to bring closure to the upset or give it
meaning we look for a reason—"I must deserve it"; or
blame—"I don't deserve it—it's not fair"—to understand
it. The conclusions we reach as we try to make sense of

the emotional upset become strong influences on our later behavior.

Confusion

This is the third factor in vulnerability and is often a part of first impressions and emotional upsets, but it may also occur by itself. Confusion is actually a state of anxiety about a clash in our concepts, beliefs, expectations, thoughts, or realities. When confused, we're pushed to formulate new beliefs or meanings that accommodate whatever is perplexing us.

There are those who are not concerned about conflicting data, either because of psychological health or to escape responsibility. At the other extreme are those who anxiously seek immediate closure and cannot rest until the question is put to rest. Most of us fall somewhere between these two.

Brainwashing

This is an example of programming that is used by two types of agents: political and commercial (otherwise called advertising). Brainwashing is a purposeful and conscious attempt to alter our beliefs and to implant a new set of behaviors—whether it's about buying soap or adopting an ideology.

Hypnosis

Hypnotic trance and suggestibility hardly need to be elaborated on here.

Unconsciousness

Whenever we're unconscious we're vulnerable. This is because we're never truly unconscious. Our "conscious" mind is simply unaware of what's going on—whether from injury, sleep, astral travel, or surgical anesthesia. The so-called "unconscious" mind never sleeps. It continues its functions of maintaining the body—taking in information and acting as best it can to keep us alive. Hypnotic research has revealed our ability to recall some of the comments made by medical personnel during operations—when we're supposedly unconscious.

Prenatally

The vulnerability to programming during the prenatal period has already been discussed in Chapter 4, "Womb for Improvement."

These are all situations or conditions that past-life therapy and hypnotic research have shown to be times of suggestibility. Things that are said or done by others during these times assume special importance in our desire for closure and can influence us in the same way that posthypnotic suggestions do after trance.

All of these states of vulnerability have two things in common. First of all, we can only be programmed for things we are capable of doing and to which we are predisposed. After all, we can't adopt everything we hear in trance, or on TV, or when we're upset, or in the operating room. However, already existing tendencies or potentialities may be triggered or reinforced at such times. These are also the times when karmic lessons or patterns may present themselves.

The other condition that all these states have in common is that the ego as I define it, is not able to perform its duties of discrimination. When we cannot discriminate what belongs to us and what belongs to the environment, it means that our "ego boundaries" are not adequate. Thus, we internalize external events and suggestions as if they were our own experience. We become a psychological sponge for whatever we may be prone to accept.

Such programming can explain a lot about human behavior. Indeed, some theorists consider the unconscious mind to be basically a "stupid" computer that only absorbs what's put into it. I don't entirely agree. The patterns in our behavior reveal organizing principles that go far beyond this kind of mindless programming.

COMPLEXES

The organizing principles through which we reveal our deepest patterns of behavior are called "complexes." In the deepest levels of the mind, the organizing principles are referred to as "archetypes." It is through these complexes and archetypes that karmic patterns and past-life impressions are communicated to the conscious mind and to life. Simply defined, a complex is a subsystem of functioning that has been split off from our ordinary consciousness. It then operates relatively unconsciously and autonomously.

It is erroneous to think that only the cognitive part of the mind is able to process information. The emotions have their own system of coding, communicating, and changing information. They're also one of the bridges to past-life experience.

Physician and researcher, Stanislav Grof has looked at complexes in a special way. He refers to the "COEX," a term he coined from "COndensed EXperience." This is a modern derivative of Carl Jung's idea of the complex. It implies that the intellect isn't the only system of data collection, processing, association, and retrieval. There is, through these emotional patterns and associations, a parallel operation of thinking with the emotions.

Thus, emotions should no longer be categorized simply as reactions. They should be given the status of an active function of experiential processing. Emotions are part of our sensory system. They help us collect information about our internal world. It is this perceptive ability of the emotions that Netherton uses to access past-life material through focusing on the emotional data (feelings) and their somatic concomitants (bodily sensations).

In everyday life, when we have an emotional reaction, we think of other events that provoked similar reactions. For example, if someone makes us angry, we think also of the other times he angered us or we were treated in a similar way. This is a partial accessing of the COEX—the complex, the core experience, the trapped emotion.

The various forms of therapy have their own ways of dealing with such emotional coding. Freud sought to do it through free association, which he expected would de-repress unconscious material. Jung used his form of association, a word-association test, and active imagination. Even the cognitive therapists seek the uncovering of "illogical unconscious connectors." Many use dreams.

The effectiveness of the past-life experience in regression as a therapeutic tool rests on the ability of a client and therapist to be able to reach core emotions and memories. We do this by taking the emotional reactions at face value (as explained in Chapter 14, "Getting in Touch with Your Past Lives") rather than attempting to deter or distract from them through interpretation, making references to the present "realities" in order to detract from the inner experience, or to control them by means of relaxation. These emotions are accepted as being perceptions of something, of another valid reality that's trying to make itself known.

The very act of accepting the emotions as valid constitutes a therapeutic leap, in that the emotions are no longer considered the problem but rather the means of traveling to the place where the problem originally occurred so that the learning experiences stored there may be re-solved. Therapy involves the releasing and reintegrating of the energy and the impact of that core experience.

The psychological mechanisms most involved in past-life experience are those of our periodic vulnerability to programming and the presence of unconscious complexes of emotionally charged memories.

AN ACCOLADE FOR CARL JUNG

The more I thought about it, the stranger it seemed to me that the fathers of psychotherapy could have neglected or missed such a significant set of concepts such as reincarnation as well as such an effective means of bringing about changes in behavior or relief from suffering. Of course, the state of knowledge at that time wasn't as rich as it is now. But then again, was anyone even looking in this direction?

Of the early investigators, only Carl Jung seemed objective enough to take an open-minded look at such possibilities. In fact, his interest in the investigation of parapsychological phenomena was one of the points of disagreement that led to his eventual break with Freud.

Jung gave the general concept of ''rebirth'' much importance. In a 1939 address, he put forth the idea that rebirth is one of the archetypal experiences. In this paper he delineated five forms of rebirth. These included metempsychosis, reincarnation, resurrection, rebirth, and participation in ritual processes of transformation.

In his autobiography, *Memories, Dreams, Reflections*, written nearly twenty years later, he says he has no answer to the question of whether karma is the outcome of his past lives or the ''achievement'' of his ancestors. However, he says:

> I could well imagine that I might have lived in former centuries and there encountered questions I was not yet able to answer; that I had to be born again because I

had not fulfilled the task that was given to me. When I die, my deeds will follow along with me—that is how I imagine it. I will bring with me what I have done. In the meantime it is important to ensure that I do not stand at the end with empty hands. (Page 318.)

Not only did Jung give personal credence to the possibility of living again, he also put it in a context of general purposes congruent with his overall concept of self-development—the "self" for Jung refers to a special concept that includes much more than the conscious ego. As he put it, the self "meditates" an earthly form (the body) whereby "it can pass through the experiences of the three-dimensional world, and by greater awareness take a further step toward realization." (Page 324.)

Later he says, "Unconscious wholeness therefore seems to me the true *spiritus rector* of all biological and psychic events. Here is a principle which strives for total realization—which in man's case signifies the attainment of total consciousness." (Page 324.) He considers it man's destiny by attending to the contents of the unconscious to "create more and more consciousness." (Page 326.) Compare Jung's comments here to "The Karma of Completion," in Chapter 10.

These comments show us Jung's personal affinity to ideas of rebirth and reincarnation. They also show how the concepts of reincarnation discussed in Chapter 11, "Implications," fit in very well with Jung's idea that the purpose of the process of life is self-realization. In Jungian terms, this means to have increasing realization and expression of the greater Self beyond the ego.

CHAPTER 9

METAPSYCHOLOGICAL CONNECTIONS

THE SPIRIT COMES BACK—AND IT COMES BEARING ALL OF its memory images. These memory images appear as impressions that remain generally unconscious. But they may emerge as patterns, in spontaneous activity, and under hypnotic conditions. They also emerge in what is loosely called "karma"—that is, in the working out of those images in the events around us. These events may seem to be coincidental and accidental, yet they reveal themes. They begin to form a pattern.

We have themes of victory, of inhibition, or recklessness, of self-defeat. Unconscious guilt may create a theme of self-sabotage. Themes also emerge as attitudes: the way we feel about women, men, the authorities, or the common folk. These are all attitudes that have been programmed into us in this and other lives.

These thematic patterns speak of the continuity of living. Just as the days are separated by our sleep of the night, our life continues on quite recognizably. Through the imprinting of the womb and birth experience, certain of those themes receive emphasis by virtue of the emotional content contained in them. And so the past lives related to that emotional content become easily accessible through the events of this life that provoke those very emotions.

Indeed, certain events will be created or sought after that will provoke that very emotion so that what is unresolved from previous experiences can be dealt with once more— not as karma, or punishment, or a repetition compulsion— but in an effort to resolve or complete the gestalt so it can all be left behind. The case of phobia in Chapter 17 shows a theme of falling that began in a past life, was reinforced prenatally, triggered in a childhood event, and finally presented again for resolution by virtue of Howard's job.

If we wish to explore the existence of karma in our lives, our success depends upon two things: the emergence of patterns, and our ability and courage to recognize those patterns.

Theosophy speaks of the human being as a combination of body, personality, and soul. There is the soul, which is transcendent and apparently unchanging. There is also the personality, which arises out of the current life and breaks up at death, leaving seeds for the next incarnation.

Rosicrucian writings suggest that there is the soul and the soul-personality, in addition to the body, of course. They, too, believe the soul to be perfect. However, for them, the soul-personality enters into each incarnation and develops or has lessons to learn. My experience, and that of other therapists, attest to the survival of enough of the tendencies and sentiments from one life to another to support the idea of a continuing personality, whether we're conscious of the continuation or not. An angry man in one incarnation is likely to be an angry person in another until that anger is played out, released, assuaged, or transcended.

Simply put, it appears that the conscious mind dies at death—but the unconscious mind lives on, carrying the patterns, impressions, and attitudes from past living.

THE SOUL'S ENTRY

There has been debate among reincarnationist circles about the time of the "entry" of the soul into the physical body. Some writers say the soul joins the body at birth, some say at conception. Some, of course, believe that occurs somewhere in between.

The idea that the soul enters at birth has been based on psychic observations and memories and interpretations of sacred writings. But so has the idea of earlier entry. Some of my clients spoke of moving in and out of the body during pregnancy. One man insisted that his soul entered the body at five months of gestation, although he had memories from conception.

From these observations I have postulated that there are three or more different memory systems that our consciousness may tune into. One is the standard neurological one found in the activity of the brain. This neurological memory function, however, is not fully available until rather late in the pregnancy. One obvious memory source is the soul since it carries the memories over from past incarnations.

The third memory source I'm suggesting functions around events related to the physical body. Perhaps it's centered in the cells of the body, in undiscovered molecular chains or combinations. Perhaps it operates through the "etheric double." I prefer to call it a "cellular memory," regardless of whether it's based in the physical cells or in those of the energy surrounding the body.

When the soul attaches itself to the body, regardless of when, it gains access to these neurological and cellular memory systems and identifies them as its own.

As I hoped to show in Chapter 4 on prenatal influences, a physical body is genetically and prenatally selected to best express and develop certain aspects of the karma of the soul-personality. This happens in much the same way that, in the physical world, we choose a car or other means of transportation to meet our individual needs. And eventually it no longer adequately serves us and we trade it for another.

MODELS:

To graphically picture this whole process, of the influence from past lives onto the present as well as impressions made in the present which may later be expressed in future lives, I've developed two ways of representing the on-going nature of interrupted living that we call birth, death, and rebirth. One way uses a linear model and the other a more circular one. Hopefully, they both can help the reader grasp these concepts, especially if they're new or unfamiliar.

First, let's look at the linear model. Here are the points for birth and death:

BIRTH   DEATH

●   ●

Between the points that we perceive as birth and death, there is a line of consciousness, that represents the way a materialist views the span of life:

BIRTH   DEATH

●————————●   —the line of ego-consciousness.

With psychoanalytic, hypnotic, and past-life research,

we can extend at least part of this consciousness back prior to birth:

Now, when one life follows another, it's obviously not the conscious, sense-based, ego-identified aspect that continues on. The connecting function between the lives is the unconscious mind. Impressions from the past life are absorbed into the unconscious and emerge into the consciousness of the next life:

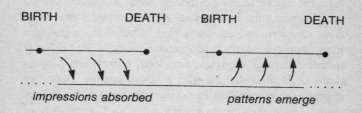

impressions absorbed   *patterns emerge*

Over time, there's a constant interchange between the conscious and the unconscious minds. This interchange is greatly simplified here:

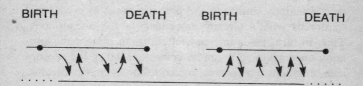

All of the thoughts, emotions, sensory data, and events an individual experiences in one life filter into the unconscious mind. They may remain there as fairly objective, uncharged memory data. However, in the event of traumatic situations or karmic attachments, a complex is formed. According to our earlier definition, a "complex" is a part of ego-consciousness that has been split off from the ego and then stays alive with an autonomous life of its own.

These complexes resonate to thematic or emotional similarities. In addition, each complex bears the stamp of the event that formed it. The images of the traumatic event are the framework that holds the emotions until they are released. When the complex is resolved, the energy contained in these emotions is released and becomes available for conscious use, and the memory is no longer "charged."

Thus, while the conscious mind seems to be the tabula rasa, the empty slate theorized by some psychologists, the unconscious mind contains all sorts of images, emotions, data, expectations, and complexes. Therefore, in the later lives, material in the unconscious memory makes itself manifest through thoughts, emotional complexes, inspirations, skills, dreams, and other memory images. They may appear as daydreams, night dreams, or situations. Most any repetitive situation or experience has a high probability of being related to a complex or to past-life influences, although its importance may be nil.

A more accurate rendering of this process is shown in the interaction below. The forward motion of the process is often arrested because of unconscious actions creating new situations similar to the past-life event in a way that reinforces what's already embedded in the unconscious. This, in turn, leads to renewed efforts to present the situation once again so it can be corrected. All of the sensory data, emotions, complexes, memories or situations, dreams, skills, and desires form into patterns:

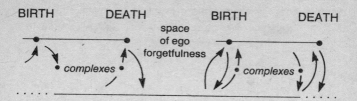

The circular representation below should be more meaningful to those who believe in the simultaneity of time. This is the concept that asserts that all time is NOW and that we're living out all our lives simultaneously.

In this model, the Self can be seen to weave in and out of the span of time and yet always returns to itself. However, our normal consciousness only allows us to be aware of one or perhaps a few of the points on that great round. Thus, our consciousness travels, as it were, around the circular path, becoming aware at one time of childhood, at another of past lives, and at still another of only the present. As we travel this circle, some patterns are repeated, some eliminated, some altered, and new ones are formed.

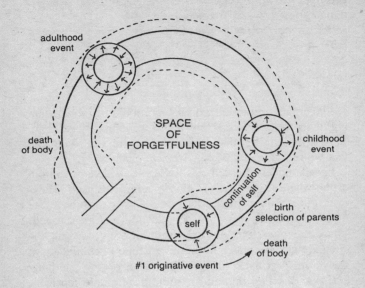

There is an originative event (#1) which becomes the origin of the psychological imprint which will seek later expression. Its memory images, emotions, and meanings form a complex or pattern that impresses its particular pattern onto the Self or unconscious mind. That Self goes on and, in that life or another, arranges a similar situation. Some secondary reverberation is likely to occur during childhood or the prenatal period—most likely both—of the coming life. Later adulthood relationships or behavior will reflect the earlier pattern. Now, we often mistakenly attribute the cause of our adulthood patterns to those that were impressed upon us in childhood. Actually, however, the influence of the originative event in the previous life brought about the childhood and later events.

Past-life regression allows us to cross that space of forgetfulness to the originative event and to discharge the trauma in the context from which it sprang. To do so is an act of consciousness expansion that momentarily includes more of the points that make up the total self. In other words, in making the connections across that space of ego-forgetfulness, the Self is both consciously and unconsciously expanded and becomes more whole.

Linear time, as represented by the apparent sequence of events, and emotive or simultaneous time are joined in consciousness during such a process.

CHAPTER 10

METAPHYSICAL MEANINGS

Karma is the stepchild of reincarnation: acknowledged but not quite felt as one's own. We usually think of karma in terms of pain, suffering, punishment, lessons, or compensation. Any of these may indeed be part of karma; but we seldom hear someone exclaim, "What a beautiful day—it must be my karma!"

As I mentioned before, everyone talks about karma but few people do anything about it. This is partly because the various concepts about the function, operation, and purpose of karma are seldom clearly delineated or defined.

The negative or Saturnian connotations with regard to the word "karma" are acquired over time and reflect more of a wish to avoid responsibility than to acknowledge its purpose. At its Sanskrit root, karma means "action." Action is certainly a fairly neutral word and seems quite different from the usual ideas of restriction or limitation attributed to karma.

It's important to me to be clear about these issues because I consider past-life therapists—and other therapists, perhaps even ministers, rabbis, and priests—to be in the "karma business." We, as past-life therapists and metaphysicians, are addressing ourselves fairly directly to the lessons, needs, and compensations from past living and the result that such living has had on the soul. The concepts that the therapist and client hold about the nature and purpose of karma will greatly affect the therapy and influence its outcome. There are significant differences between ''balancing'' and ''union,'' between ''understanding'' and ''release.''

WHAT IS KARMA?

Basically, karma is that which connects our present conditions in some way with our previous actions. However, if this concept of karma is to be really useful, we need to know how it functions in our daily lives. It's one thing to speak of idealistic cosmic purposes and connections that may transcend centuries of time, but what is that to those of us who need to get up in the morning, put on clothes, feed ourselves, earn a living, and engage in sometimes rewarding, sometimes painful, sometimes boring interactions with others?

I've already mentioned the number of patterns that can exist in anyone's life—patterns of emotions, habits, dreams, attractions, or situations. Even our physical body is made up of a particular combination of patterns. On one level these patterns enable scientists to recognize that we belong to a particular species. On another level, the patterns form the very personal features that allow our friends and acquaintances to recognize us.

As I see it, karma has several aspects. They may be viewed as:

- The karma of compensation.
- The karma of balancing.
- The karma of cause and effect.
- The karma of completion.

Most writers focus on the first three aspects of karma. I will mention them, but in the context of their purpose—the final act of completion.

THE KARMA OF COMPLETION

A significant element in our makeup is the inner impulse to complete parts of a pattern that may be missing or unfinished. Educators call this ''forming closure.'' Gestalt therapists call it ''completing the gestalt.'' I usually demonstrate this by writing out words with missing letters:

REINCA NAT ON   or   J NU RY   or   M RCH

Even though they don't really say it, we read these examples as REINCARNATION, JANUARY, MARCH. We spontaneously fill in the blanks.

I also use the phrase ''LIFE B4.'' As you see this, you automatically translate it into ''life before,'' and because of the context—a book about past lives—you assume it refers to reincarnation. You are correct. It's also my license plate.

Without any action on my part, but by virtue of a process operating wholly within you, the reader, two additional steps are taken to arrive at the recognized meaning. You made B4 into ''before'' and then you added the meaning of past lives.

A more dramatic example of this impulse for completion is evident when familiar music is interrupted. Most of us have had the experience of hearing part of a familiar piece of music and not being able to hear it all the way to the end. And then it may run through our minds for hours—sometimes until we later hear the complete piece.

In my lectures I play a few notes of ''Twinkle, Twinkle, Little Star.'' No one is particularly concerned when I play just the first few notes. However, when I play the entire piece except for the last couple of notes, expectation hangs heavily in the room, and many listeners will finish those last missing notes in their own minds. There's always a sigh of relief when I finish the song—and it all comes from the desire to complete what is recognized as belonging to a specific pattern.

These examples demonstrate the fact that there are, once again, patterns that we recognize; and when they're seen to be incomplete, something within us motivates us to make a move toward completion. Also, the closer to the end of the patterns one gets, the stronger and more compelling becomes the urge to make it whole.

Of course, the patterns I used here as examples have been acquired or learned. Karma, on the other hand, refers to a greater pattern and impulse toward completion.

THE DEVELOPMENTAL CONTEXT

All I've said thus far about karma bears little resemblance to the traditional expositions of it being "pay back," balance, or causality. For those who may be new to these concepts, I'll review them shortly. But first I'd like to put these different views of karma into the context of what psychologists know about the development of morality in human beings.

Writers and theorists may speak of karma in lofty terms, but a close examination of the way they explain it often reveals fairly elementary levels of moral development. Although great pains are taken to avoid the appearance, karma always seems to turn up as a variation on the theme of reward and punishment.

Lawrence Kohlberg, a psychological researcher, has found that our moral development occurs in six predictable stages. In summary, they are:

Stage 1: The morality is based on simply the avoidance of punishment, or obedience.

Stage 2: Morality is pragmatic. Other people are recognized only in terms of their reciprocal usefulness to us: "You scratch my back and I'll scratch yours."

Stage 3: Here, morality has a more interpersonal value and we seek to be the "good boy—nice girl" through approval from others.

Stage 4: Morality is based on the importance of "law and order" in which one invokes the principles of authority, duty, and order.

Stage 5: At this level, morality recognizes the relative nature of personal values and places moral judgments at the level of a social contract or agreement. The moral force has validity because a majority has agreed to it. This is a legalistic orientation and the basis for the United States constitution—an agreement based on the consent of the governed.

Stage 6: Here, morality seeks universality through universal ethical principles. They are usually rather abstract, such as reciprocity, equality, and rights that are expected to be universally applied. And even with the ideas of universality, individual conscience is expected to hold sway over external authority.

Obviously, fewer people reach the highest levels than remain in the middle. An interesting fact is that we can only seem to grasp the idea of the level that is one stage above where we are. If it's more than one level away, it seems incomprehensible to us.

You may note how the earlier stages rely more heavily on the power of external authority to bring about what is essentially obedience. The last two stages recognize the power of individuals to determine their collective values as well as the expectation that we will be moved to moral action on the basis of something within us—our conscience.

Returning to our discussion of karma, the concepts related to Kohlberg's earliest stages are those that say we are punished or rewarded for our past actions. This implies that some external agent keeps a cosmic score and then doles out either pleasant or unpleasant consequences. This is the Santa Claus of karma who makes a list and checks it twice . . .

A somewhat higher level of thinking involves the "eye-for-an-eye" concept. If I do something wrong, I can expect to receive the same thing back (pay back). "As ye sow, so shall ye reap." If we do good deeds, we benefit—in this life or the next. The implication of this concept is that someone suffering in this life must have done something wrong in the past to deserve the present misery. When we carry this idea to its extreme, it makes it difficult to start any new karma because we're always reacting to the past.

The karma of balance attempts to go beyond this eye-for-an-eye compensation. If the ideal is balance, we have the opportunity to make up for something done in the past either by doing good in the present or through creative suffering. This is akin to the Roman Catholic principle of purgatory, where one must suffer in measure to sins committed. Time may be reduced through good works or the prayers of others.

It's a popular idea to think in terms of the karma of balance in order to give meaning and justice to the suffering that apparently innocent people undergo. However, if balance and compensation were the only overriding elements, we'd have to be careful not to do too much good in this life for fear of having to make up for it later by doing bad or by suffering. That is to say, if the ideal were a homeostatic balance, anything that moves us out of a state of neutrality is going to have to be compensated for—whether good or bad.

Make no mistake: Compensation and balance do play a

part in karma. However, they're only part of a greater purpose.

A somewhat more objective and less moralistic, less judgmental viewpoint is the karma of cause and effect. Those who promote this principle point out that we're simply receiving the benefit—pleasant or not—of what we've done in the past. This is close to an eye for an eye but lacks the personal pay back connotation. The karma of cause and effect is portrayed as an almost mechanical return of energies sent out. This is analogous to Kohlberg's Stage 4, with its emphasis on impersonal law and order.

I've presented these ideas of karma almost as caricatures in order to show how any one of them is inadequate without considering their part in the greater scheme of things. However, each does play a valuable part.

Most of the ideas I've mentioned thus far imply some external agent doing the balancing, or deciding the means of compensation, or bringing back to us the consequences of our actions. At least, that's the way the principles are usually used. This is not much different from the ancient legend of the three Fates: each had a task in the measuring, cutting, or doling out of fate to us mortals.

THE NEXT STEP

One of the reasons the above aspects of karma don't go beyond the simple punishment and reward system is that the crimes or blessings we perform are seen as being for or against someone separate from us. That is, we view it all from a dualistic standpoint that suggests human beings are isolated, separate, and circumscribed within the physical boundaries made apparent to us by our sensory limitations. If we're taking action against someone outside ourselves, then it stands to reason that something else outside of us both will bring justice.

A higher perception, akin to the principle of universality, says that there is one universal soul, often called the "over-soul," that unifies humankind. More recently, some writers have identified an oversoul as referring to a collective unity of a group of individuals but lacking its universal nature. Jung recognized the existance of the "collective uncon-scious" which psychologically served a similar function to the original concept of the universal oversoul.

From this monistic vantage point, a crime against another person is equally against oneself—against one's own share of the oversoul. The real punishment is the experience of sep-aration that occurs when we take ourselves out of the har-mony of universal living. Because of this separation there's no further need for retribution, punishment, or teaching.

What appears to be lessons or punishments are the expression of the pain of the individual at having been psychologically separated from the source. At the same time, these manifestations of alienation, these unpleasant events, occur so that there's an opportunity to correct or re-unite with them.

For example, if I commit a "sin" against another, I cloud my connection with my own inner source of light and love. My unconscious mind then strives to bring me into contact with similar situations so I may then act dif-ferently in order to heal the split I've induced. As long as I fail to re-solve my felt separateness, my unconscious mind tries faithfully to bring me as often as necessary to the point where re-union is once again possible.

This act of re-union brings what is religiously known as atonement (or at-one-ment). It establishes some openness to a state of grace. Thus, these karmic residues are not sent to bring us pain but are a reflection of pain that already exists inside of us because of our false perception of sep-aration from others and from our Source.

Many people carry out actions that bring them repeated pain because somewhere in the soul-personality a pain is seeking to be released by creating a more conscious awareness of its presence. The pain is a mirror to the inner self—a reflection of our disharmony—held up so that the corrective action may follow and thus ideally return us to peace and unity. The purpose of the pain is to cause healing to take place.

We sometimes find our consciousness to be quite stubborn through natural disposition, karma-producing attachments, or unfortunate programming. When we're rigid, a great deal of pain is sometimes necessary to bring us to the point of paying attention. But when the old false patterns are given up, the new life entering our world is often felt as a conversion experience. The very act of altering rigid ego boundaries is used by cults and self-development seminars where participants are taken beyond the limits of resistance through intensive social events, fatigue, or overwhelming indoctrination.

At the point of conversion we're flooded with the grand experience of union, oneness, forgiveness, atonement, and bliss. After such an experience we usually look at things differently—at least for a while. This erasure of our habitual thoughts and reactions allows a fresh examination of things—or an openness to the group's dogmas. It is, at its essence, a group context for an hypnotic state of altered consciousness and suggestibility.

Grand as it may be, we're not likely to be made perfect by this alone. Therefore, the inner self will seek a still higher level of functioning. I mention these activities of groups to help bring to light the desire and pull toward those experiences of unity in which our separateness is—if only temporarily—bridged.

Now, as we become more sensitive to our unity with others, we may be struck by more subtle types of pain. This is a tuning so that we may become aware earlier of when we're out of the flow of things. This is much like what happens when that interrupted piece of music nears its conclusion. The closer to completion, the easier it is to recognize, and the more we're drawn to complete it.

Naturally, in going through these many experiences and lives, we become exposed to and learn to exercise in a very real sense all of the various attributes of living. The person who at one time may be the expression of a great deal of power will at another time be subject to that very same energy. We are at different times kings and peasants, perpetrators and victims.

Karma is not necessarily about suffering what we perpetrate. Rather, by a process of experiencing both polarities, we may expand beyond the compulsive reactions of either— to exercise genuinely free choice. Thus, one can go beyond the concept of a polarized balance, which implies seperate elements, to eventually achieve a state of wholeness. In this way, the balancing is a means to an end—it is not the end in itself.

It's almost as if someone cast before us all of the traits and attributes of life, and we spend our incarnations living out, trying on, picking up, and collecting them for our use. Sometimes we get stuck or attached to a particular one that requires some adjustment later on. But we eventually establish a balance between ourselves and the outside world that reflects the balance and integration within us. This in turn allows us to transcend the polarities and to have an experience of the "All."

Past-life therapy fits with this schema in being a more conscious act of collection of these aspects of ourselves that have continued to exist in pockets of emotion, attachments, and partial memories. By becoming aware of them we bring them closer to conscious realization. We can release their energies into consciousness so we may be more integrated and so that all of the various paths that we have traveled throughout our many lifetimes may be brought closer to functional integrity. It's a process of re-collection, or recollection.

Attachments also serve to keep us enslaved to false ideas or in contact with people of whom we could be free. Attachments are not only of love or lust—hatred is one of the strongest of attachments. Love attachments are more easily completed because of the acceptability of consummating a relationship. There are many admonitions against the expression of negative feelings. Without a way to deal with such unpleasant feelings, we try to avoid, sublimate, swallow, or project them—and so form a complex in our unconscious mind that will seek to express itself later when we least expect it.

In general, therefore, we see that karma operates through the mechanisms of the programming effect of separation or attachment. The purpose and end result of karma is not just to balance our actions, or to recover, lose, undo, or accomplish something. These are all means to the end—that end being to clarify the consciousness and make it knowledgeable and free. ''And ye shall know the truth and the truth shall make you free'' (John 8:32).

Ultimately, there is in each individual an often unconscious awareness of the wholeness of perfection. Being droplets of the consciousness of the Holy One—made in God's image—we interact with others. And through those interactions with the rest of creation, we move toward reflecting that totality of Being. ''Know ye not that ye are gods? . . . Be ye therefore perfect [whole], as your Father which is in heaven is perfect [whole]'' (Matthew 5:48).

Some inner meanings are learned, such as language, signs and music. Others are universal and come from the heart of the Divine Source via the Self: the karma of completion.

Past-life work helps point out to us our own particular meanings and the way they've developed through the various paths taken by the Self in its journey toward realization.

STATE-BOUND MEMORY

While these patterns and past lives are pervasive and close to the surface, they're often difficult to remember spontaneously. Conventional psychology has discovered an explanation for this problem in the principle of "state-bound learning." When you learn something or have an experience you remember it best when you're again in the same state of mind in which the learning or event took place.

For example, when you're angry at someone, you're more likely to think of the other things that person has done to anger you. Experiments have shown that when we learn something under the influence of alcohol, we remember it best when again intoxicated—the same is true of sobriety, of course.

It's a matter of whether a memory survives the act of moving from one altered state to another—as though a boundary lay between these mental states. As we cross these boundaries, memories can be left behind—like the amnesia after a party. Of course the memories still do exist—apparently encoded in or connected to the original mental state. We just have to find the right key to unlock that boundary. Hypnosis and meditation are two ways, so are emotions and patterns.

The death that intervenes between lives is certainly an "altered state." When state-bound learning combines with our cultural biases to erase such memories, it takes a brave soul to acknowledge them—or an innocent child. Children around the age of three or four seem most likely to recount parts of past-life memories that are often dismissed by their more realistic, but ignorant, adult caretakers as "fantasy."

CHAPTER 11

IMPLICATIONS

THIS CHAPTER IS A LOOSE COLLECTION OF THOUGHTS AND observations about the implications the various concepts and experiences presented throughout this book suggest to me. Reincarnation, karma, programming, and the very concept of a surviving soul-personality have important ramifications in psychology, religion, metaphysics, and I hope in everyday life. In short, it does make a difference.

IMPLICATIONS FOR PSYCHOLOGY

The implications of Netherton's approach—as well as Milton Erickson's—for the accessing of the unconscious are that the ego boundaries are not so impregnable as they're often portrayed. There's no absolute or general need to have the ego put to sleep, as it were. The most important thing seems to be giving ourselves permission—permission to do what is well within our capabilities. This giving of permission allows us to go beyond habitual patterns of re-action that we have learned to believe are limitations.

This image material coming out of the past and out of

the unconscious mind is labeled early in life threatening, dangerous, unrealistic, or maladaptive. Naturally, we then avoid such behavior—the entertaining of these image-memories and ideas. In addition, in a culture without a belief in nonmaterial realities or reincarnation we rarely hear others talking about them. As a result, we think we're the only ones with such experiences, and perhaps more importantly, we fail to develop the communication tools to be able to express what we experience.

Further, valid inner events are relegated to that murky unconscious world that is then seen as nearly unaccessible. In other words, a barrier is erected to keep these memories and ideas out of awareness. When we have some otherworldly experience, we look elsewhere for an explanation. This new model of the mind, or at least of its extent in time, shows us that we have resources and memories undreamed of—or should I say only dreamed of—by more repressed members of our society.

In short, how can we investigate or refine our inner experiences if the majority of people—especially "realistic" scientists—don't want to talk about it, avoid it by calling it something else, such as delusion or wishful thinking, or we lack the words to give our experiences expression? How could we talk about a screwdriver if we had no word for it?

The anxieties or resistances that people have encountered when trying to go beyond this social and psychological boundary is not a function of that boundary, nor is the anxiety a fear of the eruption into the consciousness of something threatening. Rather, the anxiety itself is the eruption. That is to say, the usual interpretation of an intrapsychic anxiety is that some idea or emotion is close to the surface of awareness and we're afraid of letting ourselves know what it is. Therefore, the anxiety is thought to be about knowing something we already know.

However, what I'm saying is that the anxiety is part of

a memory from the past—a memory of an event that was truly threatening. A phobia of heights, for example, is not related to the future—a fear that something will happen—but is the reactivation of a partial memory of having fallen in the past. The eruption of such feelings indicates that we've already gone beyond that so-called boundary.

To say that our anxiety is symbolic or displaced which could be true, is to ignore the reality of the feeling. The symbolic features of such feeling events are added after the originative event. For example, a woman who fears male authorities may be told that she's really afraid of her father. However, my contention is that her association of her father with male authority is just coincidental and that some earlier experience with authority engendered the fear. Things can be begun in this life, for sure, but they seldom have the impact that past traumas load into the symptom. The events of this life are usually too mild to account for the size of the symptom.

This leads us once more to the idea that the symptom is the emerging substance of the partially conscious complex or COEX, the rest of which is available for exploration if we go into the symptom. Palliatives such as relaxation, drugs, or positive thinking, among others, can be effective in replacing the traumatic complex if they can assume the strength and impact of the originative event, and if the individual is able to let go of the attachment that caused the problem. In other words, new learning replaces old.

METAPHYSICAL IMPLICATIONS

In addition to the serendipitous improvement of psychic abilities, one of the metaphysical implications of past-life therapy is the origin of what we commonly call "consciousness" or the "mind."

The mind is often thought to be a product of the brain.

That is, the activity of the brain—with its nerve firings, electrochemical transfers, and hormonal changes—claims to be the father of our being conscious. However, out-of-body experiences, psychic events, and memories of past lives all suggest the existence of a mind or consciousness that is separate from the brain; that we have consciousness of our brain activity rather than consciousness coming from it.

We commonly speak of the two brain hemispheres and the act of activating the left or logical one or using the right or holistic one. Indeed, brain research shows that when we use one or the other of these hemispheres, there's an increase in brain activity there. However, using the same data, we could say that the mind is using that hemisphere as an act of perception. Let's look at how this works for the rest of the body.

If we concentrate on or use any part of our body, there's a natural increase in the blood flow in that area. In order to use our arms, nerves fire and blood flows to carry out our wish. Similarly, when we want to use our brain in a certain way, we activate that part related to that activity. In the physical realm, the brain collects data provided by the senses and makes it all sensible. The brain makes sense data sensible by perceiving patterns. Thus, the brain is our sense organ of this higher function of consciousness—the functions of pattern recognition and of knowing.

This theory of the mind/brain suggests that the brain is a sensory organ for the perception of patterns. When the brain and mind are both fairly clear and well functioning, we may perceive realities in both the material and psychic worlds—we perceive the patterns of the world as well as the patterns behind these patterns. It's simply a matter of changing the focus of the brain, our organ of perception, the way the eye changes focus for near or distant objects; or the ear, through mental activity focuses on one sound or another, screening out what is not important at the moment.

The different areas of the brain have been shown to have localized functions such as language, speech, movement, and memory—these are the specialized sensory instruments for those specific purposes. They're much like the rods and cones of the retina of the eye, which share the task of vision. Color blindness does not mean that colors don't exist—only that our sensory instrument has failed to see them. Similarly, when an area of the brain is damaged, we're less able to perceive materially and to act on the data available.

Most of us know more than we've been taught, told, or seen. We have drawn conclusions and discovered patterns. We know more than sensory data has shown us. Thus, the brain not only receives data but also produces information that goes beyond the physical sensors. If we think about the function of memory, we see that current knowledge doesn't so much depend on present sensory data as on the mind's "knowing." Precognition remains the same principle in the opposite time direction. Perhaps precognition is the perception of a subtle pattern that tells the perceiver what will follow.

RELIGIOUS IMPLICATIONS

There are hardly any religious doctrines that are truly incompatible with the idea of reincarnation. Most disagreements are based on the end of life or the final outcome—whether we go to heaven or hell, to attain nirvana, to be with a savior, to dwell in the presence of God—or simply nothingness. None of these outcomes inherently prevents the possibility that many lifetimes might be lived before we go to a final reward. Even the idea of the resurrection of the body might occur with the last body inhabited—if that refers to the physical body at all.

If doctrinal belief requires reward and punishment, the lower functions of karma will suffice: We can find the wailing and gnashing of teeth in many incarnations along with hellish events. In this sense, our soul visits hell or heaven many times and may spend years in either one until it achieves union with its source again.

I raise this issue not to challenge these religious beliefs but to assert that reincarnation does not detract from them— unless someone wants a whipping boy or a straw devil to point to, the way Hitler used the Jews, or Romans the Christians, or Christians the heretics.

In addition to these doctrinal concerns, there are also implications regarding the changing content or focus or areas of experience that religion has been willing to include within its province.

Psychotherapists, especially psychiatrists, have begun to assume much of the role that was formerly exercised by the priesthood. The priest used to have great power in declaring whether parishioners were part of the fold or were to be excommunicated and ostracized from the community. Physicians took care of the body, and the priests cared for the soul—sometimes to the detriment of the body. However, the modern age has witnessed the decline of this absolute power of the priests.

Nowadays, it's the mental health workers who tend to take care of the nonphysical needs of the bulk of society. The class of professionals given the largest amount of power is that of the psychiatrist. Psychologists also carry a portion of that status, but it's still the psychiatrist who generally carries the high status of the medical aura. After all, it's the M.D.s—whether physicians or psychiatrists— who wield the power in hospitals. It's also their testimony that helps the secular authority declare a person sane and part of the real community, or insane and therefore possi-

bly in need of the ostracism and treatment or confinement.
I use the terms ''sanity'' and ''insanity'' very loosely here,
recognizing that they are not psychiatric but legal terms.

The more recent emergence of past-life therapists and
similar metaphysical workers goes a step farther. Who else
will speak in terms of the karmic debts of the soul and
perform the ministrations necessary to help remove those
debts? Furthermore, it's the metaphysicians and past-life
therapists who speak of forgiveness and grace in a practical
way—as if they had real meaning in this earthly life.

I doubt that the mental health professionals intended to
assume the role of the priesthood. However, for whatever
reason, by some process the magic that either left the functions of the religions or was driven out sought residence
with the groups or professionals who would to some degree
attend to the needs of the soul. After all, psychology is
named after the soul, and the psychotherapist is, as indicated by the origin of the word, the one who is charged
with the ''care of the soul.''

Human beings seem to want magic somewhere in their
lives—not the magic of superstition and the belief in weird
powers, but the experience of belief, whether it be to believe in science, or in the state, or in psychic powers, or
guides, gurus, priests, rituals, deities, or even law and order. This apparently innate drive to be connected with
something greater than ourselves seeks an expression,
whether personal, social, ideological, or religious.

Most religions form their identity through the way they
communicate to their god—through their rituals and prayers
and the form of their worship service. There are very few
religions known for the way they receive God's answer.
The ritualized ones, of course, adopt the premise that God's
response has already been given in the past and there's little
to do other than carry it out. Many current religions, however, seek God's answer in signs, in speaking in tongues,

in shaking, in revelations, in visions or in the inspiration during the Quaker meeting.

Let me digress a bit here. As I prepared Chapter 28, "The Tricking of Zeus," I felt it necessary to precede the past-life material with an apology for the fact that it dealt with mythological figures. Now, however, I'm struck by the implications of my need to do so. Most of our religious traditions already teach such things—at least to children. It's standard Sunday fare to read about angels, spirits, knowing about things going on at a distance, visions, communication with guides and spirits, the competition among gods (Jehova and Ba'al), and the basic idea of a reality other than the material sense-based one.

Why should it be surprising to the traditional church goer that someone would actually seek to experience any of these phenomena? It makes me wonder if we reserve that world for the childhood teachings of Sunday school, like fairy tales. I suppose I would gently challenge the religious to begin taking steps to believe—in a very real sense—in what they profess, read about, and discuss on their day of worship.

Perhaps it's the loss of this expectation of the supernatural that has led to the decline of the traditional ritualistic groups and the increasing interest in the world of charismatic, pentecostal religious activity, revivals, psychic phenomena, and pagan forms of worship. That desire for direct communication with some manifestation of the divine source and the greater magician will be sought by most of us wherever we think it can be found—or allowed. This then is an admonition to our brothers and sisters in the long-standing religions and cults to get back in touch with the spirit from which they sprang. (See fuller discussion in Part IV, "The Evolution of Christianity.")

Like the prodigal son, these institutions have left the fold of the father, ventured into the world to experience its fruits and material products, and found themselves to varying degrees bankrupt. Those that are not bankrupt, spiritually speaking, have remained in touch with their source. And, like our own individual cycle, they too have had an incarnation of their soul and must be reminded of the origin of their life.

It appears that past-life therapists and metaphysical healers are, in the truest sense of the words, the best current expressions of ministers and psychotherapists (caretakers of the soul).

CHAPTER 12

"FREEDOM THROUGH WORK" MARIA'S NIGHTMARE

THIS CHAPTER IS LARGELY A TRANSCRIPT OF A PRESENtation before a class in Jungian psychology. Since one of Jung's archetypes is that of rebirth (see "An Accolade for Carl Jung" in Chapter 9), I was asked if I would present my concepts of rebirth and reincarnation. Another student, Maria, said that she had some information from her own life that might be of interest in my efforts. The term "student" might be deceptive here since most of the these students were individuals already in a profession and seeking continuing education or to change fields.

Maria was a psychotherapist, married, and the mother of two children. She told me she had noticed patterns in her life—and inconsistencies—that intrigued and plagued her. We will examine them in more detail as I describe her experience, but let me summarize them now as recurrent dreams of the Holocaust, the Nazi genocide of the Jews, and an unexplainable interest in people and things Jewish—despite her white Anglo-Saxon Protestant background. We agreed that a regression might be the best way to demonstrate to the class in the clearest manner just what reincarnation was all about.

167

Her session was remarkable in the number of spontaneous therapeutic connections that she made while the session was in progress. It was also remarkable in the way that it demonstrated the attempts of the unconscious to correct attitudes of the conscious mind that were in error—such as her thoughts about continuation of life; as well as to compensate for previous, uncompleted situations—not having had time to cry.

The regression was done in my office prior to the class presentation. In the class I presented my account of the session with a tape recording of it and some commentary.

This is a story about a journey—the journey of a person who outwardly appears to be a blonde-haired, blue-eyed southern Baptist but who inwardly feels Jewish and associates with Jews. Recurrent thoughts and emotions erupt from her unconscious, centering around the loss of such "pretty people" during the Holocaust. Her life has been, as we shall see, a struggle to unite pairs of realities: the inner Jewish self with the outer Aryan self; euphoric and painful feelings; the conscious and unconscious minds; the temporal and eternal; life and death; meaning and meaninglessness; adulthood and childhood; trust and fear; celebration and grief.

It is a journey that attempts to fill what appears to be the chasm between these dichotomies—a gap that is otherwise filled in her life with anxiety and uncompleted images.

It is a journey that is in one sense universal because these are polarities that very few of us escape. In another sense, her journey is unique in the way these dichotomies take shape in Maria as an individual.

Whereas most sessions require my intervention at the end in order to help make the connections of inner and outer patterns that have occurred more conscious and comprehensible, Maria has many conscious realizations as they happen.

For this very reason she's a noteworthy example of the

advantages of the conscious techniques developed by Dr. Netherton.

The first forty-five minutes of the session were, as usual, spent in a discussion of the patterns of dreams and nightmares, waking images, untaught knowledge, attractions, fascinations, friendships, obsessions, and the anxiety that comes to fill the gap between the dichotomies I previously mentioned. The second forty-five minutes of the session covered the regression material itself along with some spontaneous observations.

It is of interest here to note that Maria has written a fair amount of sensitive poetry—some of the meaning of which she discovered only after the regression. To me, her poetry was the latent content of the past-life images, which were making themselves manifest.

Whether you wish to believe in reincarnation or not, you cannot escape the powerfully influential and organizing function served by the few images we examine that Maria experienced in depth. Nor can you deny the therapeutic nature of the results.

Maria comes to us with an awareness of having long been attracted to Jewish culture and being fascinated periodically by Jewish men with certain distinctive features. In addition, she had suffered from nightmares several times a week for most of her life. And she collects lullabies and children's songs, some of which have had very special meaning.

I would like you to be aware of two themes that become significant in terms of things left uncompleted in Maria's current life. One is a philosophical question regarding the ongoing nature of life. The other is a personal uncompleted act of crying. Note particularly the phrase that came from her lips during the discussion before the regression: "Had I had time to cry . . ."

KARL: You mentioned being anxious. In fact, in one of the classes you said you had a feeling. What was that feeling?

MARIA: I used the expression "fear and trembling."

KARL: And then just now you said . . .

MARIA: I'm physically frightened. That's a problem I
have anyway. . . . During the years I lived in
Boston I had more and more dreams of the Holocaust. I had specific dreams of being shot. I
had a brother in the dreams . . . I didn't know
if that had been suggested by my friend [a lecturer on Jewish history]. I wrote it off that way.
But they were very specific dreams. And then I
watched the television commentary on the Holocaust and I got very upset.

I later moved to Baltimore. I was sitting on my
porch one day, and I was trying to do my emotional work over losing Boston, my friends there,
making the move, and losing a special friend that
was like losing my father again. I had been with
him when his illness finally took his life. So I
was sitting on my porch, and I said to myself,
"Now don't worry; if you work on this [meaning
the grieving, the loss], if you work on this you'll
be free."

Just then this powerful screaming image came
to my mind:

It was a white sign that said: "Freedom
Through Work". [Her voice intensifies] And I
said, "NO! It's a lie! It's a lie!" It was the sign
on the top of the Jewish "work camp." I said,
"It's not true that you'll be free through work!
This is a death camp! It's not true!"

So there was this powerful association between the statement I was trying to give myself,
which was meant to be comforting [if you do
introspective work you can be free of your
problems], to the horrible form of that saying,
which had been a total lie.

I still dream about being hunted to be killed.

My husband compliments me about my blond
hair and blue eyes—and I hate it. It's no quality
of my soul that my hair's blond and my eyes
pale. I think I married a man who had the
blackest hair and the brownest eyes of any white
man in Tennessee.

KARL: What we would describe as the symptoms: the face, the anxiety, the terror . . .

MARIA: . . . and the euphoria. There had been about five times in my life when I had seen a specific face that absolutely trips me out and causes euphoria.

One of the most striking examples I think back to was when I was ten or eleven years old and this man whom I didn't know from Adam came to my parents' home. There were twenty-five people there and as soon as I saw him I said, "Oh, Ma, look at him! Isn't he gorgeous!" I made him sit down and pose, since I liked to draw—made him sit for a portrait—very bizarre behavior for a ten year old. It was graciously accepted by my family. But it was that absolute recognition that this kind of face caused—the instant euphoria. This Jewish face . . .

KARL: . . . and the euphoria. Rather than something to try to escape, these symptoms are an attempt to complete something that was only partially done at another time. It's like the formation of a psychological complex: In a trauma some part of the ego-consciousness gets split off and assumes an autonomous life of its own. What I'm saying is that when that splits off, it does so with the imprint of that event—the event that caused it. As a result, that event stays alive in the unconscious mind.

You can look at the thematic material in just this life. It happens not only in feelings, not just in the terror that somebody gets in the night, or the dream. It happens in physical reality—you set up events to express those themes—whatever they are. Look at the number of father images you've lost in just this current life—five.

MARIA: One could say that I've had five fathers: a biological father, two of his brothers as surrogates until they died, a stepfather, and a paternalistic therapist.

KARL: You [your spirit] unconsciously know what the life is going to be like before you come into it.

> The broad outlines are already drawn because of past karma. You came into this family that has a fairly predictable outcome—the loss of men. You have relived that loss five times. You have also relived the damage to a child; inflicting pain, the alleged kindness with pain in medical situations, and the deliveries of your children.

We're referring here to a number of events in this life in which she was supposed to be taken care of by medical personnel—but they cut into her foot without anesthesia and let her go through a "clinically violent" delivery—twice—without any medical intervention. She had, in a sense, been victimized by people who were supposed to be taking care of her:

KARL: What we look for in my interviewing you like this are the repetitive experiences. Of course, certain words and phrases that you've used already obviously [to me] came out of another reality.

MARIA: I'm ready to work. A great deal of pain came up about four minutes ago. I choked it down. It was when you said we were going to go back there.

KARL: I didn't say that. You said, "I have a feeling we have to go back there." You already knew what was needed. Now, what was that sense of pain you said came up?

MARIA: A release pain, of wanting to cry. Not so much a physical pain—just how I would have cried if I had been there; if I'd had time to cry before they shot me.

This was said before any regression material had been consciously elicited and before any other information arose that would have given her more of an idea of the events surrounding her dream:

MARIA: Unlike the fairy tales that Jungians talk about, it's hard for me to see the happenings of the Holocaust as part of yin and yang, or part of all of life that I can accept. Something in me does not see that as a necessary contrast for people's good potential.

Please note how I lead her to focus on the pain. I'm not being reassuring or comforting. There comes a point where I challenge her, which serves the purpose of raising the level of intensity of her feelings even more. You'll see this when I say, "Here, there's nothing to cry about."

MARIA: I had this dream where I was with my brother, and I said to the soldiers, "It isn't right for you to shoot us." And they said, "So we'll shoot you first." I was facing things without control in my life but had the belief that I should have control; that it was a universal moral principle that people should have government over their own lives and bodies.

KARL: Maybe you do?

MARIA: One other point is coming to me. What I feel I'm crying about is my reverence for the lives of the people who died. In this life [the current one] one of the things about me is that I have a sense that helps to make my therapy work when I help others. Despite the lack of skills or training, I have a phenomenally deep and enthusiastic reverence for the lives that come into my office—a feeling of celebrating their lives that comes very naturally to me. It's tied in very much right now with what I'm feeling for those lives that were not reverenced. [Her voice becomes shaky.] It seems very wasteful.

KARL: You're already there. You're having an experience of another reality while you're sitting here. Here, there's nothing to cry about. There's nothing sad in this room.

MARIA: [She begins crying] Well, not right here today, but that kind of thing still goes on right outside.

KARL: You're there.

MARIA: I don't know where I am. I'm not in my mansion in town with my two healthy children . . .

KARL: I'm going to ask you to close your eyes and remain in touch with that part of you that's weeping. I want you to be aware of the fact that your unconscious mind is already in touch with the life situations that are the ultimate source of this grief and sadness, and it has been trying to make itself known to you for some time. Connect in with that weeping. Describe what it feels like.

MARIA: [Sobbing now.] So hard to talk. The thought keeps repeating that, "They were such pretty people." [She continues sobbing.]

KARL: Say that again.

MARIA: All right. They were such pretty people.

KARL: Again.

MARIA: They were such pretty people. [Becoming more calm.]

KARL: Once more.

MARIA: They were such pretty people. They were very pretty people.

KARL: What are the next words that come to you.

MARIA: Just images of people. I don't think any words. Just little children and grown-ups and pretty brown eyes. And children not understanding why they were being hurt. The grown-ups understood it little enough, but at least they had probably seen some evil. . . . Not the children; they couldn't hate. They were unbelieving; they were just so surprised.

KARL: As you connect fully into the physical reality of being there, be aware of the fact that this phrase comes from some other time and some other place. You can be there, where this phrase comes from.

MARIA: But I don't want to be there.

KARL: Say that again.

MARIA: I don't want to be there. [She becomes upset again.]

KARL: Where is it you don't want to be?

MARIA: [Replying immediately] In the forest with the

pit!

[Crying] I don't want anybody to be there.

KARL: What do you know of the pit?

MARIA: That's where they shoot the people. In the dream with my brother we weren't in the forest. The pit—maybe I know that scene from a movie—maybe. In the dream, my brother and I were in the street like near the place where people came out of the sewers in the Warsaw ghettos when they tried to get out.

KARL: You don't want to be there.

MARIA: I want all those images to go away. But then I would be like the people who refused to deal with the Holocaust and said that it didn't really happen or that they didn't participate in it.

Here was a trap for her mind—she has confused the act of forgetting the images with failing to honor the people there.

MARIA: That would not be honoring the people that died. Remember the others.

KARL: Go back now to where this got locked in, so that you can be relieved of your attachment to it. It was that sense of sorrow that they were such pretty people. And as you recall to your mind the sense of thinking or saying this to yourself, what physical position comes to mind?

MARIA: I'm standing up. Oh, I just had a comforting thought. One of the things that I'm thinking when I think about the Holocaust is that I keep saying the sense of wastefulness and the loss of the pretty people—but that's a denial or an ignorance or an inability to believe that those very people who were killed it's possible were not killed—not their spirit.

In the session, we went back over this scene in the forest a number of times. Then we moved back in time to an experience of a little girl looking for her father:

KARL: We'll go back to when you first had an aware-
        ness that something beautiful was about to be
        destroyed. Give me the first phrase or words
        that come to you.

MARIA: I'm trying to look for parents; trying to look for
        a father.

KARL: How old do you feel?

MARIA: Four. I don't see a father there. I don't see any-
        thing.

KARL: Where are you looking?

MARIA: In a city . . . like an old European city. An old-
        fashioned city with narrow streets, little houses,
        side-by-side houses, walls of houses. I don't
        see any people there.

KARL: What are you doing as you're looking?

MARIA: Looking out the window, looking for people.

KARL: Give me the first thoughts . . .

MARIA: It's cool, and the street is just not very busy,
        and I don't know where my parents are. Music
        is there somewhere. . . . Music has a magical
        power. He knew how to sing or play a stringed
        instrument. I'm sorry, I can't remember.

KARL: Is this child male or female?

MARIA: It's a girl.

KARL: What is she feeling?

MARIA: Patience and hope. She's not frightened—yet.

KARL: Going back a little more to where she last saw
        her father . . .

MARIA: I'm just looking for a face, a pretty face.

We went through this experience of watching and waiting for the father to come home, and then we went on:

MARIA: I remember a lullaby. It had the verse in it
        about: "Maybe it's raining where this train must
        ride, but all the little children are snug and warm
        inside." It always brings up the image of the
        children who were not snug and warm inside—
        going to the camps. They were not—[she
        pauses, and then excitedly goes on] they were
        going to morning town in a way, weren't they?
        That thought keeps coming back: That's what

I've been denying! The song said the children in the song were going to morning town. I couldn't believe that before. I thought they just stayed in the pit. But I've met some of them, haven't I?

KARL: I'm going to mention a phrase, and I want you to tell me where it fits here, or what comes to mind.

MARIA: O.K.

KARL: If you work on this you will be free.

MARIA: It doesn't hurt anymore. I see the forest and the children going past the shooting, past the dirt, and they are free.

This realization related to one of her poems about the philosophical question of whether a tree falling in the forest is a reality without anyone to witness its passing. Similarly, she struggled with the question of the children's ultimate survival—she had not witnessed their passing before, only the end of their bodies. The children were their own witness. Thus, the issue here was her mistaken idea that the lives of the children ended there in the pit. This does not remove the tragedy of the event, but it does eliminate some of the false ideas surrounding it. Her unconscious mind further seeks to correct her failure to see their "passing" by reminding her that she saw her stepfather die peacefully, and he evidently saw something beyond; and by later in the regression witnessing her own passing. We ended the tape recording at this point and she and I made some comments to close the class.

MARIA: I felt I was not honoring the people I was remembering because I was denying their triumph. When I said I didn't see them when they died, I thought to myself, "Indeed, I did." I had seen my stepfather die in my arms on Father's Day. Just before the end, he clearly came to life and saw something beyond the physical that comforted him and calmed him as

he gave up the struggle for breath and peacefully expired.

KARL: This theme that, "I did not see them go on"
starts correcting itself by recalling the fact that
she did see her stepfather look through her and
into another reality at that moment of death. We
then went to another past-life situation where
she, as a child, was shot by the Nazi soldiers.
It was the source of the recurring dream. This
time we went through it more completely. She
was shot in the chest.

At the end of the regression session, Maria commented
that her chest had been hurting all week. This is a demonstration of the responsiveness of the unconscious mind:
When you plan to do something like a regression, the unconscious mind is ready to give you that material. Her
painful chest was part of the past-life memory of being shot
there.

Rather than being the retentive agent Freud projected
onto it, the unconscious mind is very helpful in trying to
compensate for these errors. Once more, the errors that
were addressed here were: the philosophical one of whether
there was life after death—whether the children went on;
and more personally, the incomplete act of crying. In the
situation of seeing the pit, she had had to withhold a great
deal of her crying. Then, as a child, she tells us, "Had I
had time to cry before they shot me . . ."

This regression had many personal meanings that have
already been discussed. In addition, the nightmares that
had occurred twice a week disappeared.

MARIA: To me, the key—the personal meaning—of what
you did for me and with me was to tie together
the triumphant images with the tragic images
and to help me realize that it was a continuum.
And that since it was a continuum, the trium-

phant images in fact negated or obliterated what
I had kept as an unresolved tragedy.

Maria's unresolved tragedy of having personally in her
previous lifetime witnessed the slaughter of the Jews in the
Holocaust left her painfully grieving in this life, while at
the same time seeking those very people she had thought
lost. She had believed that their death would be the end of
these people. Ironically, however, she lived on to continue
grieving, not realizing that those for whom she grieved did
also.

Her grief, reinforced by the unconscious images of the
killings, became an act of virtue since she felt that forgetting the images was a failure to honor those who were lost.
Although the regression didn't remove the tragic nature of
these events, nevertheless, it alleviated some of the unnecessary responsibility and pain associated with it. Maria's
nightmares ceased.

PART III

TECHNICALLY SPEAKING

CHAPTER 13

THE THERAPY IN
PAST LIVES

THIS SECTION IS PRIMARILY FOR PSYCHOTHERAPISTS OR laypeople who might be interested in some of the technical aspects of past-life therapy. Anyone contemplating past-life therapy or regression may find it helpful. It puts what appears to be a radical treatment into its true relationship with more "traditional" therapies.

The fascination of past lives brings interest and mixed reactions whenever the subject is broached. But after the dust of sensationalism settles, after the excitement of self-exploration or simple novelty wears off, after reincarnation is accepted as a natural part of life—what's left? In other words, when it's no longer entertainment, how can we use it?

Of course, there are always the philosophical questions—the love of wisdom, the nature of humankind, the purpose of life.

My initial introduction to past lives was theoretical. But then came the idea of using it for therapy. After all, if part of our behavior comes from previous lives, then that prior life would naturally need to be added to the equation of our present-day identity. If we have created our own reality, then many events in this life must be reflections of our own past actions.

Freud and others assert that childhood events have lasting and profound influences on our adult life. Past-life therapists include childhood as one of several conditions in which we're vulnerable to being influenced. Many of these influences come from past lives. The importance of the consideration of past lives is best expressed by a story I often tell in lectures:

> The town drunk was down on his hands and knees under a lamppost at night, obviously looking for something. A policeman came along and asked him what he was looking for.
>
> "My keys," replied the drunk.
>
> The officer, in much better shape than the other, could plainly see there were no keys there. Curious, he asked, "Where did you lose them?"
>
> To the officer's surprise the drunk pointed down the street and said, "Back there."
>
> "But if you lost them down the street," asked the policeman, "why are you looking for them here?"
>
> "Because," came the drunk's shaky reply, "the light's better here."

If the problem lies in another life, childhood exploration is only looking where the light is better—not where the "keys" lie. Going to the source of the problem provides a much quicker resolution or at least understanding of the difficulty.

I hope to show that competently done past-life regressions can be profoundly helpful in psychotherapy, that there are more ways than standard hypnosis to access past-life material, and that past-life therapy bears more similarities to traditional kinds of therapies than is often thought to be so. Sensational as it may seem, past-life therapy could be viewed as little more than a reorganization of many other therapeutic techniques. The only sensational aspect is that the images arising in the clients' minds are attributed to real past-life events. As I show later, those images can be handled much as in standard treatment. Even the belief in past lives is not necessary for the effectiveness of the technique.

FUNDAMENTAL DIFFERENCES

Psychologists and psychotherapists have long sought the roots of habits, emotional complexes, or other behavior in early childhood. To use an analogy, the client's history is much like a large tree with its leaves and branches and roots lying on the surface of the ground of its being. Most therapies deal only with those roots that are visible above the ground, and are satisfied to take years of exploration there.

These visible roots, however, are the result of older and more deeply buried roots. What is visible is not the cause but the effect of previous events. I believe that past-life work goes to the roots that lie beneath the ground, without which even the ones on the surface would not be visible or viable.

This isn't necessarily a condemnation of traditional therapy. One can almost always look into the childhood of an individual and say, "Yes, there's a pattern that first becomes evident to us in the childhood years." However, the family pattern and childhood traits are the expression of previously established tendencies. The family was chosen by the incarnating soul in order that certain patterns might be expressed and/or resolved.

An important way to view the process is not so much that we live through a succession of discrete lives. It would be more accurate to say that we live one long eternal life that is interrupted by a change of body, time, and place, somewhat the way we change clothes and roles in this life. We leave one role behind for a while in order to carry out another more effectively. Our role of worker is put aside when it's time to act like a parent. Parenthood is temporarily set aside when it's time to relate to our spouse.

This endless life is much like one whose days are interrupted by the night's sleep during which we have all manner of strange "out of body" experiences and visions that we often forget the next morning. We forget more of the days of this life than we remember. Even though we may forget many events from day to day—our attitudes and beliefs, decisions and emotional reactions tend to be relatively consistent. Thus, there is the surviving personality core that carries on through the forgetfulness of days and lives.

REGRESSION VS. THERAPY

Past-life regression deserves a special place among the techniques of psychotherapy. Past lives do not have to be considered in a strictly therapeutic context. Regressions can be undertaken for curiosity, self-exploration, or similar self-enhancement purposes. Take a historical regression, for example. Here, the subject is usually more interested in or directed toward information—facts, dates, the names of people and places. On the other hand, a regression undertaken for the purpose of therapy is more focused on the subjective experience of the person. The time and place of traumatic events are not so important as their meaning to the individual's life. These meanings are what take external events and turn them into internal programs.

To be sure, therapeutic results often occur during historical regressions since they often bring new meanings to old habits.

Clients may not always know what the practitioner's approach is by what he labels himself. In many cases it makes little difference. But in some, the uncovered material may require the intensive reworking and integration that only a true psychotherapist can provide.

THE PURPOSE OF THE PROBLEM: THE PURPOSE OF THE THERAPY

The Nature of Symptoms

In any health care worker's office, people usually arrive with a complaint. They have a "symptom." Much of the treatment effort is directed at relieving the symptom. Many treatments are criticized severely for being more oriented toward the relief of the symptom than toward eliminating the cause.

In my view, symptoms are not just an element of life to be avoided at all costs. Rather, they should be explored. When you're presented with a physical or psychological symptom, it's not therapeutic to simply cover it, talk it away, or relax it. The symptom is a message. It's an attempt to call attention to something—an effort at self-correction.

The symptom may be looked at as a unit of currently unconscious experience seeking to emerge into consciousness in order to increase that consciousness. It is, in fact, an attempt at unifying parts of the mind. This is part of the genius of Netherton's techniques. He gives the symptom its due respect. It is recognized as an attempt to point us in the direction of the solution. As may of my examples have shown, when we focus on these symptoms and their associated emotions, the message is more clearly received along with the attending images.

When this message is accepted, the work of the symptom has been completed. The split in the mind is healed, and this eliminates the need for the symptom. This isn't "faith healing," and it won't automatically change bodily defects, but it does improve functioning.

Past-life regression also implies respect for the symptom in suggesting that it points to a root cause. It respects the constructive function of the symptom by taking it seriously as a reflection of concrete events. It is more than a neurosis.

In short, the symptom points to the source and the solution. Our task is not to cover or destroy the signpost, but to make it unnecessary by heeding its direction.

The Purpose of Therapy

It seems patently obvious to state that therapy is undertaken to solve a problem, relieve a pain, or in some way to live or feel better. However, some therapists believe it's enough for the clients to adjust to their problems. Therefore, many therapies are undertaken for the purpose of understanding the cause of the problem. Very often I hear people say, "If only I understood why I have to suffer through this I'd feel much better." Indeed, this is a valuable and genuine use of therapy based on the traditional idea of insight.

A more comprehensive approach is to seek more than an understanding of a symptom—to expect a change in it. It's one thing to say, "I feel better because I understand why I overreact to things." It's something altogether different to say, "Not only do I understand it, but I no longer feel the necessity to react that way."

This hairsplitting distinction causes some confusion in many therapy efforts. Many clients as well as therapists stop at the point of understanding and expect the change to come about all by itself.

The purpose of regression therapy is to follow the symptom to its cause and to release the client's attachment to it. It's not always so easily done; nor is it always accomplished. But one can see how Joanne's unspeakable thought in Chapter 7 and Howard's phobia for heights in Chapter 17 lost their grip on these individuals. Joanne and Howard had come to past-life therapy in genuine distress and in need of more than understanding or insight. Fortunately for them, their needs were answered.

CASE STUDY: BURNING ANGER

This is a case in which memories from both the present life and scenes from past lives present themselves. Of course, conventional psychotherapists would have been contented with exploring those of the present childhood.

Jared came to my office neatly dressed in a three-piece suit in spite of the heat of the day. He answered my questions thoughtfully, often taking a moment before answering. His neatness, thoughtful answers, and precise way of speaking belied the nature of his main complaint: loss of control of his anger. He talked of a history of suppressing his anger that would, nevertheless, explode in temper outbursts. In arguments he found himself unable to control his tone of voice.

The automatic nature of his anger response was especially evident in his statement that he was unable to back down from an argument even when he knew he was wrong. He couldn't give in or admit his error, especially in his marital situation. He had recently lost his job, and his marriage was very seriously faltering.

Years of suppressing anger had left Jared with stomach problems and a constant state of tension.

As I asked for more details about the anger outbursts, he was able to say that just before feeling the anger itself he would feel scared. Instinct told me that as we entered the past-life experience we'd encounter one of two themes. On the one hand, he might manifest a lot of unpleasant, festering anger. On the other, his control might assert itself and leave us with nothing to work with at first. But as you will see, the pressure of the anger and the need for control interacted in such a way as to give us some isolated scenarios, releasing pockets of emotion, but without sufficient context to give us a clear delineation of the issues as they manifest in the present life. At least, not until the very end.

We entered the regression by focusing on Jared's feelings of anger, which because of our discussion, he was already feeling. He felt his anger through sweating, queasy feelings, tension, and nervousness. We also included in this focus his immediate antecedent feeling of fear.

Jared's first past-life awareness was of himself sitting, hunched over, crying. He was in a panic that he'd let go and be uncontrolled. He was afraid of what he might do. He was also crying in my office as he described himself again, sitting in a chair with his ankles crossed, hunched over, resting his head in his hands.

This intense experience expressed both Jared's fear of losing control as well as his insistence that, "I must be in control." But we didn't find out why. My suggestion that we go into the past for the source of this anger led him to a pair of childhood memories from his current life. One was a fight he'd had with a friend about something that so angered him he felt he could have killed the friend. The other memory was of having beat up a neighborhood bully because he'd picked on Jared's brother.

Using the additional intensity of these feelings as a bridge, I suggested that he once again look for a past-life answer. He then described the feelings of being in a war with the hatred a soldier feels toward the enemy. "I'm running. I see someone with a rifle and a bayonet."

A suggestion to go further back to the source of that hatred of the enemy led us to a woman making advances to him. This made him very uneasy; he felt that it was wrong. Nevertheless, he gave in to her, expecting negative consequences. The scene then jumped into one where he found himself being punished for failing to conform and again having to fight in order to defend himself.

There were some additional scenes, again without sufficient context for us to draw parallels to Jared's present life. Although we had not accessed a complete past-life sequence, we nevertheless had begun to draw to the surface the thoughts, images, and feelings involved with his primary conflict over the expression and control of his anger.

Some of the motivating experiences of the anger were present, such as having to defend himself, to defend another (his brother), as well as the war. The control issue had broadened to include sexuality—temptation was coupled with the expectation of punishment because of his involvement with the woman.

Nevertheless, I wasn't satisfied, so I asked Jared to tell me his worst death.

He immediately responded, "Something during the Inquisition. They would lower him into boiling oil [note the third person reference here] and when he passed out, revive him. . . . They would be taunting him, asking how long he could take it before he would give in."

I asked if that were him and his response switched to the first person when he said, "I'll die first." As he went on to describe the death, rather than the expected feelings of gruesome pain, instead his feelings were those of "pain and triumph." I asked him what he needed to say to those men of the Inquisition, and he immediately responded, "I did it! I won!"

We'd already run over our time in the session and so couldn't pursue further any of the scenes, themes, or meanings. However, we'd evidently tapped into something significant since Jared reported that his stomach now felt less tense. In addition, that final scene tied together a number of the themes we'd encountered. One was the necessity to not give in, coming actually from a time that religious convictions made him feel that he would rather die first. Unfortunately though, victory was measured in terms of being totally self-controlled, not giving in—even to the point of death.

Other than these insights, the results of the regression are unknown as I did not see this client again.

CHAPTER 14

GETTING IN TOUCH WITH YOUR PAST LIVES

IN THE PREVIOUS CHAPTERS I'VE DISCUSSED PATTERNS and the accessing of past-life memories without telling how this is done.

Most people assume that past-life material comes to us only when we're in a state of hypnotic trance. However, this isn't necessarily the case. We've already seen in Chapter 2, "The Images in Your Head," some of the examples of spontaneous memories through dreams and déjà vu.

I specialize in difficult cases. The people who come to my office have often attempted to get in touch with their past lives with hypnotists but were unsuccessful. Some were unable to achieve a trance under the method used or, once in the trance, received nothing or only confusing impressions.

One such example is Samual, the 41-year-old athlete and engineer, who had attempted during several sessions with a hypnotherapist to become aware of past-life material. However, each time they tried, the client would begin shaking and grimacing as if in great pain or intense emotion. He strained and felt compelled to draw up his knees. With the particular hypnotic technique that the therapist was using, these physical contortions served as stumbling blocks to both therapist and client.

My training with Dr. Netherton and in Ericksonian hypnosis prepared me in what is called "utilization." I saw that these physical contortions weren't really obstacles to our purpose but were the attempts of the unconscious mind to communicate to us the events as best it could. Therefore, rather than trying to have the client relax further or in any other way resist what he was picking up, I instructed him to actually increase his movements and repeat them. By this conscious act of "embracing the symptom" we began bringing into consciousness the words and images that were related to these involuntary and unconscious movements.

It all became clear. The grimacing, the muscular contractions, the drawing up of his knees were vivid portrayals of the regression images. They were the movements of a woman pushing out a baby in an abortion. Her guilt was so overwhelming it made the act unspeakable.

An additional interesting fact occurred in his regression. He and his family were of middle European extraction and spoke more than one language. The words that came to him during the regression were from a dialect which he would not have used but did understand.

If someone—you, perhaps—came to the office of a hypnotist or past-life therapist for a regression, what might you find? Your experience could be as varied as the number of regressionists in practice. Nevertheless, there are some strong similarities among the few methods of accessing past-life memories.

HYPNOSIS

Most people naturally think of hypnosis as being the one means of reaching so far back in time into the unconscious mind for these memories. Hypnosis, however, is not the only way—it's not always the easiest way, nor is it necessarily the most therapeutically effective way. It seems to be the most common way. Here's an example of how it might be done.

You'd come into the therapist's office and I hope have any questions answered. For the session, you would be placed in a comfortable position on a couch or chair and the hypnotist would begin. Some form of induction would be used to put you into trance, to help you relax, to remove the obstacles allegedly presented by the conscious ego, and to otherwise prepare you for the release of the forgotten memories. For example, you might be asked to close your eyes, breathe deeply, and then to relax various parts of your body until you become very much at ease. On the other hand, you might be asked to gaze at a flashing light, a spinning disk, a spot on the ceiling, or even your own hand. When this concentration is combined with the hypnotist's suggestions of tiredness or relaxation, it helps you to enter a hypnotic state.

When the therapist is satisfied that you are sufficiently in an altered state of consciousness, he or she may then give you suggestions to recall past-life material. Normally some symbolic set of images is used to take you back, for example, counting, visualizing travel through time by means of a bridge or tunnel, or seeing time go backward by going upstream.

In the chair, in the trance, and hopefully in a past life, you're then given further suggestions to move your consciousness forward or backward in time to gain additional information. The therapist may then have you either view the life from a distance as though you were an observer, or to actually re-live many of the events with their emotions and ideas. The way it's done depends mostly on the training and courage of the therapist. While the reliving process can be the most anxiety provoking for both client and therapist—especially if either one is afraid of strong emotion—

it's usually the most therapeutically effective. There are techniques that can be used to allow the client to go through and relive the most difficult of situations without being overwhelmed.

Many therapists tape record the session for the client. Being in an altered state reduces the memory of the regression.

After going through the regression, the client should at least gain an understanding or explanation of his or her current predicament. Often he or she also finds a release from the compulsive nature of the problem.

The use of hypnosis to do this work has particular advantages and disadvantages. Some of the advantages are that people who are afraid of what they might see or hear of feel, or who are concerned that their ego might distort the experience, can find refuge in the hypnotic sleep. However, I consider such anxiety or self-distrust to be symptoms—they're better addressed directly than circumvented. Sometimes in hypnosis, however, people seem to provide names, dates, and places more easily.

Some of the problems encountered in the use of hypnosis come not from the nature of hypnosis but rather from the training and techniques of the therapist. An Ericksonian hypnotist or Neurolinguistic Programming (NLP) practitioner would have less difficulty than the traditional formula-oriented hypnotist who does the same thing with each and every client. In hypnosis, the prerequisite condition on which all else depends is the establishment of the trance state. If the individual is unable to relax or concentrate, becomes somnambulistic, or suffers from amnesia, a traditional hypnotist may find himself at a loss and unfairly judge the client to be resisting.

SEMIHYPNOTIC TECHNIQUES

A new class of procedures has been developed whose proponents usually go to great lengths to say that they're not using hypnosis.

In these techniques, your regressionist gets you suitably positioned, then suggests various visualizations or feelings such as expanding or contracting, floating, turning off parts of the body. Although the proponents deny using hypnosis, these procedures serve the same purpose and have very similar effects: An altered state is induced; there is dissociation from the physical body; and there is the suggestion to enter into a past-life experience—regardless of whether the practitioners refer to their activities as a time-lap, consciousness expansion, or altered state.

The primary difference between these techniques and classic hypnosis are the expectations of client and regressionist. Both usually carry the self-fullfilling expectation that the client will not fall under the control of the therapist. The regressionist assumes more the role of a guide or perhaps alter ego. To my mind, the situation is the same with hypnosis—only the expectations are different.

I have used semihypnotic techniques in both group and individual settings with consistent success.

NONHYPNOTIC TECHNIQUES

The Netherton Technique is probably the best and most genuine expression of the attempt to access past lives without the need for producing a trance state. The fact that you can have past-life memories without hypnotic induction and without being put into a trance is astounding to many. But it works—and very effectively.

When a client enters the office with a question or problem, he or she is already in a regressed state. The client is acting as if he or she is now in that past-life situation. If you're living according to the conditions of another reality, you're partially in trance. It's the same as operating under a posthypnotic suggestion.

Thus, rather than trying to induce an altered state of an already altered state, Netherton believes that this person is centered in the the time and place from which the programming emerged and thus gives permission to complete that situation. The procedure is to focus that person more completely on the source of the problem by paying attention to the symptom signposts.

For example, if the person comes to the office with an anxiety, rather than teaching him to relax or putting him into trance, the therapist has him focus his attention on the anxiety itself. He's asked how the anxiety feels, where he feels it in his body, and what it feels like. This type of focusing on the symptom is akin to the hypnotic process of "deepening" the already regressed state. Associated images and words from the past begin to come into the client's mind. In this way, then, the past life is accessed.

This summary is too brief to do justice to Netherton techniques as he's also developed a set of methods for releasing traumatic material and for detaching oneself from the difficulties. I'm only presenting his alternative induction method here. More of the releasing techniques are presented in his book.

The basic difference between Netherton's techniques and the others is the premise that the person is already in a trance state. Therefore no additional induction is necessary. No therapist-oriented procedure is interposed between the client and his unconscious mind. He's already in touch with it. The task is to temporarily bring him more completely in touch with it so that something can be finished. Although trance isn't induced prior to the past-life memories, trance usually develops as a by-product.

Therapists familiar with hypnotic phenomena in everyday life will recognize that the trance state occurs spontaneously with the intensive use of memory. The Netherton Technique, then, is an associative one—it operates on the natural associations of related material in the mind. This conforms to Jungian theories and principles of the operation and structure of the mind.

If I were to give a descriptive name to Netherton's process, I would call it "Associative Integration." Not only does he provoke past-life memories, and trance, through mental associations he also uses masterful methods of integrating those memories into the life of the client.

Like the NLP practitioners who say that anyone is hypnotizable if we can only become aware of an individual's particular needs in trance, I say that past-life material (memories, words, images, attitudes) is accessible to anyone—if the regressionists have sufficient tools and techniques at their disposal to meet the individual needs of their clients.

DISCHARGING THE ENERGY

Hypnotic and nonhypnotic therapists allot varying amounts of time for these sessions. Some prefer forty-five minute sessions. Others prefer two or two-and-a-half-hour sessions. Mine usually run two hours. Many hypnotists use conditioning procedures prior to the regression. This may require a preparatory hypnotic session and then practice with a conditioning tape before the regression session. Netherton's assumption that the client is already in trance eliminates the need for such conditioning—but only if the therapist is able to recognize the signs of the preexistent trance.

For the hypnotherapist, the regression begins with the induction and ends with the awakening. Therefore, the therapist's task is to be able to induce a trance, deal with the material that emerges, and bring the client back into the present.

Using the Associative techniques, the therapist is able to recognize the patient's questions or symptoms of anxiety, pain, pattern, or compulsion as evidence that the regression is already in effect. In this way of looking at things, the therapist's job is to get the person out of the trance of regressive living and into the position of conscious choice.

In either instance, with or without hypnosis, the desired outcome could be the same—to be free of some problem or question. The distinctions that I've been making in this chapter would have little importance except for those clients who undertake their work with a therapist who might be unable to provide for that client's individual needs.

After going through a regression session, the client and psychotherapist are faced with a wealth of new material from the client's unconscious mind. Those memories may be left as pure experience—the client may be left to figure it all out alone.

They may discuss what it means. They may rework some part of the regression, as Netherton does, to discharge trapped energy or to create new patterns. The client may be taken through the major events again, or even more than once, in order to help desensitize him to the traumatic parts of the past life so it doesn't bother him any more. Sometimes this reworking does not have to be done. It depends on the purpose of the regression, the wishes of the client, and the talents of the therapist.

Even traditional psychotherapists are able to make use of the themes that are generated in regressions—for example, rejection, punishment, wielding of power, frustration of efforts, achievement, abandonment, or religious conflict. One of my clients regularly used the dynamics that were uncovered in our past-life therapy sessions in her more traditional group-therapy treatment.

These past-life images are as open to interpretation as dreams are for those therapists who prefer an analytical approach.

PSYCHIC READINGS

Psychic readings often produce indications that current problems may be related to past-life events. Even though clients may not be consciously reliving their past lives, being told of a concrete cause for their difficulties can help them understand why things are the way they are—if they believe in reincarnation. However, there's the ever-present pitfall in which one may abdicate responsibility and assume a helpless stance in the face of one's plight—blaming the unchangable past or karma rather than making the necessary effort to change it.

Many times, however, such readings put individuals more closely in touch with their inner experience. It can be a process of opening to oneself. After all, opening to one's inner self is the goal and benefit of past-life exploration.

CHAPTER 15

COMPARISON TO OTHER PSYCHOTHERAPIES

Past-life therapy is definitely not in the mainstream of psychotherapeutic thought, practice, or even acceptance. All too few professionals have taken a serious look at past-life therapy and what it has to offer their clients and themselves. There are a number of reasons for this. For one, schools of therapy don't usually teach their students to look in depth at competing sets of ideas, unless they do it critically. Second, past-life therapy is a new kid on the block whose worth and metal is awaiting proof and demonstration. Also, this new kid appears to have developed outside of their territory.

Third, whether they admit it or not, in the West there's strong religious and cultural bias to disregard such sets of ideas. Any concepts relating to past lives have traditionally been the province of foreign cultures, occultists, fortune tellers, psychics, and other such outcasts of accepted (meaning "approved of") practitioners.

Finally, even traditional psychotherapy is still feeling the lack of confidence that comes from the fact that it is itself a new institution. Psychiatry is new to the medical world; psychology as a separate effective discipline is only recently being accepted. Mental health counselors are now on the cutting edge of psychotherapy; some states recognize them and many do not. Psychiatrists are physicians who receive specialized training in the medical and psychotherapeutic treatment of mental disorders, often specializing in the neurological or biochemical causes of emotional problems. Psychologists are not directly involved with the medical aspects of emotional problems but may be specialists in the areas of diagnosis of learning disorders and emotional problems, the measurement of intelligence, and psychotherapeutic treatment of individuals, groups or families. Most states have some mechanism for licensing psychiatrists and psychologists. Mental health counselors, recognized by licensure in some states but not in others, specialize in counseling and psychotherapy of individuals, groups or families. There are also psychiatric nurses and licensed clinical social workers who also share in the therapeutic pie. In this struggle for recognition and acceptance, few therapists are courageous enough to allow themselves to be identified with controversial techniques and concepts, or even to investigate alternative practices objectively.

Indeed, some psychotherapists may experience ''concept shock'' at having to consider adding non-material realities, past lives, and prenatal influences to their therapeutic treatments. They may also find rejection from their more traditional colleagues.

In addition, there's subtle snobbery on both sides. If the traditional psychotherapist is seen talking to or investigating the occult areas, or the occultist is seen hobnobbing with professional therapists, they're often regarded by their colleagues as having sold out. Sometimes there's a money vs. service split. This kind of behavior is evidence not of any intellectual or scientific orientation, but rather of a clearly emotionally based, self-protective system of belief.

In the history of psychotherapy, the classic example of this dilemma is that of Carl Jung, who wanted to investigate the phenomena that were then labeled "psychic." Freud, brave as he was in other areas, could not tolerate this interest, and so the conflict contributed to their eventual parting of the ways.

To be fair, there is a growing body of psychoanalysts, psychologists, physicians, hypnotherapists, psychiatrists, counselors, and other helpers who recognize the influence of past lives and are not afraid to deal with them.

If we are able to erase these theoretical and philosophical biases, what might the various schools of psychotherapy see in the hypnotic and Netherton types of past-life therapy? In other words, if it somehow could be proved that there exists only this one life, what principles used by these various schools would still explain why past-life therapy works?

Again, let me assert that there are three basic acceptable facts involved. First of all, there are patterns that become evident in our thoughts, emotions, and behaviors. Second, there are images in our minds, conscious or unconscious, that are related or attached to those patterns. Finally, addressing these images can result in significant changes in the patterns and behavior. The major arguments among the various viewpoints are over the origin of those images and the most efficient form of correcting painful situations.

However, if we could get professionals to address not the belief systems but the therapeutic interaction, what might they say?

Let's imagine that a round table of professional psychotherapists have heard a presentation of the principles and seen a demonstration of a competent past-life therapy session. How might some of the more traditional psychotherapists explain, from their own points of view, what transpired in our imaginary demonstration?

Who rises to speak first?

BEHAVIORISM

In such situations, the action-oriented behaviorist is often the first to speak and will usually focus on what is observable and what precedes and follows any behavior of concern. He might say that we've established a format in which the client is positively reinforced for expressing feelings and opinions that in the past have been suppressed through punishment or negative reinforcement. The therapeutic change comes about by means of the "desensitization" that results in a weakening of the anxiety response. This desensitization is accomplished by taking the subject through (reliving) a traumatic situation that at one time provoked an anxiety response.

In addition, by the use of mental images, the subject has been taught to engage in "cognitive rehearsal" by seeing himself in other situations and acting in alternative ways. This cognitive rehearsal expands his repertoire of available behaviors.

In these ways anxiety states are reduced by breaking the conditioned link between the anxiety response and the imagined situation; new and more effective behaviors are invoked by cognitive rehearsal and reinforced. Positive self-affirming statements replace negative ones by virtue of the recognition that the client has lived through a difficult situation. Finally, guilt (negative self-accusation) is alleviated by seeing the fault or blame placed elsewhere or shared.

RET (Rational Emotive Therapy) is one branch of behaviorism. A proponent of RET might say that we have uncovered some of the "illogical unconscious connectors" that have been keeping us from acting in our own best interests.

PSYCHOANALYSIS

The Freudian would focus on the idea that we have put the analysand (the client) into a state of mind that permits, through association of ideas (although not quite the "free association" of Freud), the searching out of internal images and memories. This results in the reliving of repressed emotions that have been unconsciously motivating the previous behavior. In bringing that repressed material to consciousness, the trapped psychic energy is then released to ego control. As it is released through the images, the process of insight occurs.

The neurotic conflict becomes symbolized through the use of the past-life idea in such a way that does not require the superego to punish the individual for the otherwise normal impulses of the id.

Part of the foundation of psychoanalysis is the "analysis of the transference." This refers to the way the relationship develops between the analyst and the patient, and the misdirected, or projected, emotions and expectations that occur. For example, a female patient may begin to behave toward her psychoanalyst as though he were her father, expecting him to pay special attention to her, take care of her or to exchange intimacies more appropriate to a father-daughter relationship.

In regression therapy, the analysis of the transference is indirect; it's projected onto the images produced in the session. The unresolved projected feelings of anger, love, hatred, sadness, and so on, are then worked through symbolically. The emotional charge is then "decathected," drawn back into the person rather than attributed to others.

JUNGIAN ANALYTICAL PSYCHOLOGY

The Jungian might say that the regression therapy is based on the process of active imagination, a technique of building a fantasy around an emotion or concern, and the amplification of the images through making associations to them. On the therapeutic level, this allows one to activate or release energy previously tied up in complexes to more conscious control. This frees the libido (psychic energy) for other use.

By bringing these images into consciousness, and integrating them into the ego, the ego becomes more whole and more identified with the larger archetype of the Self, that inner principle organizing our behavior and psyche. In addition, repressed or unacceptable traits, impulses, and desires (the personal shadow) are symbolically integrated into the ego, improving our internal and external reality orientation.

With the implications of the transpersonal or spiritual elements implied by past-life regression, the spiritual drives are allowed more healthy expression and so are not distorted into neurosis.

The psychic phenomena that occur around a course of depth therapy are evidence of the interconnections of the ego, the personal unconscious, and the collective unconscious. These connections result in events of a synchronistic nature. Synchronistic events are those "coincidental" happenings which, although a connection between them is not visible, they, nevertheless, have special meaning. For example, the client may have a dream about a bear and, during the following day, receive a gift of a bear in the form of a pin and then go into the therapist's office to find a new picture—of a bear—decorating the wall. Although there is no evident connection between the dream image and the next day's events, the fact that they occur so close in time and have a recognizable identity give them meaning. It is an interesting fact that the more we pay attention to such coincidences, the more they seem to occur.

Ego projections, in which we take our own feelings and attribute them to others, are withdrawn and placed back within us. This permits attributes that we have disowned in the past and split off in order to deal with them are returned to us so that we have a larger number of available attitudes, behaviors, and energy.

LOGOTHERAPY

Logotherapy is concerned with meaning. The Logotherapist might say that we have given meaning to the patient's suffering by seeing in a past life some cause for this pain, or, in karma, some reason. This reduces the suffering and makes it more worthwhile. It becomes part of a larger picture. In addition, there are implicit meanings attributed to this life through the past-life connections. The Logotherapist could say that the therapeutic outcome emerges by taking what seems to be unrelated and purposeless elements—such as physical symptoms, suffering, unpleasant situations—and giving them meaning, relationship, and purpose by putting them into a past-life context.

PRIMAL THERAPY

The Primal therapist might say that the images have been useful in provoking trapped primal emotions so that they may be re-experienced and released. These trapped emotions have been locked into the attitudes, emotions and physiological reactions of the body. In the catharsis of expressing and releasing the emotions, their trapped energy is freed from its crystallization.

ADLERIAN INDIVIDUAL PSYCHOLOGY

The Adlerian might say that we use the images to expose the person's habitual life-style. This would show him how he's been dealing with his feelings of inferiority and drive for power. This new awareness allows him to attend to the task at hand more adequately. Even more important, it allows him to accept responsibility for himself and his situation. The drive to power is met by the feelings of increased ability to handle various situations, if only symbolically. The "social interest" our natural inclination is to be a useful part of a social group, is fed by giving a social context to what had seemed to be anomalous feelings or behaviors that were not useful in the person's current situation.

TRANSACTIONAL ANALYSIS

The transactional analyst could point to how the images represented various "transactions" between figures representing the parent, adult, and child functions. Through the therapeutic procedures, these functions are reconnected with one another and realigned so that we begin to function more completely and are better able to respond appropriately in adult-adult, parent-parent, or child-child communications rather than crossing the transactions in inappropriate ways.

GESTALT THERAPY

The Gestaltist might see in these transactions—the "conversations" that are set up or occur in the past-life memories between various people—a reflection of a process of interchange often taught in Gestalt therapy. It allows the elements of the mind to speak their messages, thereby making them more conscious.

In addition, the kind of work that Netherton does would be seen as "completing the gestalt," which promotes the resolution of the conflict. This is the process of finishing something that was left psychologically undone (see "Karma of Completion" in Chapter 10). As these unresolved and incomplete gestalts, or patterns, are completed and integrated, people are better able to attend to the here and now because they feel less compelled to act out unresolved material.

FOCUSING

Eugene Gendlin's "focusing" technique bears much similarity to the way Dr. Netherton may begin a regression by having a client concentrate—or "focus"—attention on a part of the body in which emotions or feelings are being physically experienced right then. The inner sense or feeling of one's problem is focused on rather than our thoughts about it. Importance is given to a sense of physical shift in bodily awareness during the process, as well as the words and pictures that may develop out of a feeling. The completeness of the session is often judged by returning at the end to awareness of the physical sensations to test whether the tension has been released or whether something else is presenting itself. The changes in these emotion-related sensations are monitored throughout the therapy session.

NEUROPSYCHOLOGY

If we could get a neuropsychologist to address imaginal processes, he might explain the effect this way. "What you've done is to take advantage of the connection between electrochemical processes and imaginal and external behavior. In so doing you have inhibited the production of anxiety-producing chemicals and stimulated the output of the brain's natural morphines, the endorphins. This leads to a more peaceful state of mind, which allows one to be more open to other possibilities in the various situations that one encounters. In this way new neural pathways are laid down, resulting in altered patterns of behavior.

"Integration would occur at the juxtaposition of linear processing (via verbal labels and causal attributions) and simultaneous processing (via images and emotional factors)."

GUIDED IMAGERY

Anyone trained in guided imagery obviously recognizes the use of the images and the emotional charge they carry. Experiencing the images helps release these emotions and integrate the energy into the consciousness. In addition, there are the healing experiences that often happen after reliving a death or when we revive memories of pleasant lives or situations.

REBIRTHING

The rebirther might attribute the success of the technique to the fact that we make available the possibility of reliving the birth experience. Although regressions are done in a different way and from a different perspective than traditional rebirthing, they still help the client remove or transcend the traumatic aspects of unconscious birth memories.

HYPNOTHERAPY

The hypnotherapist would look at the altered state in which the client would be more suggestible and would have easier access to unconscious images. The technique is a use of age regression. Emotional scenes are produced that allow abreaction to occur, the process of bringing unconscious emotions to the surface and re-experiencing them, as well as the catharsis that discharges suppressed emotions. At the close of the session, the therapist gives embedded or covert suggestions that the subject will be free of the problem, feel less anxious or less compulsive by virtue of this metaphorical journey.

Providing a past-life context for current emotions reduces the pressure of our conflicts by means of dissociation: The conflicts or problems are attributed to a distant situation and thus removed from immediate concern.

Doubtless, my presentation of the traditional—and not so traditional—schools of therapy was unfairly brief. Nor is this list exhaustive. My purpose was not to give a complete catalogue of comparative therapies but to show where past-life therapy fits into the various schools.

CHAPTER 16

THE BEGINNING OF A
THEORY OF THERAPY

WHEN WE CONSIDER THE LAUDABLE AND BENEFICIAL outcomes of undergoing regression experiences, one wonders why it works at all—especially since it doesn't depend on a belief in reincarnation. What difference does it make that someone comes to my office, reviews or relives dramatic and sometimes traumatic events, and leaves freer of some previously ingrained symptom?

I believe that there are a number of possible explanations. Those who do believe that we have had past lives can recognize how many events occur that are traumatic to us because we don't have a large enough picture to gain a positive value from the experience (see Chapter 10, "Metaphysical Meanings").

As we go into a regression, we have to access a certain "soul consciousness" that has been influencing us as well as the emotions that have slipped out of a past context and spilled over into the present because of some incomplete or unresolved factor. During the session, these gestalts and trapped emotions are vented and the entire situation is examined from a larger perspective.

The therapeutic part of the regression process is to go

back and re-collect (recollect) whatever needed to be completed or returned to its place. We go back in time with the current consciousness as well as with the company and assistance of the therapist so we can re-examine, re-live, re-process, and re-solve the difficulties to which we'd become attached. In so doing we discover, for example, that for various reasons we've fallen pray to the suggestions and influence of others during times of vulnerability. In a regression many of my clients find themselves generating and releasing anger that should have been expressed during another century. Sometimes the unexpressed emotion is one of loss—or of love. These unexpressed emotions are often the cause of many current psychological symptoms.

In all cases, the resolutions come from experiencing the situation more completely and in releasing its energy. It's this sense of completeness that allows us to be relieved of our attachment to the situation and the eruption of its symptoms into our present reality. It's one of the ironies of life that what is incomplete calls us back—and our going back allows us finally to leave it.

When we experience a situation more completely, we can better determine or discriminate whatever feelings and ideas actually belong to us and which ones we wish to be free of. That is, under stress we may have taken upon ourselves someone else's karma, opinions, beliefs, or values; or made a judgment against ourselves or someone else that wasn't warranted.

The regression gives us an opportunity to go back and do it over, to make a new decision. The programs that we picked up psychologically at times of vulnerability can be left behind as simply someone else's opinion and not a judgment about our real nature.

Thus, whatever made these influences so powerful is depotentiated, and we reclaim our ability to decide for ourselves the meaning of the situation and to have more mastery over our current behavior. We come to the realization that there is no real inhibition to the expression of our emotions, but that we decided at some point that we didn't want the consequences of expressing them—or sometimes even the responsibility of deciding. In any case, we come to a position of being able to choose rather than being driven by fear or compulsivity.

A symptom is, after all, only seen as such because it appears to be inappropriate. It is this inappropriateness that gives rise to our judgments against it. When we have unexpected feelings about our situation, or someone, we worry about those feelings. However, when we can find a reasonable and concrete cause for those feelings we're much less concerned. Furthermore, when those feelings can be placed in a context, and as it were, attached back into the past and left there, we not only have less worry about them but they don't bother us any more. It's as though, via the regression they were placed back where they belonged all along.

If you want to look purely at the imagery involved without reference to reincarnation, there are still a number of possible explanations. To assume that it's the inner images motivating us, regardless of their origin, still places the regression imagery into the central focus. If we view these images as motivating and suggestive forces in the psyche, we can access them and bring them into consciousness. This places their motivating force under more conscious control. In effect, they are a visual or somatic representation of future suggestions that would otherwise seek completion in the outer life.

The regression experience allows for the experiencing and release of these scripts so that they need not be carried into the outside world. Therefore, the unconscious programs of failure, self-defeat, unpleasant relationships, or self-punishment can find an expression, safely, in the context of the therapist's office. Experiencing these programs consciously in this way, the client is then able to recognize the patterns when they occur on the outside so that more choice may be exercised to alter or interrupt them.

Using an energy model, one would say that the images are crystallized emotions or structured psychic energy that can be released by bringing the images more into consciousness. Thus, the symptom may be looked at as a blockage of psychic energy that has taken a form mimicking sensory data. By releasing the emotional energy that is tied up in the images, the client realizes benefits that include less rigidity, more available energy, and less emotional upset.

Ultimately, past-life therapy could be viewed as an act of "associative integration." Thus, seen as imagery or energy, we could allow the therapy procedure to assume a current-life context free of any reference to or belief in reincarnation. This points to the importance of the personal metaphors that motivate us, usually unconsciously.

In short, this type of therapy is basically a clearing of the conscious mind so that the unconscious images that stand directly behind the sensory world and our symptoms can emerge into our awareness. In so doing, the incomplete gestalt, the karmic debts, the metaphors can be relived and relieved.

TRUE PSYCHOTHERAPY, OR "CARE OF THE SOUL"

First of all, let's look at the client's experience of going through a regression. Many of the anecdotal accounts have already listed the benefits of the therapy—the release of emotion, the reduction of anxiety, the increase of creativity, and the increase of psychic ability. In almost every case there's an expansion of one's self-image to include the unexpected elements of the regression imagery.

One of the experiential effects is the discovery or realization that one's self goes much deeper than we would ordinarily have thought. Even if one does not believe in reincarnation, there's still that experience of the deeper level of the personality, which is the repository of all those images. This deeper self is also the organizing function that forms the images into the series of remembered events.

Again, the end result could be the understanding of a problem or finding an explanation. One might also be more comfortable with accepting blame or responsibility for the present-life predicament. A current unpleasant situation may seem to be justified because of past "bad deeds." However, this kind of faultfinding is not effective therapy, it simply reinforces the structure that allows the person to remain attached to the problem.

The goal of past-life therapy is not to get lost in the movies of the mind, but to free ourselves from their influence. Nor is it to substitute one problem or set of beliefs for another. One may still choose to remain in an unpleasant situation but to do so out of choice and with a fuller realization of the consequences.

The therapy does not eliminate the individual's capacity to feel love, hurt, sadness, anger, or anxiety. Rather, it frees these emotions so they can become the health-maintaining signals they were meant to be. The overall self becomes more in control rather than any of these less complete elements.

Ego functioning is enhanced. With the way "ego" is often used negatively in metaphysical conversations, I should clarify what I mean. In regression therapy, the proper functioning of the ego is enhanced without the much-maligned "ego-attachment" that is the real cause for concern. These proper functions of the ego are twofold: first, accurate data collection—being able to discriminate what belongs to us and what belongs to others; and second, effective decision making.

Simply going through the regression process itself is an

act of opening oneself up to awareness of both inner and outer realities. To produce something creative from within, to order it, to check it against external reality, and to give it all new meaning is a process of training in clarity of mind. One learns to "report without resistance, existence."

Past-life therapy can also have important implications for the way in which the therapist treats the client as a human being. First of all, more power is given to the client. Validity is given to the client's experiences rather than to the therapist's interpretations. Healing is seen to reside within the client and not to come from the therapist.

There are none of the implied moral judgments one finds in conventional diagnoses. In fact, a diagnosis is generally unnecessary since the task of regression therapy is to find the context from which the problem came, not to assess the degree of "fit" or appropriateness into the present.

There is obviously more respect given to the conscious and unconscious worlds of the client. Rather than being reduced to complexes or diagnostic labels, the feelings and images of the client are taken almost at face value.

Past-life therapy tends to be briefer than traditional talk therapy because of its intensity. It's more experiential than intellectual.

Here's a list of some of the noted benefits of past-life therapy:

- The imagined context—memory images—surrounds and binds the emotion.
- Conscious and unconscious minds are united, while the function that allows us to tell which is which remains active.
- Right and left hemispheres of the brain are activated and integrated through the use of both language and image.
- Meaning is given to otherwise baffling events.

- Through the concept of karma, we're given responsibility for our situation.
- A direction for change is often indicated because of the implied lesson needing to be learned.
- We're given some sense of a place in the greater scheme of things, while still maintaining our individuality.
- Trapped energy in the psyche is freed and integrated for more conscious use.
- Psychic abilities often improve and meditative states deepen.

THE NETHERTON TECHNIQUE: IS IT OR IS IT NOT HYPNOSIS?

A basic problem with the controversy regarding the use of hypnosis is that people speak as though hypnosis has some existence as an entity with clearly identifiable features, dimensions, and regular results. In fact, there is no entity known as hypnosis whose outcomes can be clearly predicted. I'm not saying that hypnosis does not exist. Rather, I feel the term now covers such a broad area of human functioning, and its own experts so disagree about its nature, that the term is no longer specific enough to be as useful as it was when it was used in its earlier days.

Hypnosis refers to either the behavior of the operator in inducing a trance or an altered state in another, or the behavior and experience of the subject who goes through some altered state of consciousness.

The questions of who's in control and what states of consciousness have been produced—memory or amnesia, access to unconscious memory, induced hallucinations, and posthypnotic suggestions—depend not on the imaginary entity called "hypnosis," but on the behavior of the subject. Again, that is not to say that hypnotic realities do not exist, but rather, that they involve several dimensions or factors of consciousness that get lost in the labeling.

Even in a history of hypnosis we find reference to such diverse activities as "stroking" or "the royal touch" for healing in previous centuries, the "fluid" of Mesmer's "animal magnetism," or the trance, or suggestibility, or metaphor. Modern practitioners and therapists fall prey to identifying with one of these aspects, defining the rest in terms of that one, and calling it hypnosis.

Each of these manifestations represents a discrete phenomenon or function of the mind. Any or all may be in operation at one time. You may slip into a trance state. You may have a trance with suggestibility. You may be rendered suggestible without the induction of trance—as advertisers well know. A lover may be entranced by the other—seeming to be under the other's control. However, while entrancement and unquestioned obedience can come with emotions of love, they can also come with participation in military and paramilitary groups.

As if to emphasize my point, there are already schools of healing specializing in one of the above attributes of hypnosis. Stroking and the royal touch have been replaced by "aura healers" or healers using "energy flow." Altered states are promoted in relaxation training for stress control. Constructive hallucination is taught in various guided-image modalities. Suggestibility with trance is used in habit control such as smoking or weight control. Neurolinguistic Programming teaches the art of suggestion without necessarily inducing trance. It's no wonder that the boundaries and core of hypnosis have become blurred.

To be fair, part of the problem also arises from science's simple lack of knowledge about the nature, functioning, and capacities of the mind.

Now the question of whether regression is achieved with or without hypnosis would be a moot one if it weren't for the fact that, because of preconceived notions, people who have difficulty producing trance are then unfairly judged to be blocked or unable to have a past-life experience. Part of the irony of the situation is that this often occurs in the very people who might benefit the most from accessing other parts of themselves. The use of the Netherton Technique has shown that people who are hypnotic failures (who do not produce predictable trance, do not lose consciousness of their surroundings, or do not respond to hypnotic suggestions) can still gain access to and have very poignant and moving experiences.

The problem is not whether the client is hypnotizable, but whether the therapist is able to find the key in the client's behavior or the technique that will allow unconscious knowledge—the past-life memories—to become manifest. Indeed, some people do not identify with any image-making activity in themselves. For these people, their trains of associations can be used to access dynamically significant information.

But is the Netherton Technique hypnosis? I would have to answer, "Yes and no." There is no induction into trance, but an altered state does occur as a by-product of the accessing of memory. The focusing acts like an induction, turning the attention of the client inward.

However, there is what I consider to be a crucial difference. With Netherton's techniques clients maintain a consciousness that seems able to look both inward and outward at the same time. They are not lost in a trance. Nor do they become dependent on the hypnotist to be able to remember additional lives. That is to say, clients do not learn to associate past-life memories with trance and are therefore better able to learn to access them on their own.

CHAPTER 17

A CASE STUDY
OF PHOBIA

"CAN YOU SEE MY HUSBAND?"

It was a former client of mine now asking assistance for her husband.

"Howard has a problem with heights," she explained, "and a new job that requires him to climb." There was some urgency to the request since he would soon have to climb the tower once more to man the observation booth that was part of the job. In the meantime, he had other duties—and time to worry. I gave him the first opening I had available.

Phobias **tend** to be rather gratifying to work with for a number of **reasons**. For one thing, the problem is quite clear and **specific**—the phobia is of a particular object or situation. The feelings of anxiety are easily provoked, and the images come quickly. Thus, the problem can be focused on rapidly, the regression is normally dramatic, and the relief unmistakable.

Howard had no particular belief in reincarnation, but he was desperate for a solution to his problem. He began his session by telling me of the time he had to climb a tower to gain access to an observation booth. "I thought I was going to die," he said. "I didn't think I was going to make it down."

Howard's phobia was specific to climbing and being in an exposed high place. He had no problem when he is inside a building. He described being "fascinated" while at the same time being terrified. "It's an impulse to jump, and I wonder what it would feel like to fall."

Howard's history indicated that he was an only child. There was one previous pregnancy just prior to his birth. That child was full term—but was born dead.

We began the actual session with a description of the most recent incident—Howard climbing the tower.

> I'm dry in the throat. I feel the increasing fear. It's like time stopped. My heart is pounding. I'm going to fall. I felt I couldn't hold on. I couldn't go on any longer. Each step was like climbing a mountain. At the top I felt like jumping. I wondered what it would feel like to fall. It's almost like a desire to experience that fear—to give in to the whole thing.
>
> The camera girl mentioned that I was sixty-five feet up. It's like it snapped. I thought, "I won't be able to do it. I'm going to die. I won't see my loved ones again." I was afraid I'd freeze and have to be carried down. I just couldn't see myself climbing down.

Out of this description, given the sound of his voice and his body posture, the phrase that seemed to carry the strongest charge was, "I'm going to die." Therefore, I began the regression by having him focus on that phrase.

> I'm going to die. [Repeated several times.] I'm young and like in a fall. I'm headed toward the ground. I wish it would come soon. I want to get it over with. But I can't make it. It's so far down. I'm going to fall. I can't hold on. It's so slow—like I'm floating. It seems like there's no bottom to be reached. I'm sort of hanging in space—falling—but really to nowhere. I'm falling but not getting closer to the

ground—like floating into eternity. Then the words
come, "Relax, you'll be all right."

As will become evident later, this was the event he'd
been living over and over through the phobia. But the last
phrase pulled him into the memory of an event that occurred in this life. At around the age of five or six he
recalled using a ladder to climb a tree on his uncle's farm.

> I climbed to the top. But then I realize I'm very
> frightened. I thought it would be fun, but now I fear
> I'm going to fall. . . . I can't come down. I can't make
> it. I'm going to fall. I hear myself saying, "Please come!
> I can't stay here anymore! . . . Hurry up! I'm afraid
> I'm going to fall."

He clung to the ladder until his uncle came up to retrieve
him and bring him down.

Here's an example of a childhood event that turns out to
be traumatic and would by many therapists be indicated as
the cause of the later phobia. However, it indicates to me
that a fear of heights was already in operation. The event
of climbing the ladder and going to the top of the tree was
not traumatic in itself. The pain and fear came from the
provoked thoughts about falling and dying. Without this
mental agitation, the whole incident would have been unremarkable. This is an example of a preexisting program
brought to light—and to new life—by childhood events.
The childhood incident acts as a trigger.

Therefore, I indicated the need to go back in time to that
fear of falling and dying. This led Howard to a memory of
being in the womb.

> It's warm, soothing, relaxing. It's like floating. I'm
> hearing the words, "Be careful. Don't fall." It's either
> my father or the doctor—definitely a male. My mother
> is climbing stairs, taking it very slowly, one step at a

time. The fright comes on a stairway in her home. She slips and starts to fall and just manages to hold on. She starts thinking, "I'm going to lose this baby—just like the other one. I fell. I killed the baby. If I wouldn't have fallen, I would have saved the baby. It's all my fault."

Howard's mother was expressing guilt about the loss of the first child even though there had been no known injury to the fetus from that fall. I asked Howard if he could go back to the source of that guilt carried by the mother. He said:

It's in the hospital. She realizes there isn't going to be a baby. She thinks back to that fall. I'm inside my mother and afraid of the hospital. Something was wrong. That's why I was here. Somehow I know I'm going to die. It's all very tense, and I feel my fists clenched. I'm trying to stay alive. My toes are drawn together and my eyes are closed tightly. There's fear. Something is wrong. My body is drawing up into a knot. I'm trying to make myself safe, to ward off the danger. I'm feeling closed in, like something's wrapped around me very tight—holding me in. I can't breathe and things become tighter. But then things gradually loosen, become more relaxed and I'm floating, warm and safe. Then I have the feeling of falling. It seems rapid, endless—dark and endless. I hear a male voice and I feel like it's time to perform—time to breathe. I should be on my own. But there's the doctor's voice saying, "He's dead. She wanted him so much, but he's dead. We can't do a thing."

Howard's entity or consciousness had evidently been attached to the stillborn fetus who failed to survive birth two years before his birth in this life.

What we have so far is an adult experience, a childhood event, and a prenatal occurrence from the present life, all of which involve the sensation of falling, the fear of falling, and thoughts of dying. In addition, we have the prenatal memory of a pregnancy immediately preceding his own, which did indeed involve a death associated with a feeling of falling, as well as the mother's memory of having fallen while she was pregnant.

Howard finally seemed ready to go back to the primary cause of this pattern in order to find out what was seeking completion, and what had locked him into repeating and reexperiencing these events. Therefore, I suggested that he go back to the time just before the feelings of falling became so prominent. He described being:

> . . . on a cliff. It's very high, overlooking a beautiful valley. I'm right near the edge. One inch closer and I'm gone. It's beautiful and I'd like to float down to the valley and be like one of the birds. . . .
>
> I'm a small boy about eight or ten years old. I'm dressed in short pants, shoes, and a shirt. It's warm and summertime. It's a hot, beautiful day. I get one step too close and I do fall. It seems to be very slowly—falling. I tense up, waiting for the end. I know it's coming and I can't do anything about it. . . . I seem to still be falling. I never feel the bottom. I've been falling forever, like there's no end.

Howard experienced a fall that should have taken only a few seconds as "falling forever." It happened to him— as it has happened in other people's accounts of death by falling—that the soul or entity left the body prior to the actual physical death. Although leaving the body can act as an avoidance of the physical pain of the death, the person frequently fails to fully experience leaving the event. Therefore, the sensation of falling forever gets locked into the unconscious mind and seeks repetitive expression—until the act is completed. The purpose is to try to complete what was left unfinished—to effect closure. We did this in the regression session when I asked him what his body experienced after his consciousness left it:

It was like an explosion. My feet hit first, and I'm almost torn apart. It was like every bone was broken. The body is there rejected, abandoned, and unwanted. It's hardly recognizable.

Having fallen from the cliff would account for the particular form Howard's phobia had taken, but his report indicated to me that there were additional factors to be considered. Specifically, his description of the body as it lay there, "rejected, abandoned, and unwanted," indicated that there was more to this event than just an accidental fall.

I instructed him to go back to the situations that had set him up for this event and asked his unconscious mind to give us the words of rejection that he had internalized. Howard's response was "We didn't want you anyway." With that phrase he began to describe an event in the boy's life. Once more, the rejection began in utero:

. . . before I was born, as soon as my father found out my mother was pregnant. They had to get married. He berated her: "Why weren't you careful. I hate you. You should be careful. I'm going to leave you."

She had already had a child by another man several years before who [the child] was very jealous of me. My mother was disgraced and ashamed. I could hear such words being said about or to her as, "tramp" and "You're a fallen woman."

This rejected young man, who had internalized yet another prenatal form of rejection, grew up in a family in which he was further rejected, in which there was a lot of fighting, and in which he was materially and emotionally neglected. From a particular incident he related:

Leaving the house. It's a beautiful day. I look at the cliff and want to jump, but I can't. Actually, I'm afraid of falling. I want out—out of the situation, but I don't

really want to die. I stand on the edge of the cliff and
freeze. Nobody cares. I'm thinking that I never want to
go back to that house.

Thus, at that moment of feeling totally rejected as well
as rejecting his family and never wanting to go back but
being afraid to either run away or to jump, he is indeed
frozen. Although it was his original intention to throw himself off the cliff, he couldn't bring himself to do it. Just at
that moment, however, his foot slipped and he fell.

Howard never consciously got to make the decision.

My analysis of the situation was that there may have still
been some lifetime prior to the one of the fall whose karma
he was playing out. It seemed to be a script of rejection.
Nevertheless, what we had covered seemed to adequately
address the problem for which he had come: the fear, feelings, and fascination involved with falling.

Yet, there was an unanswered question in my mind about
what linguistic connecting links might lie between the fallen
boy and the later stillborn child. I asked Howard if there were
words or attitudes preventing that later birth. He responded,
"Don't fall. Be careful." This suggested to me that, as he
was about to be born and he was beginning the process of
"dropping," that often-described feeling of falling, triggered
the previous reaction of leaving the body. In a sense, his fear
of dying by falling brought about the death. To fearfully
leave the body in order to avoid physical trauma should be
distinguished from ordinary out-of-body experiences. The
former is an act of escape and incompletion, while the latter
is usually an effort consciously undertaken to expand one's
awareness.

Howard's regression was exemplary. It contained nearly
all of the elements possible in past-life programming:

• There was the prenatal programming of rejection during the previous life.

- There was the prenatal programming of fear of falling in the present life.
- There was a childhood trigger event in climbing the tree.
- There were incomplete actions—the decision about whether to jump, and the leaving of the body before the death—that were played out again and again until they could be resolved.

It was this incompleteness that made for the fascination Howard felt about falling. He was stuck or frozen in that fall and needed a way to complete it so it would not result in another death.

This true regression account also shows how in two to three hours Howard was able to be released from a lifetime—or lifetimes—of programming. Not long after, he successfully made his climb to the observation booth without fear or discomfort. As fate would have it, his job then changed so that he would no longer have to face the tower again.

The account was closed, the lesson had been learned, and fate was not going to ask him to repeat it. By bringing these unconscious memories into his conscious mind, Howard was clearly able to free himself from his phobic reactions. In so doing, he was then able to return himself more completely to the present so that he not only did not panic at the heights, but he could let his feet dangle over the edge and enjoy the view.

OF TIME AND KARMIC MIDWIVES

Many people believe that time is simultaneous—that all our lives are going on at the same time—and they wonder if that doesn't contradict the principle of having one lifetime after another. While it seems fashionably enlightened to deny linear time in favor of the concept of simultaneous time especially given the popularity of the Seth material, my belief is a little different. Because of the obvious influence I see our past lives having on our present life, I feel that it would be absolutely true to say that all our lives are happening psychologically in the present.

However, I do not accept one concept of time over another or say that one is true and therefore the other must be false. When I walk, I put one foot in front of the other, one at a time. That is one of my experiences. But I have also known occasions in which time and space disappeared. That is another of my experiences. I feel no need to deny either, for to do so would be to ignore a major portion of life as we know it.

The distinction is valuable, though. Think of the two brain hemispheres. As most brain research shows, the right hemisphere of the general population functions in simultaneous time. The left hemisphere operates in linear time. Both are realities—and unless we take both into account, we're operating with half a brain.

I'm often asked how clients, such as Howard, find me in such a timely fashion. I believe this is because by the time they walk into my office, they have within themselves realized that they want to pass through this pattern and be done with it in their lives. I've often mused about how the same set of actions can bring some people luck and others very different results. Since I believe that the healing comes from within the clients and not from me, I must also believe that my influence is modest. I just happen to be where the clients are when they're about to get rid of their problem. I'm a karmic midwife. When someone calls me, something has triggered it. This means that something has emerged into their consciousness crying, "Help. I want some attention."

I don't heal. My greatest influence is when I am sensitive enough to help the client to merge with his or her own place of inner healing.

PART IV

THE EVOLUTION
OF
CHRISTIANITY

CHAPTER 18

THE PREPARATION
AND TEACHING

SUPPOSE FOR A MOMENT THAT SOME OF THE GREAT FIG-
ures of history were alive today. Imagine that, instead of
laundered accounts of history strongly influenced by political factors, we could look through a window of time and
see directly through the eyes of those who observed the
events themselves.

In a very real way we can do just that. Great historical
figures, no matter how far back in the past, still live in the
memories of those with whom they came in contact. It's
ironic that although this section supports many of the traditional Christian beliefs, it's likely to be the subject of
controversy. This is because of the use of concepts relating
to reincarnation to provide that support; however, it does
call into question the position that reincarnation and traditional Christianity must somehow be at odds.

PREPARATION

This is a story of the personage who became known to
us as Jesus. The expectation of the coming of the Messiah

231

is still a Jewish tradition. In fact, many cultural traditions looked forward to the advent of a savior.

The coming of Jesus was foretold, expected, and prepared for by those who accepted him as the Messiah. Biblical tradition reports that the Magi, who were astrologers, saw ''His star'' and so knew to begin their journey. Of course, there were people closer to the Holy Family who were also making preparation.

Our story begins with the subconscious account of Lance, a twenty-three-year-old hair stylist:

Astrology was part of it. There was simplicity in the life that we led in preparation for Jesus. People before me created the organization and I was brought up in it. Faith prevented me from questioning. It was definitely a minority, believing in Jesus Christ. It was a secret society—[we were] not supposed to let anyone know what was going on. It would be a threat to the standards; it would disrupt. We have knowledge that was not revealed to other people, like reincarnation and the universalness of the Spirit of Christ.

Our diet was different, too, from the others. We were vegetarian. We believed that people who abused their bodies through sexual misconduct or overeating became vulgar. The organization was in the countryside, not far from Rome.

I was born an unwanted twin and given to the Essenes. By age fourteen or fifteen I was part of a group of chaste virgins studying the entrance of Jesus into the world. We were junior priestesses who would serve. We engaged in reading, studying, and self-control of our sexual desires. There were ceremonies with smoke and fire; that was part of the preparing of Mary to make the situation easier for her to come into the world. Our rules were for us to stay, and to not leave the community. There were three wise men who were indirectly related. They knew they would help prepare.

We pitied the other people for their religious beliefs and gods. We taught reincarnation. We [the women] stayed together and were rarely involved with men. The celibacy was part of our sacrifice thought to help us in maturity. Sex was not seen as bad, but it was not the ultimate fulfillment. In addition, that sort of fulfillment could be had in a later life. We engaged in much meditation, prayers, and self-respect. We subsisted mainly on fruits, nuts, and vegetables. We were admonished to, "Look within yourself and you'll see the truth." There was mainly the desire to progress as a soul rather than the suppression of sexuality.

This Essene sister became curious about the rumored feasts and orgies of the Romans and, contrary to the rules of her group, stole away and was caught by a guard while she observed a party at the house where her twin had been reared. She died in prison, considering the time to have been wasted since she could have been serving instead. She felt an aloneness but did have the satisfaction that the knowledge she had attained could not be taken from her. Even when she sought the satisfaction of her curiosity, she maintained their ideals of "beauty in my simplicity—plainness but richness."

On a personal level, Lance was reminded of his earlier experience of belonging and purpose. In addition, in a larger context, we see how this Messiah came into a particular community, which helped prepare him for his eventual destiny.

Perhaps through enough regressions, we will gain more firsthand knowledge about the early years of Jesus. Our account here, however, resumes with a client's encounter with a matured teacher.

TEACHING

Hardly an ordinary man, Jesus' ability to influence people either for love, anger, or fear has been traditionally taken for granted. There was fear at the loss of political power and fear and anger at the alleged blasphemy. The effect of that profound influence remains alive to this day nearly 2,000 years later when a middle-aged man in my office was moved to tears as he described this scene:

Jim saw himself wearing leather sandals and a robe tied with a striped cloth. He lived around fruit orchards of figs and dates. His residence was square and "sparse but adequate," made of light clay, like the soil. He lived there with his family—his parents, his sister, and her son.

At mealtime there were prayers to Jehovah, and his thoughts would often turn to God. He would like to know more things. "There are many things I don't understand. I want to live the right life—obey the commandments and know my part. . . . I'm a grape harvester."

Because of his desire to learn how to obey the commandments better, he sought those teachers available to him. During his time, there was one particular teacher drawing large crowds with both his manner and his teachings. We find this grape harvester in the crowd:

> We are listening to Jesus and there is a great feeling. God cares for us no matter how we are. He is so wonderful. It's the first time that I actually feel a part. He brings meaning into my life. I want to touch Him but he's too far away.
>
> I have a feeling that is strong, uplifting, and gives me peace. There's a warm sensation moving from my stomach to my heart, and when I cry [as he was doing in my chair] my head feels light. It's crushing, yet a relief. There is such acceptance; accepting all that's around me, even the soldiers. It's a feeling of being each and every thing; a feeling of love for everything and that everything has love for me. Even me—a servant—is important in the eyes of God. I don't feel like a wretch.

This grape harvester hungered for the teachings he found in this man. But what of the conflict in those who deeply believed in the traditions of the Hebrews? Some called the actions of Jesus the fulfillment of the Jewish law. Others saw Jesus as a threat to the Roman and Jewish traditions. Regardless of which side one's family might have chosen in this conflict, those who chose to take a different route were in danger of suffering a loss of their own tradition and the esteem of their family.

Not all of the conflict was with political authority. There is always the internal conflict, as shown by Elizabeth, a young Jewish caterer whose thoughts even today are consumed with religious issues that would dissolve the sharp distinction between the Christian and Hebrew traditions by her emphasis on certain basic overriding principles.

Elizabeth's religious conflict has come down to her through the ages to this life. She was raised in Judaism but felt a pull toward Christianity some six years ago. Going back into her past, she found herself with people in white robes in caves by an ocean:

> I felt I was a child, close to the people but not completely understanding what they were doing. They looked so much bigger. There was a loving and open atmosphere. These people worked well with nature and together. They weren't constricted by their environment. They taught that Jesus was love, and I see a person who is an expression of that love.
>
> They were healers. That man—people are around him. I don't know what they're doing. They are putting some type of robe on this person. There's no need for words. I see myself following, just to be around him.

Could it be that Elizabeth's attraction to Christianity, despite her Jewish upbringing, derives from these till-now-forgotten memories? Her conflict today is remarkably similar to that of the original followers of this Teacher, as has been shown in history—and in the life of the grape harvester.

It began as inspiration but was to become controversy and persecution.

CHAPTER 19

CONTROVERSY AND PERSECUTION

CONTROVERSY

Jesus inspired not only illumination, action, brotherhood, or love but also controversy. As the grape harvester who was filled with the Spirit at hearing the teachings of Jesus observed:

> The great feeling became clouded; it came from the people in the town. Their talking confused me. It's about the teachings of Moses and about what the Master said. There's turmoil inside of me now. I don't know whether to believe the feelings or the logic. They are refuting his teachings; saying he's one of Satan's. Others say, "No, because he heals." They say he has no power to forgive sins, that he blasphemes, that only God can forgive sins. I love the word of God, but I'm not sure what He wants me to do. I want to think of God as loving and forgiving, but some of the teachers make Him sound hateful. [I asked him what finally put these arguments to rest and he replied:] The feelings inside—they tell me that God was a god of love. He forgives sins.
>   They talk of healing and many are excited. Some hate him, and many don't know. I see men talking with my

236

father, and they're waving their hands. It's important. Eventually I, too, am accused of blasphemy, of going against God's words. I'm afraid, yet I'm not.

Someone takes a sword and stabs me. I want God to forgive him. I seem to move through a tunnel. There's a bright light and I'm drawn to it. I'm drawn to the presence of That which created me. . . .

More of the grape harvester's experience is presented when we look at his impression of the teachings of Jesus a little later.

Concurrent with the time of Jesus was another charismatic figure whose life became intertwined with that of Jesus. This man was John the Baptist. His suffering, of course, was not directly related to his involvement with Jesus but rather because of his own political importance. At the time, he had such a following of his own that the authorities were afraid to act against him. But as often happens, these political considerations were superceded by Herod's infatuation for Salome.

As reported by Darlene, a fifty-seven-year-old executive secretary, the charismatic Baptist was indeed also able to move people:

I don't know if I'm supposed to lead or to follow. I'm in awe of something so great. I'm in awe of a power, a goodness, something very great. I just know that there is a mightier power. I've always known . . . It's a great person—John the Baptist. He's a follower, but he also leads. . . .

But he's gone now and I don't know what to do. I don't know if I am supposed to lead or to follow, and I'm afraid I might cause someone to be killed. And now something has happened. Something happened to Jesus. He died, and it's lost.

By then, after I die, I am all mind and no body. . . . It's like a happy state—light, very light and all-knowing.

PERSECUTION

The martyrdom of John the Baptist brings us to the subject of the sufferings of the followers of Jesus during the early years—until they attained their own political power and began their own persecutions.

Let's begin with an account given to us by Delia, a school teacher:

> In a market square, I see slaves and prisoners being carted away. I am feeling fear, sorrow, and helplessness. I am unable to help; and I fear also that I might be taken away. . . .
>
> A man stands before me. It's a non-Christian religious figure warning me that I'll be discovered, punished, and killed. I'm dragged away by guards who say, "You are wrong and you will be punished." But I don't care. I am taken to a place of public execution and it is announced: "This person has been found to preach against the church and must die."
>
> I am burned.

Unjust accusations abound in times of religious controversy. People try to justify false judgments by portraying Jesus as a politically dangerous rabble rouser. His innocence, however, is asserted by Emma, a forty-two-year-old administrator. Her life becomes one more example of that suffering:

> There was a long trip, but I'm meeting my husband at last. He's been here in Rome. I don't like Rome because there are too many people and it's too noisy and too crowded. But this is where he has to be and my duty is beside him.
>
> Oh, no, my husband has become a Christian! It goes against the gods and must be kept a secret. I just get here and now he tells me what they're going to do. The troopers expect a lot of trouble and must go to Judea. I don't want to go but the wife's place is beside her husband so I go to Judea, too.

It's hot in Judea. Judeans want the Romans to leave, and the Romans want the Judeans to accept Roman things. There's going to be trouble.

They crucify him—the man called Jesus. They shouldn't crucify him. You can just look at the man and see that he hasn't done anything wrong. But the Jews don't want him either. My husband wants to give up his command. He can't consciously be a Roman and a Christian. . . .

We're always running and hiding now and if we don't get away, we'll be crucified too.

We do get away to Athens for a while. And then we go back to Rome because our families are there. I don't want to go back to Rome because it's too dangerous. The emperor is mad. Caligula is crazy. He throws everybody to the lions and we'd better watch our step. . . .

Things are O.K. for a while, but then somebody suspects us. One of the servants is a spy looking for Christians. We've got to leave. . . . We don't make it, but the children are safe. We and others are herded into the Coliseum. I don't want to die a martyr. I don't want to die this way. It doesn't do any good to resist. No matter what you do you end up out there with the lions.

In the arena, it's us and the lions. I lost all track of time. It was terrible. We couldn't fight them. They were too big. . . . But then there is peace—peace and tranquility—no more fear.

Jesus was a man who inspired fear in the powerful, love in the sinners, humility in the proud, anger in the weak, and hope in the downtrodden. He continues to speak to us through the memories of those who witnessed his teachings.

We also see the continuing controversy that exists to this day between those who become inspired by elevated teachings, but because they're not part of the present religious or political establishment are labeled "products of Satan" and suppressed.

One wonders what the fate of this Jesus would be were he to appear these days in the midst of those religions and sects who claim the "One True Way."

CHAPTER 20

THE TEACHINGS

Some of Jesus' teachings are given in the Bible. And others reach us through our window in time providing special impressions that some of the forgotten but fortunate ones of the past can report about the man they took to be the Messiah. Seen in a new light and from a very personal level these firsthand accounts of this Master's teachings are free of the cultural biases and predispositions of those who have jumped to interpret Christian doctrine for us.

This man Jesus talks of loving one another as oneself—that "What you are here is of great importance to reaching that state of heaven, that peace." We won't be accepted only for what we believe. I just seem to know that to follow his way will be difficult and lonely; and that many are called but few are chosen. I need to be an example—that is the test. The test is to be able to die for one's faith.

Jim, who was the grape harvester in his past life, reports the impressions of his feelings and the teachings that he either heard himself or heard discussed by others:

My feelings inside tell me that God is a God of love. He forgives the sins and He wants everyone to be His. He is our Creator, our Father, and our Friend. He lets it rain and makes the sun to shine on the wicked as well as the righteous. . . .

God is inside. The body is the temple of your soul. There is so much importance in the synagogue for worship and sacrifice. I'm happy because I know that the worship comes from the heart and not actions. What is important is to think of God. It's the surface that can fool you. My station doesn't mean anything—it's what I am. [I asked him what that is.] I am what I am in spirit, a part of God.

My subject adds self-consciously to that last statement, "I can't understand that."

This is an example of how the consciousness from the past life has picked up part of the philosophy of monism, or oneness. His current-life consciousness has been conditioned by thoughts of duality and is confused by the expression of what he believed in the previous life. His statements made sense out of the logic presented in the past life. But, being conscious and having the ego present in the regression, he recognizes it as different. Such events as this—something being apprehended as "ego-dystonic" (not recognized or accepted by the ego) yet inspiring—indicate the presence of philosophies that have no known root in this life. In other words, this vignette is highly unlikely to be a product of fantasy since this life's experience forms no basis for its construction.

Naturally, since these teachings bear similarities to well-known biblical passages, they prove little in themselves. However, until similar reports come from cultures unfamiliar with Christianity, these will have to suffice as mainly inspirational reminders of the wisdom that is available in the universe of the unconscious mind.

In my practice I have had no account as yet of the later events close to the end of Jesus' physical life. Morris Netherton, however, reports data regarding the crucifiction. My chronology must jump to a much later time, when the Church has become an institution.

CHAPTER 21

THE INSTITUTION

As HAPPENS IN MANY GRASS-ROOTS MOVEMENTS, THE original leaders die off and the "true followers" begin to establish a structure, an organization, in order to perpetuate what has come down to them. Simplicity and inspiration often give way to dogma and formalism. Ritual may or may not retain its original numinous nature. What follows here are two accounts, one of a monsignor who saw things in purely political terms in his time but was aware of better ones. The other is an account of a pope who, perhaps because of his great compassion and concern for the people, also retained an awareness of the roots of ritual. Thus, by the time of later leaders, the traditional inspiring and pristine origins eventually give way to the "Church." Once a collection of true believers, the Church had become a political entity.

Niles, an attorney in this life, gives us this account:

I am a monsignor in the Vatican in Rome. I serve the Pope. I'm referred to as "Your Reverence." Essentially, I'm a secretary who kept records.

Politics is used for advancement. Sex is too, but not

by me. I am very straight, strict, and feared. The Pope
listened to me. I wanted to be a cardinal. He could have
made me one but he was selfish. . . .

Another Pope, Pius the Tenth, however, walked between two worlds. He was a good Pope.

The vested interests of political power, tradition, authority,
and the felt need to be protected from competing beliefs not-
withstanding, I in no way want to impugn the sincerity of
those who were involved in the organizations of the Church.
Any large organization with a long history may show us times
of corruption as well as sincerity.

Witness this account given to us by Alex, a thirty-five-
year-old psychotherapist, whose memory images showed
him to have been a Pope. He says of the masses of people
he wishes to serve:

There are just so many of them—so many of them
with so much need. I stand before them with my staff
and red-clothed bishops. I may be more aware of their
needs than they. They are satisfied with so little.

In terms of religious power, it all rests on my word;
as if the whole creation, whole new forms of being could
be enlivened by annunciating an idea to be taken up by
the impressionable and adoring affection of the people,
creating something new. The singularity of that position
is a source of great formative power as well as setting
one [me] apart from anyone else.

In the mass of people crowding around there is no
place to breathe. They press in and energy goes out. I
have that conflict of wanting to do more yet being personally depleted. There is a need to balance out.

[Here he discusses the papal position of power and
the symbolic identity he assumes by giving up his personal life.] There is this dual energy. The very public
thing of cloth vestments that are a shroud to the personal
personality that dies under the vestments so that a perfect example can be seen. And it's a very public office.
All the preparations for an appearance or ceremony are
made in private with only a few advisors.

There is in me that wish to wipe away the residue, the heaviness of so-called sins. What is in general called the "sin" is really error. My thinking is that it [forgiving sins] is more the granting the right to be happy—to say that someone else [the Savior] has already paid the price.

I feel forgiveness in my heart and hands like a blessing. Things have really gotten confused, mixing up the absolution with the blessing. The church has become like some of the old Hebrews and their laws. What was to be formulated and constructed and initiated to be a structure for the distribution of the glory and outpouring has almost become a blockage, a distraction. It has become more a sign than a carrier of that [Holy Power]. It becomes clear at the ordination.

At the ordination there is rapt attention, great celebration. The immediate things on my mind are the clothes, vestments, miter, and staff—one piece of cloth on another. . . . Certainly there could be no dancing. The energy could not release in dancing. About the only thing one could do would be to move one's hand in blessing lest the staff be dropped or the miter to fall, or the vestments be disarranged.

There are indeed reasons for these things (the vestments and other paraphernalia), but the form has become primary over the realization of the substance. Seeing all of the concern about the formal aspects [censing, intonations, etc.], I want not to be judging the precision of the performance. Nor do I want to struggle among all that needs to be done. I want to remain centered on the Source of it all. When it is done correctly, it regenerates itself. The important thing is to be able to move from the technical precision to the inner response.

A pillow is brought—an ornate cushion with what looks almost like a sword. It's too short to be a staff— it's more like a scepter. And a ring is brought. These are all symbols that allow the concentration of attention through the lines of which flow the energy and the will of the people so that it can be used for the ordained purpose. Odd that "ordination" takes the "ordinary" away from things.

There is a glow around everything—so it's not just empty words here! There is something to it! It's more than being a person; it's being a position and stepping into that position. Now there are those who have acted vulgarly in the position, who in a sense, had neither the spirit nor the precision. But I took it very seriously. . . .

[He goes on with a discussion about the contrast between the weight of the physical vestments as opposed to the lightness of the light and the glow around everything.] My main desire was to spread that light physically as in the Easter blessing. I take their almost blind faith, simple adoration and childlike devotion to and through this office and its ceremonial procedures and transmute that into a higher order and return it to them. It is that principle from which come the "orders," which is to return something taken. They give me the personal [their adoration and love] and I return to them the impersonal for which they are grateful. I felt the sense of not being able to give the personal back.

I realize that the individual personality who put on those vestments did not die. He was not really obscured—although I might say somewhat obscured by the brightness of the vision—he was there. In other times, it [the personality] would have found expression in exoteric personal life. They [the people] do want that which is fully human and fully divine. It's a bit of a balance: their extreme humanness, with divinity kept from them, leaves this [priestly] position to have to express in an extreme degree the divinity. In other words, the extreme humanness of the people is matched by the extreme divinity of the priesthood.

The people came to provide for the priests' material bounty and care. The priests should provide them in turn with the spiritual; taking their adoration and returning it with more of the divine fire as a valid exchange.

However, what I yearn to see happen is the upliftment—the people using the priestly function, not in a routinely obligatory manner but actually with both they and the priests moving toward each other so that they are risen—the people are risen—moving in station closer to that balancing. And then the priestly is fulfilled, having been filled full—having filled full the laws and their lives.

But reason interjects here that for many, because of

their idiosyncrasies and faults, the best they can do is to adhere closely to the law.

There was still that desire in me to move about the people incognito—to once again touch them. . . .

Now, at any of these points in history we could begin a new round of the same series of events: small groups of people being inspired by the moving Spirit of Divine Revelation through the agency of the Christ or the Holy Spirit, who are then persecuted by the established order, which mistakenly believes that such outbreaks of religious fervor are necessarily the works of the Devil. And so we see the mottled history that includes the Crusades, the Inquisition, the Reformation, and the birth of such groups as the Shakers, the Quakers, and the charismatic movements. Other needs find expression in such groups as the Masons, the Rosicrucians, the Martinists, the Kabbalists. The list could go on and on.

We are at a point in history when we are able to look back in time and have a perspective of the origin and evolution of that religious movement begun so long ago. We see how it mirrored the religion from which it rebelled and yet gave birth to new forms of its inner spirit.

CHAPTER 22

THE CHRIST AND
THE ABBOT:
LOVE AND JUDGMENT

THE SPIRIT OF CHRISTIANITY GREW OUT OF THE LEGAL-istic structures of both Rome and Mosaic law. As time went by, the followers and adherents devoted to that original spirit formed their own organization very similar to the structures from which they had come and yet under whose hand they had suffered. The simple life of fulfillment as lived by Jesus, along with his primary tenets to "love the Lord . . . and love your neighbor" became massive and wealthy agencies known now as "major religions."

These major Western religions have many distinctions of caste or social standing separating the clerical from the profane, and many laws and fine points of doctrine. The more legalistic followers of the carpenter turned the admonition of: "You are forgiven; go and sin no more," into the need to determine first whether the sin was a venal or mortal one that would require some amount of penance, here or hereafter, before one could be absolved by an act of the organization.

I'm not saying here that any of this is in and of itself wrong or necessarily to be criticized—times do change. A structure may be used to either give form and endurance to a spirit, or to contain and smother it. My purpose is to draw attention to the contrasts and evolution.

In that evolution, what would it be like to actually live through these stages? We have a clue in one of my client's regression experience.

CASE STUDY: CHARLES'S UNWORTHINESS

Charles, a thirty-four-year-old programmer/analyst, came to my office with a developed spiritual philosophy and an evident devotion to evolved living. He was, however, plagued with unexplainable feelings of "unworthiness," which were in conflict with what he knows to be a higher truth. This conflict between what he knew to be instinctively true and uplifting and his feelings of debasement expressed themselves in a past life as a monk. As we shall see, although the conflict took form in a monk's life, its origin began in simpler, much earlier times.

Following the usual interview and preparation, we began to focus on those feelings of unworthiness that were themselves evidence that he was already living in a regressed state. Using the Netherton Technique, these phrases emerged: "It's never good enough. . . . Nothing human beings do is ever good enough. By the nature of us we are not perfect."

These phrases made him recall a medieval church. He was kneeling, listening to a sermon from the abbot. The abbot was a "strong, pushy, dominating guy—that's how he got to be abbot. He was forceful."

The abbot's beliefs and the way he used them made a strong impression on this monk:

> He teaches that man is inherently evil. . . . Everything we do is to atone for our sins. He would say, "You are sinners; you are all sinners." It's emasculating. "There is nothing good enough so don't do anything but what you're told."

The beginning of the monk's serious self-doubts occurred because of the abbot's persistent degradation.

> I and another monk are going down steps into the courtyard, heading into the building away from the abbot. He [the abbot] is shaking his head, yelling at us for something we tried to do. We thought it good to show respect and adoration to God, but the abbot did not like it. It was of too joyous a nature, appealing to the love side—not justice and judgment. He's telling us it's wrong for us to even suppose we could do anything pleasing. Life is strictly for the atonement of our sins, not to be better or to please God—not even to earn merit. He tells us to go and do what we're told. . . .
>
> The joy goes out of life; it becomes a drudge. I have no thoughts, no hopes, no aspirations. That's all I'm doing—going through the days with no aspirations.

I asked Charles what it was that attached him to these experiences:

> Not being able to prove that the abbot was wrong. I know we're supposed to feel that God is joy and happiness.

The conviction that God is joy and happiness began early in his stay at the monastery. It came in moments of solitary prayer and contemplation on the question: "What is God?" What came of that communion were feelings of:

> God's respect for us as souls—the feeling of love between God and man—that He wants us to do what we can in joy and happiness to make each other happy.

Our monk has increasing distaste for the rote services that pale before the revelations that come in his more sincere prayer. "So I come on my own when I can so I can have quiet," he tells us.

But the years in the monastery and the abbot's insistent preaching took their toll. That communal and inspiring feeling lost the strength it once had in his contemplation. He began to doubt his convictions. His mind moved toward acceptance of the abbot's evident self-degredation. Yet he still practiced his daily meditation:

> This time I'm asking for help trying to understand why the abbot feels as he does, and why we're not good enough. I ask for help in understanding this unworthiness he preaches, but I get nothing that reinforces the idea that I'm not good enough.
> Another time, I'm kneeling. I'm deep inside myself, lost in feeling and oblivious to all around me. I can feel that goodness and love. . . . I don't have the doubt from the abbot. Just the openness. Just myself and no feeling coloring it. I just am; no self-consciousness. There is nothing to detract from me being myself. I don't have any doubt or preconceptions. . . . I am and He is. My mind seems bright, illuminated. My heart feels bright and warm, feeling the unity. It's what I call the classic state of beatific vision.

To begin the process of releasing the trauma of these events that was wearing on the optimism of the monk, I asked what he needed to say to the abbot that he had blocked. The monk responded with these unexpressed thoughts:

> It's wrong. You're totally wrong. You don't know what the hell you're talking about! Your vision of man as unworthy and cut off from God is incorrect. Don't even use the word anymore; it's degrading, diminishing, demeaning. Man is one with God because God lives in every man. Your view is totally wrong because you say we are separate and lowly. We have to be worthy because we are Him! [Charles's voice changes as he says:] It surprises me that I just said that.

Having now touched these deeper convictions of the unity of man and God, Charles moved spontaneously back in time to their source—to the events that had impressed him with these very thoughts. Notice how his doubting conscious mind at first confuses the images of two lives as well as conscious expectations about the appearance of the Teacher until he allows the images full rein:

> I have this stereotypical picture of Christ teaching and the Pharaoh Akhenaton [Akhenaton was the Egyptian pharaoh who was credited as the first to proclaim monotheism and to have established the form of certain mystery schools]. They are using those words, that "God lives within everyone of us; we must be worthy because we are Him." But I've seen so many movies. Anyway, the message is that the Father lives in each of us.
>
> The person preaching isn't the stereotype of Christ. It could be an apostle. He is Jewish-looking, dark-haired, bearded. He's talking, gesturing, saying that each one of us is God. It's really hot, and he's perspiring. He's insistent without being demanding or angry.
>
> He turns toward me and, gesturing, says, "Do you see that God has given each of us the power and the will to know who He is, to know who you are?" The way it is said implies that who we are and who He is, is the same thing. This is far out. I one time [in this present life] had the thought, "There is still time enough to know who we are—the will and power to know who He is, who we are."

Putting aside the personal factors in the regression for the moment, I asked him to focus on the teachings that were being promulgated:

> It's different from that of the abbot, of law and separation. The teaching says that we are God and He is us. It shocks some. Some call it blasphemy. It is a surprise. But that's what is unique about His teaching, and it ap-

peals to a lot of people—some because they felt it before, and to some it gives a feeling of self-worth. It makes them happy right away. Some—and I'm one—on hearing the idea itself, wakens to the feeling of being connected with God because I never grasped the separation.

This makes more sense. It's not intellectual. This is a heart feeling. . . . It's O.K. to love yourself. In loving yourself you are loving God.

Returning now to the person teaching these things, I asked Charles to tune in to the teacher. Charles was impressed with his eyes, his intelligence. "He was impressive but not overwhelming. He was a man like you, but the better side—intelligent, wise—without being removed or detached."

I asked the name of the teacher and Charles replied immediately: "Jesus."

Charles's regression is an example of the way in which an elevated kind of teaching was strongly impressed upon his inner mind and remained alive in spite of later attempts to degrade it. In addition, we also see evidence of a tradition of thought, handed down or periodically emerging, that is expressed by a minority of religious leaders.

In the beginning of the latter half of Charles's regression account we see the mention of the Pharaoh Akhenaton. Since we didn't explore the source of these impressions we can only speculate. However, it's likely that Charles was aware of the teachings of Akhenaton, probably through personal contact with the pharaoh or at least in a position to hear the monotheist's beliefs. That memory was tied to the memories of Jesus through the similarity of their teachings.

Many times the same sort of thing happens to all of us. We hear or read of an idea that immediately rings true or strikes a responsive chord within us—we feel very comfortable with it. We've probably heard it all before, just as Charles's older "knowing" carried through the ages to survive even the insistent program of a later monastic discipline and misguided abbot.

CHAPTER 23

OBSERVATIONS AND COMMENTS ON THE CHRISTIAN REGRESSIONS

Take note of the accounts of the teachings of Jesus as presented by these eye witnesses. They seem rather consistent. And they do not emphasize the obvious and popular dogmas now presented by many of the major religions with their focus on obedience, salvation, sacrifice, forgiveness, evil, and law. If these images had come from consciously known and familiar stories from the present life, one would expect that they would more closely resemble these now-popular dogmas. But they don't. Rather, there are themes of unity, of loving one's neighbor, of feeling love and worthiness, and of being one with the Creator.

Whatever their source, they do not come from well-known, safe, and socially sanctioned beliefs—which was the case when they were first spoken.

The question has occurred to me—and I have waited for a skeptic to pose it—about the number of people reporting memories of Jesus or the early Christian era. It's remarkable that such a localized geographical area over roughly a three-year period should produce this seemingly disproportionate number of regression contacts. In addition, why would five people come to Morris Netherton with consensually valid, previously unmentioned reports of an incident at the crucifiction? The odds seem to be against the relatively few who would have witnessed the crucifiction to have sought regression from the same person.

These odds, however, are only against random chance. Helen Wambach's research has already shown an 87 percent chance of encountering people in past-life regressions who we know in our present life. This shows that some principle of attraction is operating in place of randomness, which means that random distribution is hardly a cosmic principle on the level of the soul. Rather, kindred souls seek out one another.

These regression memories suggest to me that many of the people involved with Jesus in past lives are now experiencing a desire for regression. Once again they're showing an interest in a socially and religiously nonsanctioned set of beliefs. Now, as then, they're stepping beyond the material limitations of the mundane world for a glimpse of eternity, striving for re-union with the Divine Source.

Clients who experience this kind of regression find that the sources of great inspiration are no longer out of reach. The great leaders of the past who have touched many lives may possibly have touched yours, particularly those with whom you have the greatest fascination. Jesus, for example, is not just someone who lived in a remote land nearly two thousand years ago whose essence is lost to us. Rather, vivid, living memories still arise, giving direct personal experience, not only of his but other great leaders' lives.

I have on file from scattered regressions, references to other religious beliefs such as Judaism, Islam, and unnamed primitive traditions. It is my hope eventually to be able to provide similar data about these other varieties of the religious experience as I've done with the Christian.

CHRISTIANITY AND REINCARNATION

Many churches and religions speak out against reincarnation as though they were inherently incompatible. However, these are modern pronouncements made to serve the purposes of these leaders. These pronouncements arise out of beliefs or needs that came well after the Christian beginnings. At the time of Jesus there were those who believed in reincarnation and those who did not. It wasn't until later centuries that Christian leaders moved out of the reincarnationists' camp and into that of those opposing the idea.

There are biblical statements clearly referring to the return of a previously incarnated soul—the definition of reincarnation. And there are other passages that may be interpreted as referring to this going out and coming in of the soul. While the inferred references are controversial, the clear ones are not.

If Jesus had an issue against reincarnation—the prior life of the soul—I would have expected him to speak out against the question posed by his disciples indicating that they believed that man lived before birth. This incident is found in John 9:1–3 where the account is reported of the man blind from birth who was presented to Jesus. The disciples asked Jesus, "Who was it that sinned . . . this man or his parent?" They would have had to believe in prior life to have even asked the question. If it were incompatible with true Christianity, that would have been the time for its founder to refute or endorse such a notion. He did neither and attributed the blindness to other purposes. It was not even a subject of controversy for him.

Other references indicate that it was a clear expectation among the Jews of the time that the prophets would come back to earth. Thus, they indulged in speculation on who it was that Jesus was thought to be. "Some say John the Baptist, other Elijah, others Jeremiah or one of the proph-

ets'' (Matt. 16:14–15); ''. . . others that one of the prophets has come back to life,'' (Luke 9:9). Not only did Jesus
not discourage such talk, he actually elicited it: ''Who do
men say the Son of Man is?'' (Matt. 16:14). This is no
different from the modern-day speculation that we often
indulge in, wondering who we might have been in another
life.

In addition, the expectation for the return of Elijah was
given as a condition for the return of the ''Son of Man''
(Jesus). The disciples clearly believed in this idea and
brought it up to Jesus, saying that their scriptures asserted
that Elias had to come first. This was another opportunity
for Jesus to counteract such a doctrine if it were inconsist-
ent with his thought. Not only did he not do so, but he
said that it was true—that Elias had already come (reincar-
nated) referring to John the Baptist (Mark 9:11–13; Matt.
11:14; and Matt. 17:11).

So we have here very clear references to prior living,
the possibility of sinning before birth, and assertions of the
return of a previously incarnated soul. The reason why other
religious leaders condemn such beliefs must be left to them
to explain. For Jesus and his disciples, it wasn't even an
item of discussion or disagreement—they took it for
granted.

CHAPTER 24

A CASE STUDY: BILL'S SCHOOL DIFFICULTIES

A YOUNGSTER'S DIFFICULTIES IN SCHOOL APPEARS AN unlikely place for a connection to the development of Christianity. However, we find there, buried in his unconscious mind, the memory of some of the events of the dark side of the Church.

"I'd like you to see my son," Bill's mother said. "He's had a difficult time in school ever since he started."

Unlike many clients who are brought in by someone else, thirteen-year-old Bill had specific concerns of his own for the regression session. He was interested in the reasons for his lack of assertiveness in some areas; his selective memory, which was good in the things that interested him; headaches that hit him several times a week; school problems; and an unusual ability to communicate and get along with animals.

He told me that he had been taking Ritalin since the previous school year. Ritalin is often administered to children for hyperactivity, or what is now called "attention deficit disorder." When he feels bored or jumpy he said, "I have to ride my bike a lot . . . to get out my hostility."

When I asked him about the specific feelings he had

surrounding his headaches, Bill commented that when he was in his room and it was quiet and dark he felt better.

Since headaches are frequently the result of birth experiences, I suggested that we begin the session with a prenatal exploration. As we did so, however, it became evident that Bill's time in the womb had been unremarkable. His feelings there were generally of a "warm and squishy" place until the time to delivery. His mother later corroborated that the pregnancy and birth had been quite free of stress. Toward the end of the pregnancy he had begun to feel cramped and it had been hard to breathe. During the delivery he'd had the common experience of, "You know you have to get out or you'll die of suffocation."

But at last:

> It was good to be out. There was a light shining in my eyes and a bunch of people around . . . all this light."

We traveled further back in time for the source of these feelings. Bill very quickly said he was about twenty-five years of age, dressed in black. He was in a cave, trying to get out.

> There's a light and I hope it's coming from the sun. [He was looking for gold. The rope broke that he had tied to a tree at the mouth of the cave, and a "down wind" blew out his torch. His first thoughts were of grief.] Oh, my gosh [he thought], I'll never get out again.
>
> [He moved along by feeling the sides of the cave and sniffed the air to tell where it seemed to be fresher or mustier. As his eyes adjusted, he could see a little.]
>
> So I'm in a cave, trying to get to the light. I see a light and hope it's coming from the sun. . . . Getting there, there's just a little rock out of place and a little teeny opening. I'm trying to take out all the rocks. They're falling all over, hitting me in the head. I'm

trying to get under the hole so they don't fall on me so much. Finally, it's big enough for a pig to get through. I try to fit through.

I'm out! There are a lot of people looking at me with guns. They're dressed like cowboys. There are no horses around. It's in the desert. The only thing in sight was a mountain, bushes, and cactus—but no horses.

It's almost like they're expecting me. They're like traitors—they use you. At first they act like regular people, but when I said I'd been looking for gold, they grabbed my bags. I tried to duck. I wanted to get out of there fast . . . I wanted to run, but I was cornered. They shot me . . . and then there was nothing.

In our discussion before the regression began, Bill had mentioned having the idea that his head had been hurt or cut off, which could be a possible cause for his headaches. So we left these cowboys behind, and I asked his unconscious mind to indicate if there were any events surrounding his idea of decapitation. Bill immediately described himself as a female with other people around her who were "all dressed in black. They were saying something about witchcraft." She was then eighteen or nineteen years old.

My experience with regressions has often shown that women who were accused of witchcraft in the past were frequently different or had shown some unusual characteristic or talent as a child. Therefore, I asked Bill if there had been anything special about that girl when she was a child—but his answer was in the negative. So we returned to the life he had been reporting, and I asked what the girl was like:

She doesn't like to work. She doesn't like going to church or nothing like that. I like reading under a tree. It's books mostly, and stories. The accusations about witchcraft came when I read about it in a book. It was when she wasn't in church. She was reading a book. They thought she was a witch.

She was reading under a tree near a fence. . . . The

church was surrounded by the fence. They saw her through the window of the church. They came out, found the book, and grabbed her and covered her mouth.

[I asked if there was a trial, and she replied:] No, they just put me on a stump, accusing me of reading and not going to church. They said I was a witch, that I was not going to church. The others were killed and beheaded for that, and they have to do it to me.

I'm in the woods with trees. I can't see the church or that tree now. I'm in a clearing in the woods. . . . They ask me for any last words. I forgot what I said.

It was a significant time for Bill to forget what he'd said, so I inquired more about the situation, such as the tone of their voices and other details. He replied:

They sounded like they didn't care. What I said was, "This isn't fair." A guy came with an ax, and it was darkness again.

I repeated part of Bill's interview and asked him to focus on his feelings of boredom and restlessness that would prompt him to "have to get out and ride my bike." The question took him back into the cave again when he was sitting down and trying to remember the direction out. He felt the restlessness in his stomach and was thinking, "I have to do something . . . I have to get out."

One of Bill's special interests in coming to me was to see if he could find out why he had such a rapport with animals. He seemed, as he said, to be able to communicate with them. I began by focusing his attention on the feelings that being able to do that gave him. He responded, "It feels good—like I'm part of them." Using that feeling as the point of reference, I suggested he go back to its origin. His answer surprised me:

I'm an animal: a dog—no, more like a wolf. I have a master. I'm mostly a wolf, but I'm not wild, more like a house pet. I can go out and run in the snow a lot. I have other dog friends. My master is real nice—he makes me feel real good. We play around together.

I was wild once, a pup. He raised me up. As a pup we ate meat, ate it and followed our mother around. One time we lost her. She was running after some kind of animal. I chased it so far, but I wasn't fast enough. The next thing I remember, I was in this warm place with meat and a guy sitting nearby. I fell asleep. . . . He picked me up. I felt helpless at first but realized that he was nice. I felt better.

[As time went by] I wanted to be wild again. I had to go out and be wild. There was nothing to do any-more—being wild was the only thing left. I had to be part of the wolf pack.

[I asked Bill if this wanting to "go out and be wild again" was a decision or a feeling. He said:] It was a feeling. The next night I left when he was letting us out. I joined the pack. I felt good. I was out where I wanted to be.

[I asked how Bill's life ended as that wolf.] I died at night. It was in the field with the other wolf pack friends. Some people came out hunting us, and we started to run. I had bitten one of the people. I was shot in the side.

Bill's two-hour session was remarkable in a number of aspects. In his conscious life he was bright, articulate, and apparently a clear thinker. Yet in school, although his ability was evident, he seemed to hide the fact. His regressions came quickly and clearly enough for us to be able to do not only a prenatal scan but also parts of three past lives—one of which he identified as that of an animal.

But the crucial question remained: What relevence or relationship did these regression experiences have to the problems and interests he described at the beginning of the session?

With regard to his activity level, there were several in-stances of "having to get out." These occurred in the cave when he was confronted with the cowboys; when the wolf matured enough to once again "go out and be wild"; later when he was being hunted; and finally the mild experience of his birth in this life in which he felt the necessity to "get out or suffocate."

Bill's school problems are reflected in the ingrained programs indicated by the following patterns:

- In the cowboy regression he was safe until the others found out what he knew.
- In the regression as a girl, he was essentially beheaded for reading and for what others thought he knew.
- A somewhat less concrete pattern was revealed in the sequence of events as the gold miner, during which each remedy for a problem only brought a greater problem and eventually death.
- As the wolf, he was at first cared for by humans and then killed by them.

Thus, we see Bill's restlessness in closed situations, the danger of letting others find out what he knows, punishment for reading, uncertainty about the intention of his caretakers, and an attitude that, no matter what is done, there is no escape or pleasant outcome. In this life, the darkness and solitude that was Bill's remedy for the headaches reminded him of being in the cave. Although he felt lost in the cave, he was really safer there than when he emerged into the light of day outside.

Any possible beneficial results of the regressions will come as Bill recognizes that it's safe—if not desirable—for him to reveal what he knows to his teachers, and that it's safe for him to read without fear of punishment from the authorities. Hopefully, the anxiety surrounding these issues has been discharged in its original source—these past-life memories. Perhaps even the anxiety component in his restlessness can also be reduced now. Only time will tell whether Bill will choose to realize these benefits.

It may be an interesting footnote to mention the similarities between the symptoms of anxiety and those of attention deficit disorder. Although they are physiologically different, they show similar manifestations: difficulty concentrating, restlessness, irritability, low tolerance for frustration, reduced social gratification, feelings of vulnerability, frequent inability to relax. Who can really say what the ultimate source of these symptoms may be?

PART V

TEMPLES, SAGES, AND SECRETS

CHAPTER 25

THE RIGHT USE
OF POWER

Almost everyone is aware of Freudian psychology's assertion that we are largely motivated by the drives of the libido, or life energy, which are strongly sexual in nature. It was Carl Jung, however, who asserted that the libido contained not only sexual drives but also spiritual drives. An individual could become neurotic not only through a frustration of sexuality but also from blocked spiritual expression.

Religious beliefs are of great importance in healthy living—whether your belief system is identified as "religious" or not. However we refer to them, our beliefs about the nature of the universe and about humankind may be the most influential force that motivates us.

In addition, a review of most religions suggests some very fundamental and universal principles. Although there appear diverse cultural and linguistic elements, nevertheless, there are those universal features that bind us together and give credence to the assertion that, "Truth is One; men call it by various names."

In some past-life regressions we find expression of these spiritual drives and the manner in which they are molded in various societies. We may find historical information of interest, or we may find the source of your particular way of expressing your spirituality.

Thus, emotional trauma need not always be the focus of regression. Indeed, in these often intense times, the release of recurring emotional pain will be the priority for many of us. However, the exemplary regressions in this section show us the expression and possibly the origin of some of our noblest inclinations. Although it's true that most of us are struggling with issues of a basic emotional nature—such as survival, sexuality, intimacy, or social integration—we nevertheless often feel the stirrings toward a higher end, toward a destiny.

Perhaps it's an esthetic sense, seeking a more beautiful world. Perhaps it's an intellectual appetite. For some it becomes an escape from the unacceptable present. In any case, those stirrings reveal that human potential to express the spiritual drives defined by Jung.

Many of us gravitate toward and express ethical principles that are not directly related to our survival on earth as a material being. And yet such philosophical ideas emerge seemingly whole cloth from our unconscious minds when communication is established with these ancient past-life memories.

The following regressions are instructive for a number of reasons. On the one hand, they show us that we're not so distant from the ancient sources of wisdom that we so often revere, sometimes only because they are so distant. After all, the memories of the people who had contact with Jesus, the Buddha, Lao-tzu, and Akhenaton are probably walking around in new bodies this moment.

Times seem to have changed little. The best of the philosophers are still saying the same things about honor, love, and responsibility, or making the same arguments about them. And their followers sometimes live up to their principles and sometimes do not. The process of inspiration, institutionalization, and then formalism has enshrouded most movements. From this perspective, much of history seems to be the ebb and flow of spiritual drives bursting forth through some charismatic figure, only to be lost by the followers in their attempt to preserve it. Unfortunately, it seems that the conditions set up for preservation are seldom compatible with those needed for life and growth.

Finally, we see examples in these regressions of the various forms of ethical and religious expression such as individual tutelage, small group ritualism or initiation, nature religion, apprenticeship and well-organized temple teachings.

Certainly not everything from the past comes from a place of wisdom or is worthy to be emulated. However, there are many pieces of knowledge and wise teachings that would otherwise have been lost because: they were secret at the time; handed down by oral tradition; in writings that have been destroyed—such as the burning of the ancient library at Alexandria; tribal secrets; esoteric traditions; or the Native American teachings, among others, that have been eliminated by the "White Gods." Past-life regressions have shown that at least some of this wisdom is recoverable.

It is my hope that by moving clients closer to the source of their faith, both historical and within, they may experience a renewal of spirit. We may also hope to prepare the psyche for the flexibility called for in maintaining that dual stance between an appropriate amount of discipline, as well as an openness to inspiration.

It is also my personal hope to show that those whose faith rests on truth have no need to fear such new information. Not that history doesn't present us with falsehoods, but as accounts are collected, it is my conviction that the truth will emerge and endure. The only things to ultimately die will be the falsehoods and limitations so that we no longer need to look "as through a glass darkly."

That which is closest to the Source of all Being will of course be most transcendent and immanent, vital and enduring.

My goal is to move, as far as is humanly possible, toward the establishment of ultimate principles. I hope to be able to strengthen the faith of those who are truly in touch with their God so that whatever is false in their own belief and practice may the sooner drop away.

There are those who find it essential to focus on the differences among the forms of expression of religious belief. However, although I recognize these differences, I am compelled to look at the transcendent similarities or universal principles that bind them together. After all, in any religion there are limiting elements—related to the culture in which it originated and the one that now promulgates it. There are also those elements that are eternal and universal. The latter are my primary interest. God would be a god of the universe, and any savior a savior of all people, regardless of whatever name or form God may take at different times and different places.

I add this personal reference, not to assert it as another belief system, but to avoiding any misunderstanding that I am attempting either to foster or discredit a particular sect. Again, those whose beliefs and faith are based on truths of a universal nature will welcome additional sincere information with the confidence that any parts of it that may be faulty will be the first to pass away.

Religious controversy has been too often and too long used to destroy the body in order to save the soul that had attempted to express itself through that body; or to enslave and distract our minds rather than to illuminate them. It's time we sought the highest, the noblest, and the best that human thought and belief have to offer.

CASE STUDY: THE NOBLE TRILIUS

We can often find in regression wisdom an affirmation of some of the most basic values promulgated by the highest aspects of various religions and philosophies. One such example comes from Dylan's past-life encounter with the Roman Trilius. He was tutored by his mentor and taught certain ideals on the right use of power.

Trilius was a young soldier who was to eventually assume command of a "godforsaken outpost" along Hadrian's Wall in Britain. After his tour of duty he returned to Rome to gradually rise up through the bureaucracy. His particular duties involved the procurement and distribution of food. This responsibility was of great importance in maintaining social and political stability and peace.

Although it was normal for the aristocracy to have quality teachers, Trilius was particularly fortunate in the quality of the relationship that developed between him and his tutor. The tutor recognized Trilius as being a kindred soul. The usual forms of admonition, insufferable lessons, and platitudes were unnecessary for Trilius. Since little really needed to be said, the teaching was very concise. This was partly because of the relationship between them and partly because of the nature of their personalities and character.

As noble Trilius said:

> It's a good feeling. He's not talking down to me; he's talking to me. He respects me even though I'm younger. He knows I'm a lot like him and what I'll evolve into. My character is that kind of character that develops into his. His personal strength is everything to me—and he sees that in me.

The tutor's task was to draw forth or remind Trilius of his true inner nature. There was no judgment upon those whose lot was not to carry out and express such high ideals since it was recognized that, "You are what you are, and you do the best you can."

Although the tutor did not espouse a belief in an afterlife, his passing did not leave a sense of final loss. Although there was sadness at the death of Trilius mentor, this wise man so personified the ideals he had expounded, whenever Trilius had occasion to turn to the ideals it was very much like turning to his teacher. The presence of the teacher lived on in the ideals. Our Trilius died a peaceful death after his years of service and a marriage that gave him two sons.

The mentor's teachings are summarized in this quote from the regression. Our session ended with a sense of communion and peacefulness that reaffirmed Dylan's nobler sense; it also gave him an opportunity to once more affirm his sentiments for his tutor by completing the expression of his gratitude.

At the end of the regression Trilius needed to say:

Thank you. I'm thanking him for what he told me, but more. I lived the way we discussed. I'm thanking him for confirmation of what I was. I'm saying in agreement that we were right in what we thought and what we believed; thanking him that he was what he was.

Imagine the quality of our own politics if our leaders were to embrace and live up to these ideals:

Never use power to do wrong, which means to capriciously harm other people. For if you do, the wrong will come back to you a thousandfold. For it follows that the proper exercise of power brings security, stability—and that is our utmost duty.

CHAPTER 26

THE INITIATOR

THIS IS ANOTHER OF ALEX'S REGRESSION'S, THE SAME psychotherapist who had found himself a pope in Chapter 21, "The Institution." This particular lifetime was from much earlier and simpler times. We were concerned here with a feeling Alex had of heaviness in his chest, relating at least in part to his practice of psychotherapy, as well as events in his personal relationships. The heaviness in the chest took us to ceremonial preparations that included a heavy and ornate breastplate. Note the comparisons Alex spontaneously makes between the "modern" papal circumstances and those of this ancient initiator:

I have an impression of a chest plate made of stones and gold—it's very heavy. This role I'm in has to do with a passing down of an apostolic succession type of thing. It looks Egyptian with blue lapis stones and carved stone surroundings.

We're making these ceremonial preparations in private with only a few assistants. But unlike the papal experience, there will be only a few recipients. That's the way it is—there are only a few in preparation and a few in receipt of the initiatory rights.

I'm most aware of the breastplate right now. It has a name, but it escapes me. The breastplate is where things are symbolically centered—analogous to the papal ring.

The purpose and vestment is in the initiatory power to raise the recipient to a different sort of consciousness—a different state. I do not have the lonely feeling as when [I was] Pope. The preparation and expression are done with the same small group so that the discrepancy that seemed to be there in the other one [papal] is absent. The energy that's received and passed on is more easily pictured by me to be received by the few people who come to receive it. For the Pope, thousands come to the Easter blessing.

The breastplate could be taken off. Even though the weight of the breastplate was physically heavier, the weight of the responsibility of the papal vestments felt greater. In fact, it was held to be of considerable value for the Initiator to divest himself of it—to not be invested continually in that position so that the energy wasn't what we would psychologically call "habituated to." Thus, the taking on and putting off of the breastplate and the position, the going out and the return, kept it ever new—in the sense of keeping it "new" and "knew."

It was important to be the singular Initiator and to give up for that time the most obvious aspects of personal identity, like moving into a stream or flow, and then stepping out so that the rest of the life that was there could have expression. Even though more primitive in surroundings, things seemed more complete and full.

I recall a picture from a book by Manly Palmer Hall that seemed to be part of the ceremony. The picture is of a person hanging on an X-type of cross beside a ceremonial stone sarcophagus. It represents the rising to a new life through the death of the personality. It wasn't to be the elimination or the death really of the personality, but removal of the dross. This would allow the personality to go higher. In time comes the raising up of life—the promise of the eucharist, which wasn't always carried out.

Thus, Alex—who is still helping people to rise to a new level of consciousness through psychotherapy—was struck by the differences between the ceremonially elaborate and sophisticated papal duties and the more intimate and, for him, complete experience as the Initiator.

I have in my library the book he referred to by Manly Palmer Hall. It is called *The Phoenix*. We looked through it for the picture and were both surprised by what we found (on page 160). The picture was different from what he had seen in the regression. Obviously, Alex's past-life memory was stronger than that of the present one since it was probably more accurate.

For Alex, the personal importance of this regression came in the realization that, like this ancient initiator, he must learn to take off his breastplate of responsibility and relate to others in more ordinarily human ways. He grasped fully the fact that his personal effectiveness and power as a therapist would be best maintained not through constant exercising of the therapist's role, but rather by adopting that role when it was called for, and when it was not, by renewing himself through other human interchange.

This regression was a major step that, over the course of several years, led him to much more satisfying relationships with men and women who were equal to him, rather than just those needing his assistance.

CHAPTER 27

THE RELIGION OF THE OLD PEOPLE

Mara was seeking the source of a significant relationship. In the regression, this young woman gave an account of having been a man in her/his previous life who had met his wife at the yearly fair in County Cork in Ireland. During that life, he eventually suffered an accident that caused a fatal injury. Our excursion into the secret religion of the "Old People" began unexpectedly when I asked Mara to go back to the time of that wedding.

The groom described a clearing in the woods with an altar and a gray-robed priest of the "Old Religion." His bride was of the Old Religion, and she was pleased to have this wedding in the clearing and in their tradition. It was known as the "Old Religion" because it was the one that "had always been there." As he said, "The Church tried to drive it out and so they met in secret. And we were married in secret, deep in the woods."

During the wedding ceremony, the priest spoke words in the melodious language of the Old Ones that my uninitiated client/groom did not understand. They put wreaths of flowers around each other's necks and drank an unidentified liquid. The ceremony ended with vows, after which they knelt, placed a flower on the altar stone, and the bride kissed the stone.

Their families had come from far away and they enjoyed music and dancing. Later, the couple went into the village to be married so that "the county would believe" that they were married.

As the groom, my client had a preferrence for his wife's religion over what he had seen in the Church's priests. "I tried to learn their language, but it was hard to understand and she laughed at me sometimes. I guess I was dumb. We used to worship together in our home, but we had to keep it a secret or we would have been driven out or punished." In their worship, they burned fragrant flowers and herbs and "sent up prayers."

He spoke of his efforts at trying to follow the religious activities and of being accepted in spite of his difficulties. He never did learn that language, but I asked what it sounded like. There was a long pause of inward listening. Then came the reply: "I can hear a prayer, *'Lan Hoch Thiln . . . Lan Hoch Nin, Sin Han Hoehn Sin Hagen.'* It's hard."

Our somewhat simple subject (in that past life) had not quite realized that outsiders were not often admitted to the activities of the Old People. His bride's judgment and fondness for him, however, were considered sufficient in the eyes of the others. "She said I was one of them and just didn't know it. She could tell. . . . She knew I was touched by the gods. She saw that they found favor in me. She just sensed it."

At the time of our subject's fatal accident, not long after the marriage, he was aware of leaving the body and staying in spirit in order to help his bride through her grief and through the preparation of his physical body.

He described the preparations according to the Old Religion:

She washed it. She wrapped it in linens and bindings and she said prayers and annointed the body. And she had to call the [Catholic] priest in the village. He came and I was buried.

Then the Old People came and dug up the body, and took it away to the altar in the woods, and laid it out and lit fires. Then they took the body to the cave where their own are buried. And no one knew that the other grave was empty.

The Old People knew I was with them throughout the ceremony, and when they placed the body in the cave and said good-bye to me, I was able to leave.

Further exploration revealed that this couple was together again in a later life with the roles reversed. In this later time, it was he who was to teach her. She was not ready, however, and she left him.

I instinctively felt there was still something missing here. I asked Mara's unconscious mind to return her to the event from which arose her need to teach and to be taught, to guide and be guided.

I was surprised by her response:

When Zeus left the temple, the people were lost. I tried to guide them. I tried to make them understand. And they still lost all hope. They were shallow; they couldn't understand.

I tried so very hard to make them understand that there was a reason why He didn't return, why the light was gone. Everything was gray. There was no brightness. The people had no brightness, no life. I tried—I just couldn't reach them by myself.

CHAPTER 28

THE TRICKING OF ZEUS

In the Western Judeo-Christian tradition there are stories of the experiences of the faithful that include contact with angels, with Jehovah, with apparitions of departed prophets and, of course, the return of the crucified Jesus. These accounts include the transmission of knowledge, advice, commentary on current events, and even as vigorous an activity as wrestling with an angel.

Such accounts are accepted with little thought about how divergent they are from normal reality—or how similar they are to other stories such as are found in these regressions.

Recall that other religions also speak of the manifestations of their gods, or of prophets or messengers. This should give us both an expanded view of what is possible as well as some humility about our ''specialness''—especially when we try to base that specialness on supernatural events. Many similar events have been shared by quite different people.

The Greeks had their collection of gods who lived on Mount Olympus. The gods and goddesses were seen as very human—they had personalities, jealousies, and struggles with each other and with humankind. They plotted and tricked and were taken advantage of themselves. All of this needs to be kept in mind when reading the following account since it addresses acts of divine trickery, jealousy, and limitations as conceived by that culture.

This is another regression of that same soul who was involved in "The Religion of the Old People" in Chapter 27. At the beginning of the regression Mara finds herself in a garden. She was a female then, a priestess in a beautiful temple of very white stone, pillars, and a lot of steps. On the inside, the temple is very open and there is an altar with "The Flame."

It was one of the priestesses' responsibilities to keep that fire burning. Other duties included helping others, taking turns cooking, and assisting with the worship. Her main duty, however, was to keep the fire going.

This temple, she said, was dedicated to Zeus. They worshipped by offering prayers, and taking a bowl with fire from their eternal flame, they carried the fire to their altar as an offering to Zeus. Flowers and fruit were offerings often brought by the people.

I asked her if it would be all right for her to tell me what some of the prayers were like. After a long pause she replied that only the people within the temple can make the offering. Outside people do not participate. I would not ask her to violate her principles.

There is a high priestess, a mature but not old woman. She wears a long white tunic with a blue robe over it that touches the floor. It floats when she walks. Her hair has leaves in it, like gold and silver intertwined. This high priestess is the only one who can take the flame, although she does have helpers.

The priestesses lived in little rooms attached behind the temple, sleeping on mats. Torches dipped in oil provided their only dim light at night.

I suggested she take time to enjoy some of her favorite prayers in silence. In this way, she was able to enjoy the benefit of this ancient memory without compromising the tradition of secrecy that she still upholds.

People mostly come to the temple for worship or for healing. The priestesses did not make frequent trips outside of the temple. However, our priestess wanted to be a physician and therefore accompanied their doctor—a woman— who went to help a sick man. As she tells it: "He was old. It was old age. It wasn't an illness. She gave him herbs and a drink to help him rest. He was afraid, upset, dying. He didn't sleep but he rested after the treatment; he wasn't upset anymore."

In addition to her herbal medicines, this physician also soothed her patient with words, assuring him that there was nothing to fear. This healer taught her patient that, "When a baby is born it's afraid and fights and does not want to be born. That's because it doesn't know that a whole new world is waiting there. And when it's out, it wonders why it fought because there are whole new things to look at and see." The patient was relieved and lived awhile longer before dying comfortably.

I was curious about Zeus and their beliefs about him: "He is," she said, "the Protector that watches over us. He is benevolent but can be very angry—and he likes mortal women. He likes women in his temple but does not like his wife Hera. Zeus and Hera argue and fight, so he comes to the women of the temple. Even the gods have to get away, and he knows that we in the temple love him; and we bring the flame to him. And he loves us."

Our priestess spoke of meeting this figure of Zeus as a child. She described him as very large, very white, and having a lot of light. "He called me the "Bright One" when I was little, but I can't say the name." She had been originally brought to the temple by her parents when she was just a child. She did not remember much of her acceptance ceremony other than she had been about five, and that she had had a wreath on her head.

Other ceremonies in the temple included those in the Spring when the planting was done, as well as at the Harvest. On "Flame Day," the high priestess performs a special ritual at the altar. Even the other priestesses did not know quite what was said or done there.

When she was young, "It was very bright and cheery and the sun shone." But things began to change. The festivals stopped, and not many people came to bring the offerings of fruit and wheat. People seemed to work so hard and yet not have anything extra. The government took a lot; and everyone seems to fall on hard times.

In contrast to the brightness she remembered from her youth, when she "got old and the sun shined it was still dark. The light was gone from the temple." Her voice saddened as she went on, "and Zeus was gone."

Zeus abandoned his temple in anger and did not return. The rituals were just motions. They lost their meaning.

Our priestess, now about twenty-five years old, had become the physician but was despondent because there were so many people who were now weak and tired in this bleak grayness.

She did what she could to try to minister to the people and to keep something of the old faith alive, but after two decades, there was still that barrier between Zeus and his people.

That barrier, it turns out, was the result of a trick played by Hera on Zeus out of her jealousy. As our priestess described it, this godly confrontation occurred during a ceremony in the temple at night. The flame was burning and Hera came—angry. There was lightning and thunder and trees blowing. After that, Zeus was not able to return because of some "trick."

Maintaining her devotion to Zeus until she "wore out," she finds herself at the end of that life on her bed, feverish. At death she related: "My body was on the bed, but I got out of the bed and walked out into the garden where the fountain was and sat on the bench. It looked the way it did when I was small again. And Zeus came, and it was like it was when I was small. We talked and laughed again.''

She was also reunited there with many of her loved ones.

It seems that one seldom has an opportunity to speak with gods or their human messengers, so I asked what message Zeus had for us today. This was her response:

To follow the Path . . . to guide those who need guidance; to help lead them, to help teach them. Be patient. Teach honesty. . . .

Don't wear two faces—that was his favorite—not so much physical honesty: If you are hungry you can take food, if you don't hurt anyone; but in the spirit, don't wear two faces.

Sometimes people wear two faces and they think they're helping you, but they're not to be trusted. Sometimes honesty hurts, but it's better than wearing two faces. There are people who try not to hurt by wearing two faces, and they end up hurting more than if they were honest. They try to make everyone love them by trying to tell everyone what they want to hear. And yet there are people who will never like them. They try to be kind—but kindness isn't kind sometimes. You can't be kind by wearing another face.

Healing is a way to teach, to soothe, to make them understand.

So what was this Zeus? Was this a god who is now in retirement? Was he a clever magician of the time—clever enough to return after death and appear to his follower? Was he an avatar, or an angel, or one of many divine ministers assisting the people?

Julian Jaynes, author of *The Origin of Consciousness in the Breakdown of the Bicameral Mind*, calls these manifestations of gods ''hallucinations'' resulting from one part of the mind communicating with another. We can only speculate whether such was the case or not. Other writers have theorized that there were giants on the earth, or visitors from space. We simply do not know.

My only conclusion is that, in some way, Zeus was the manifestation of the divine connection that could be understood by those people in their time and place. God's speech, after all, comes to us in our own language.

For Mara, this regression strengthened her confidence in her own spirituality. She drew from it an affirmation of her importance as a teacher today, no matter whether she lives in a temple or not.

CHAPTER 29

"TAKE ME BACK TO PLATO"

"I CAN'T BRING MYSELF TO ATTACH TO ANYTHING—unless it's totally mine." This was George's first concern. He was a young man with a sparkling personality. As we explored his concern it became clear that he was afraid that commitment "will hurt me; I'll be left alone."

His regression experience began with some events of his current life. We then went into an old life in which he had been a slave who was accidentally crushed between two large stones which were being moved. This experience of an expendable and wasted life, along with another accessed past life in which he had attempted to motivate a group of oppressed people, were the sources of a revolutionary zeal that was part of his personality. In this life, this tendency has led him to constantly want to change whatever exists—hardly a trait encouraging stable relationships or ideas.

Yet George told me that he has always asked himself the self-doubting question: "Who am I to do anything?"

In order to seek the source of this unconscious behavior pattern, I asked his unconscious mind for the words that would connect him with the source of his predicament.

"You won't believe this," George said. "The words that came to me are, 'Take me back to Plato.' "

I believed him—and that's exactly what we did. In that past life, he was young when he first saw Plato. He was impressed with Plato's knowing yet "funny" eyes. George wanted very much to impress Plato, to prove that he was "not common." He spoke of Plato's teachings, his character, and his way of life. George was frustrated by the manner of the sage's teaching. Plato considered himself not really a teacher but a "relayer" of information. He would teach what he thought, but not how he came about his knowledge.

Atlantis was one of Plato's interests.

Yet with all of Plato's knowledge, George considered him to be basically a beggar, going from town to town "with nothing set about him." Note how similar this is to George's concern about his own life now.

In the end, it was Plato's sexual interests that were the final stumbling blocks to George's desire to win approval from the master.

"Plato was so impressive with his power, his stature. He could take me anywhere—to Atlantis. He almost did. But the sexual made him seem so common."

In that life, George eventually married, grew old, and wrote about his own questions of life. The questions he wrestled with were these:

> Is anyone special—or is everyone special? What really is "special"? Are the everyday, normal things special? And who is more important than whom? I always thought that Plato was out to impress, that he wasn't special—yet he was.

In the end, George recognized his own specialness, and that one does not have to be different or uncommon to be special.

As George mellowed in that past life and began to re-solve some of his questions about specialness, he grew somewhat nostalgic for those times with Plato. He began to see more clearly how his concern over Plato's sexuality had separated him from the master and the kind of rela-tionship that he had wanted with him. This nostalgia was the source of the phrase, ''Take me back to Plato.''

With his consciousness back in the present, it was easy for George to see the way in which he had identified with Plato. He, too, wanted to know everything, and he wanted to be special. And yet he had trouble committing himself or settling down.

George's inability to become attached to anything unless it could be totally his could now be seen as an expression of thousands of years of trying to impress Plato by being ''not common.'' In addition, his admiration of Plato led to an identification with his mentor's nomadic tendencies. Like his teacher, George had few long-term attachments and an awareness of the esteem that can be had by being unusual.

Through this regression, George took a step toward re-solving his conflict over having to be different in order to be special and yet finding specialness in everyday things.

CHAPTER 30

THE LAST JOURNEY

WHILE STILL A YOUNG WOMAN, SOMETHING HAD TRIG-
gered feelings of a loss of strength in Polly's life, of not
being able to rest and "having to keep going."

As she entered the regression she reported a "doom feeling" and saw oriental symbols, paintings, and an orna-
mental sword.

In Polly's regression she found herself to be a very old
man, carrying a stick, walking on stones and dirt. He could
see mountains on the left, and fields. After heading for
those mountains, he felt winded, thinking "I have to get
there."

He passed through a village and observed people carrying water and grain—things on their shoulders and in bas-
kets. He had to stop for water. "I can really feel my
lungs," she/he exclaimed. "My lungs got heavier; I feel
heavier." He thought that if he stopped he wouldn't get
going again. He was dressed in long dark robes. "I can't
travel as well as I used to," he thought. "I'm going up a
hill to a cave. I have to bury something in the cave."

This journey to the mountains can best be understood
after considering the beginning of this story, many years

before. He was the heir of a tradition of secrets—secrets that had to do with power. He could "do things with the earth, with the sky, things with the wind, things with water. The secrets showed how to use things that grow."

I asked the old man about the nature of the secrets. My client expressed feeling "alarmed" at the question and went on to say that it was more than just knowing the formulae and "currents" in the book; it required a deeper understanding. One needed to know "how the rocks flow, and the earth flows, and the sky moves." It's only taught to those who understand after years of training, and to those who are faithful.

He himself had undergone such training. His own teacher had been very old and had handed the book down to his pupil. The pupil was honored to have been allowed to be present when the old man "died by fire," sitting on a pyre he lit himself. Such was the tradition when the old teachers were about to die. And the tradition was being carried on by this pupil-becoming-master. But for him there was to be no successful heir:

> The times have changed. My kind is being moved out. Things are not good for us now. There was one disciple, but he cut himself with a sword out of foolishness. It was my duty to pass it on [the knowledge and training]. It was a great responsibility and I carry it on my chest.
>
> Part of the training is with swords. It is very vigorous. But he [the disciple] erred because he could not control his enthusiasm. It is important to control energy in all this. His foolishness resulted in a cut in his chest. It was because he was attached to his success.

Our sage felt this keenly, as though it were his own failure to properly train the young disciple. He also felt the emptiness or the incompleteness of not having anyone to whom he could pass on his knowledge. Although there were none who wished to undergo the rigorous training, its power was nevertheless recognized. Others wanted the benefit of that power.

He tells of one time when there was an attempt to take advantage of him:

> It was a trick. It was to do something that I could not. They—a lord—wanted power. I was needed elsewhere, but he sent for me under false pretenses. It was to advance his power, ego, and self-importance. I was called a great distance for this and my refusal cost him honor. He was outraged. He tried to have me killed, but the men let me go.

The power did not come at the whim and fancy of whomever desired it, but in knowing how to work with nature. The secret of success or failure in these enterprises was to know that, "I can do many things, but I have limitations. I can not move against the forces of nature—only with them. One must know how the currents move."

Other teachings were: "To gain knowledge is to increase; to gain the Tao is to decrease. As you increase in the Tao, you decrease." It is essential to "let things flow through you." He refers here to the Taoist idea of how knowledge can interfere with being in touch with the forces around you. As one empties oneself of interfering and limiting ideas, one knows what is to be done.

These were the events, the traditions, the teachings from which he came. And now he was old, infirm, and alone with his book of secrets. "It is important who has it because of what can be done with it for one with understanding." Thus, it has been necessary to hide it. So he returns to the cave—carrying his treasure.

It is a gold box with markings and wood. This box encases the book of formulas. "I'm too old and going to die soon. I need to plan for that. I must dispose of the book with me—by fire. I couldn't die without taking care of it."

The purpose of this last journey then becomes evident: to prepare for his death, and in the absence of a disciple, to dispose of the book of secret power along with his own earthly remains. In the cave:

> I'm dressed in something different now. It's white. I've prepared a pyre. My lungs are so tired. There is the tremendous weight in my chest. I left the box, but I have the book. I sit on the pyre, and with a chemical in my pouch, I create the fire. It catches quickly. I feel the heat and then cold and then numb. I rise into the sky. . . .

Returning to the present, Polly denied any knowledge of the *Tao te Ching*, the Book of Tao. Yet the old man's teaching was indeed very Taoist. The principles of not moving against but with the "currents," the flow of things, the danger of being attached to one's success, letting things flow through you, and that "to gain in Tao is to decrease"—are markedly from that Eastern tradition that began in China in the sixth century B.C. with the life and teachings of Lao-tzu, who thought that life itself was the ultimate authority.

Such wonder workers are hardly evident in the Taoism of today. Perhaps the old tradition died out with the scarcity of worthy disciples. Perhaps they work in secret as before, not wanting the wisdom to fall into the wrong hands. Perhaps . . .

Polly's compulsion to keep going in spite of fatigue could now be laid to rest. She was no longer the old Taoist struggling toward his funeral pyre, needing to prevent misuse of the power by burning his book of formulas. Polly could begin building a new sense of hope and accomplishment without carrying the burden of the failures of that other time.

CHAPTER 31

THE TEACHINGS
OF THE TEMPLE

ONCE AGAIN WE TAKE THE STORY OF HALE AND MARY Jane, Ron and Rachel, and John and Jane, whom you first met in Chapter 6, "Relationship Patterns." We've already discussed the nature of these relationships along with their past-life origins. Our interest here is in the teachings of that ancient group to which they all so long ago belonged—and in the personality types of the instructors.

In Hale's regression we discovered that the center of these teachings was a huge temple of white stone. Two courses of steps led up to the temple columns. The temple itself was very open. "It's empty now because it's used only for special occasions and religious observances," said Hale. "This is where I received training—and where I was executed."

Members of the Egyptian aristocracy came to the temple for education in the fundamentals of living, fundamentals that emphasized the connection between humankind and their deities. Departments included the military, arts, religion, and science. Hale said:

This is a spiritual community. It works on the preparation and integration of the soul. . . .

The place has a mystical feeling. They have a strong belief in the soul, a belief in the gods, that they rule your destiny. It's an essential part of your training to know and to be on the good side of the gods.

Religious training covers all aspects of the soul—not just the ethereal but the physical and secular. The training integrates the soul and mind with the body. The temple is a place of great respect.

This temple school was run by a council of six or eight overseers along with a staff of instructors. As often occurs with significant lifetimes, my client recognized most of the council members or instructors as important individuals in his present life.

Each of the instructors had an area of special expertise. Here is a summary of their teachings as well as some of the personality characteristics of the department heads.

Ron was the coordinator. Held in great respect by the others, he carried a staff topped with a golden ball. He occasionally served as a guest lecturer, attempting to crystallize the various aspects taught there and to present them from other points of view. An effective communicator, he provided a cohesive force between these otherwise diverse areas.

Rachel was an expert in the aspects of love—all of them. The subject of her study included the physical, mental, and spiritual elements of love. Rachel herself appeared to our young initiate as rather reserved, at least in the beginning. She and the initiates had been admonished that even this sexual training is serious business. In the training of love, there was only one rule: "That we do not fall in love." Otherwise, they were encouraged to experience love from all levels, beginning with the physical and then transcending it, to "higher planes."

The initial orientation to love was through physical sex.

Sex was described as a source of energy. This was an energy to be acknowledged; it was important to the integration of the individual and to the soul. After the initial instruction in sexual positions, birth control, and the refinement of these fundamentals, initiates would demonstrate their progress by showing how this energy would then flow into a more universal sense of love.

"It gave me," said Hale, "the understanding of a more whole picture of the value of sex. It wasn't something one should be ashamed of or mysterious about. Everyone was a sexual person and should be able to explore that potential . . . to express love and to go on to a love that transcends it."

Thus their ideal was a love that would unify other aspects of the teachings—love being a unifying force that draws together opposites.

Mary Jane's department was astrology. Through the use of the horoscope she would show the probabilities and potentials in the individual's life. She emphasized that the individual must "surrender to the flow" in order to realize one's full potential, since that flow would itself direct one toward higher learning. Hale quoted her teaching in this way:

> To go fully with the flow of things you have to release yourself. You have to let go and be able to let go of your fear of the unknown.

For this temple, astrology was a tool to help the initiates measure the vast potential of the spirit, for unless they were willing to suspend fear and judgment, they would limit that potential and fail to experience the full magnitude of their being.

Jane was a stern teacher. She was the one who taught the knowledge of the gods. Initiates were expected to memorize for her the names, specialties, likes, and dislikes of the gods. It was "like a catechism." Students were expected to know the rituals, sacrifices, and methods of appeasing the gods, as well as how to summon them. Jane was a disciplinarian who drilled her students and demanded answers to her questions. Hale saw her as somewhat harsh, but his judgment may be related to his own difficulty in concentrating in this "driest of the classes."

The many gods and their specialties were reflections of the vastness of reality. The gods and their rituals were "only a way for man to make sense of that reality." As Hale said, "It's important to understand that level but also not to be bound by it."

Finally, John taught aspects of the human personality; he was their psychologist-philosopher. John's name then was Okasa. He focused on understanding the motives and inner motivations of the initiates. By beginning his study with personal motivations and limitations, he sought to help initiates gain an understanding of themselves that would allow them to transcend their limitations. "Most of the other courses had to do with ultimates and seemed so far from the young students," said Hale. "This one was easier to deal with. It helped us learn about ourselves by beginning with our own motivations and limitations and, by understanding these, to seek our fullest potential."

These were the main teachings of this ancient temple. As we saw in Chapter 6, even though their humanness overwhelmed the highest of their ideals, the basic principles to which they aspired still ring true with unusual clarity to this day.

Here is my summary of their basic principles:

- To understand the function of sexual energy so that higher expressions of love could be realized; to experience the unifying power of that energy.
- To be able to move in harmony with the nature of the cosmos and to recognize our place in it.
- To understand and carry out the basic necessities of

maintaining our relationship with the diety(ies) and humankind.

- To understand and use the limitations of our personalities and humanness in order to transcend them in a practical way.

As modern, educated, and sophisticated as we consider ourselves today, it seems that most of our institutions fall far short of even approaching these ideals of long ago.

It's interesting to note how most of the members of the temple at that time have come together once more in the present life, where in the form of a meditation group, they once again undertook to explore the fundamentals and universals in human and divine functioning.

Where are the mystery schools today? Where might these seekers have gone today for an integrated program focusing on not only the education of the individual in the arts and sciences, but also on his or her growth as a person, as a spiritual, intellectual, emotional, and sexual human being?

I believe that many of the meditation groups, study groups, metaphysical centers, and New Age centers are attempts to respond to this need for cohesive social integration of the whole individual. There are only a few institutions offering the kind of experiential examination of basic mysteries of life and interaction—experiences that become increasingly necessary in our world of television, computers, mobility, and information overload.

A QUESTION OF CHOICE

Reincarnation seems to imply that we come into a life for a purpose or lesson. But we also have a choice. We are partly drawn to a life and partly choose. Whatever we have chosen to set up at other times becomes a part of us and we gravitate toward other expressions of that pattern.

I suppose we could decide not to choose and just follow

the rules. But there's no moral choice in simply following the rules—that's really only obedience. A moral person is one who can choose, and who bases the decision on what is in his or her—and others'—long-term best interests.

Occasionally I'm asked if I also take people into the future. That process is called "progression." As a rule, I don't do progressions. My purpose in all of this is to help relieve an individual of programs that have interfered with functioning in the present moment. Observing where we may be in the future can too easily become another set of expectations—another program—that takes us out of the present. It's like a mother's saying, "My son's going to be a doctor."

In addition, I believe the future can change—otherwise there is no choice. Looking into the future shows the pattern that exists now as it will be when it's projected into the future. So a progression shows the future as it stands now—it's a probability. It's not necessarily the future that will be in existence when you get there—depending on the choices that you make in the meanwhile.

PART VI

CONCLUSIONS, IMPLICATIONS, AND OPTIONS

CHAPTER 32

REGRESSION AS VISION QUEST AND THE FLOWERS OF HOPE

BY NOW, MY BIAS TOWARD USING PAST-LIFE REGRESSION experiences as a form of therapy is clear. For a psychotherapist, the efficiency and usefulness of past-life memories warrants a very careful look at this field. Other readers, however, may have been struck with the traumatic nature of most of the material presented. Indeed, such is usually the case when we approach past-life regression through the doorway of a current difficulty. Generally we, as human beings, tend to seek the alleviation of our pain before we move on to enhance our lives and well-being.

Make no mistake, however. Past-life regression has as much potential for retrieving previous states of well-being and bringing them into the present as it has for returning current negative emotional reactions back into the past whence they came. The fact that regressions are useful for general exploration has led many people to undertake them out of curiosity. Thus, some of the cases presented made no reference to current-life difficulties, therapeutic work, or outcomes. These clients came in order to have an expanded experience of themselves, an encounter with an alter ego, if you will, and we approached it from that standpoint.

Of course, it sometimes happens that someone who comes to me out of curiosity turns out to have more serious, if unrecognized, concerns that may emerge only during the regression. This possibility alone makes it incumbent on those individuals practicing "recreational" regression to have either minimal therapeutic skills or referral resources available for the client who needs it.

Like the shamanic journey, usually undertaken for healing or empowerment, the past-life regression is, in a way, a more personal form of that journey. The client leaves his or her present reality and travels through time and encounters powerful figures within the psyche. In therapy, new relationships are established between one's present self and those psychic figures.

The regression is also similar in some ways to the Native American vision quest. The individual often prepares for the vision quest through prayer and fasting, isolates himself from his usual surroundings, and then "cries" for a vision to come and assist him with some question or crisis.

When we use regression as therapy, the client, through specific preparation—hypnotic or not—begins to focus his attention away from the present reality, isolating his consciousness, seeking the visions from within, which, one hopes, will shed light on the current question or crisis.

Thus, in a personal sense, the past-life regression can be an encounter with one's numinous self, whether positive or seemingly negative. Lest one attempt to escape this encounter with the Self on the grounds of not believing in reincarnation, let me remind the reader that these images are the contents of the client's inner world and have a life of their own, regardless of their origin.

Note in the following regression how this gardener's flowers become messages of hope, abundance, and Divine care for one client.

In the vast majority of the regressions presented thus far, trauma has emerged as a central figure in a cast of characters that also included incomplete or unfulfilled situations and painful attachments. We saw people suffering at the hands of others.

Of course, there's always that inexorable movement toward completion, toward happiness, and the idea that the universe is basically good, just, and supportive. Yet where are the regressions that give us a taste of these things?

One answer to this question is to remind ourselves that most of the individuals I see come to me with a problem—they are troubled by something. And seldom does trouble spring from truly complete and pleasant situations.

There are those regressions that are undertaken to find a source of power, a time of great strength, or to seek inspiration to help us enhance our lives. Regressions need not be confined to the release of unwanted unconscious contents. They can be used also to reconnect, to tap into unconscious resources that have been lost in time or crowded out of our awareness, not by trauma from the past but merely by the press of time in the present. These sessions can be a soul-enriching journey into pleasant experiences.

The regression presented here was sought immediately after accessing one that was traumatic for this 33-year-old male psychologist who had wanted to explore feelings of rejection. After going through past-life memories as an abused child, the following memories were brought to the surface by asking his subconscious mind for the reverse of what we had just been shown.

It's something that feels real simple. One in which there's not a lot to do. Things are simple. I'm watching the animals and tending the garden. It's someone else's garden. I take care of it there—there's not a lot to do. It's sunny, pleasant. [Pause.]

All I have to do is keep the flowers growing—and I don't even do that. All I really do is keep the weeds from overgrowing it.

They are pleased—the owners of the garden—that I work for. My mother died a long time ago. Even when she was alive I could do a lot of things. She cared for me in a benign sort of way. . . . She wasn't possessive and demanding. She appreciated the things that I did, like bringing her flowers when I was a kid, picked wild. She liked it. She gave me a hug, and I knew she liked it. I could bring her happiness. It wasn't something she demanded or depended on—when it came she enjoyed it . . . She treasured the fact that I was alive. . . . I would bring her a pretty stone or wrap my arms around her neck, give her a hug. Somehow we could both appreciate and enjoy resonating.

She could make little things out of yarn or paper or cloth—toylike things I liked. They weren't fancy. I'd play with them until they'd come apart, knowing there was always more. She'd make others. It's like the flowers of the gardener. I'd cut some off for the table, knowing there'd be more coming along—always more flowers growing.

It's real nice. She dies peacefully. There's a loss, but there is not much undone or unsaid. It's like it's her season, the end of her season. I kind of understand that. She's given me enough and gone on. I'm already doing something, working.

I don't have to worry about big things. The owners of the place really take care of the major stuff. I bring them joy through the garden, vegetables. I can kid with the cook. It's really nice. I work hard and then there's lots of time to sit and smoke a pipe and watch the worms crawl in the garden. They're almost like pets.

There's a real nice connection with the living things, and acceptance of the seasons, and how things change. I don't marry—but I fool around with the cook. There doesn't seem to be much motivation for marriage—I'm well satisfied. There is sort of a sexless appreciation of beauty and variety in a simple sort of way. I'm not a particularly intelligent person. I'm just in tune with nature's rhythms, instinctively constructive.

At the end of the regression memories, this client was advised to take that peaceful attitude into all areas of his present life. "Give the flowers that come from inside you. You have that to give . . . Be the gardener. . . . Trust that the owners of the house, Mr. and Mrs. God, will take care of the other things."*

*The words of past life-therapist, Jason Levine (private communication).

CHAPTER 33

IMPLICATIONS FOR
DAILY LIVING

IT CAN BE CONFUSING TO THINK ABOUT ALL THE EXPE-
riences presented in this book, as well as the ideas about
karma, programming, past lives, attachments, separation
from and union with the oversoul. Some people new to all
this may wonder what there is to really believe in. A number of intelligent professional people who have discovered
my past-life work have openly said to me, "Don't tell me
about it." The whole idea shattered their views of the
world, of life, and the reasons they've been following their
code of morality.

Of course, they need not have this disorientation unless
their teachers in this life have failed them by neglecting the
realities of this other world.

But one may ask, with lives through eternity, and many
roles to play, how do we stay mentally healthy and moral?
Or, to put the question another way, what has the discovery
of past-life influences, karma, and the transpersonal nature
of humankind shown us about how to live? What is The
Way taught here?

TO BE PRESENT AND TO BE REAL. This simple
statement has vast implications. To be present means to

maintain attention—to attend to what is happening and not substitute our fantasies, beliefs, desires, wishes, or delusions in place of the reality presenting itself to us. This is not to ignore our hopes, wishes, and fantasies, for that would be failing to attend to what IS. After all, our memories, desires, and dreams are part of the present. The key lies in not substituting one part of the present for another, in not drawing a narrow focus on the immediate. To be whole, the present reality includes our memories of the past as well as our hopes and options for the future.

Thus we must, as much as we can, not deny any aspect of reality but recognize it in proportion to its place in the present, for client's experiences in past lives give strong validation to the popular saying:

> What we deny comes back to us, as our shadow, in unconscious ways.

So, if the task is to acknowledge and express as much of reality as possible, how do we make any decisions? It helps to know who we are; and to do that, we need to be real.

Being "real" is a corollary of being present. When we're fully present we're also being fully real. That is to say, when we attend to what is occurring in the present moment, we must include in that equation whatever is going on within us. This doesn't mean we must act on it, impose it onto the situation, or even necessarily give voice to it. It means that we must pay attention—and then decide.

Being present tells us what's going on in the world. Being real tells us who we are in that world. With these two actions, we will learn automatically that compassion is a virtue and that unity with the godhead and humankind is both pleasurable and in our long-term best interests. We will discover the pain of separation—especially from any aspect of ourselves—and the pleasure of union.

We will also learn that dishonesty is an act of self-ab-negation, for it denies who we are. Dishonesty is an act of separation not only from outside reality but also from our own inner self. Discretion is, of course, always called for since others may not be able to handle what we could pre-sent to them—whether it's our ideas, something we've done, or a reality we see.

And there is the leading edge of our growth: finding the way to not deny that unacceptable part of ourselves. I doubt that we can really deny anything of significance in our-selves. When we try, it's expressed in unconscious ways or held for expression in a later time—or life. Thus, our unexpressed questions, like, "Why me?", our unspoken anger, and yes, our withheld love, all take up residence in the unconscious mind.

Our choice is not whether we express these things, but how: Whether we do it in a conscious and responsible man-ner, or by disowning it, leave it up to the imagination of our unconscious mind to do it for us. This is very evident in family systems where one family or group member may feel another's feelings and express another's emotions—without realizing it—much to the confusion of all. In this struggle we realize our responsibility: What we deny now will surely come back to us, and when it does, we are then the cause of it.

This should give us pause before we judge another neg-atively, for in a very real sense, they may be expressing something we deny in ourselves. Perhaps it's better to deny violent or ugly impulses, but it's equally violent to cut ourselves off—through condemnation—from those who show us these unpleasant aspects of human nature. Make no mistake: withholding condemnation is not an act of en-dorsement, nor should it prevent us from taking decisive action; but we have to recognize: "There also go I."

Through this attempt at being present and being genuine, we are put in the position to forge an integration of inner and outer worlds, to recover lost parts of ourselves, to become more whole and powerful. This integration is at the root of integrity. In its essence, integrity means a state of being complete, unbroken, and whole—hence its association to the moral principles of uprightness, honesty, and sincerity.

Being present with—conscious of—just the existence of these past-life images is enough to tell us of a reality beyond our senses and conscious thoughts; that, to be complete, we need to adopt an awareness of this indwelling altered state of consciousness and the messages that come from it. Right within our own minds is an everliving source of inspiration and inner renewal. If we should ignore it, that which is disowned will come back to us with the same negative charge with which we disowned it.

As I look at what I've written here, I have an image of some Atlas figure, bearing the weight of all the thoughts, emotions, and realities at one time, trying to see and hold them all. That's not what I mean to convey. I refer, rather, to a process of dealing with what comes up for us as it comes up—as much as we can.

COMPASSION AND IDENTIFICATION

As we begin to realize our contribution, even if unconscious, to our present situation, the differences and sense of false separation between ourselves and others begin to dissolve. When we see another's pain, we can understand their actions. When we grasp their hopes and desires, we can appreciate their direction. Again, this is not to place us in a passive position or make us wimps. Rather, if we have all our faculties at our disposal we should be able to act vigorously without losing our sense of compassion for others or ourselves.

We can recognize what appears to be a wrong act of

another and try to stop it. At the same time, we need not fall into a polarized stance, seeing ourselves as separate or superior in our righteous condemnation. Our act of integration and transcendence comes when we see the other's act as wrong, move to stop it, and still see its roots within us. Then we can be effective and compassionate, and at the same time foster the process of growth in all concerned.

When we're fully conscious, compassion comes naturally, even if we're angry, and we instinctively realize our unity with others. Perhaps that's the bottom line: to be joyfully conscious.

Perhaps this is the great alchemical work: to see all of the world as needed; to see all of ourselves as appropriate; to know our negative areas without being them; to be brave enough and yet compassionate enough to know when to speak and when to keep silent without losing our integrity. Timing and discretion may, indeed, be the "better part of valor."

Most of the therapies and disciplines—secular or religious—that help us to be genuine and present with integrity can help us to resolve and complete our karma—to be whole. Past-life therapy is available to allow us to go directly to the source of that karma.

CHAPTER 34

THE NEXT STEP

Having read this far, you've heard about the trials and rewards of past-life regression and therapy. I hope that in spite of the traumatic nature of many of the journeys, you find this material hopeful for what it may provide in your own life's process, whether for therapy, exploration, or empowerment. Perhaps you may find relief similar to the people you've read about. If you're ready, then the next step is yours.

FINDING A THERAPIST

Imagine the frustration of knowing you'd had an experience related to a past life and could find no one to deal seriously with it. This was exactly the case of Marianne, in Chapter 2, who had past-life material erupt into her consciousness. She had some idea of what needed to be done but could find no one to do it. She lived in a Bible Belt area of the Carolinas where even ordinary hypnosis was suspect. Eventually an article appeared in a national magazine about a Chicago-based past-life therapist. She wrote to him and he was able, because of my listing in a California organization's directory, to provide her with my name. Marianne was originally from Baltimore, so her mother who still lived here made the appointment for a time when she would be visiting. The problem was finally taken care of—a year after it first emerged.

Past-life regressions can be done by almost anyone with even a small amount of hypnotic instruction. However, it's difficult to tell if someone is able to competently handle past-life issues and help resolve them.

Many individuals have taken training in hypnosis. There are well-trained hypnotherapists who, as part of their training and repertoire, can perform the usual hypnotic type of regression. This involves the induction of the altered state, the evoking of regression experience, allowing the reactions to take place, and then intervening to help counteract the past-life programming.

However, there are fewer therapists who are specifically trained to work with past-life material itself, and who have a sufficient knowledge of the concepts of karma, programming and deprogramming, as well as the focusing, gestalt, and other techniques that are the hallmarks of Netherton's procedures.

There are two major organizations that may be of help in finding a past-life therapist in your area.

One is the Association for the Alignment of Past Life Experience (A.A.P.L.E). This group was founded by Morris Netherton, Ph.D., and bears the stamp of his psychological background in its goals and techniques. A.A.P.L.E. provides training for prospective therapists and publishes a newsletter. Their address is:

Association for the Alignment of Past Life Experience
1619 W. Garvey North
West Covina, CA 91790

The first association to come to my attention was the Association for Past-Life Research and Therapy. When I joined the A.P.R.T a few years ago, I was the only member in the state of Maryland and one of the few listed on the East Coast. The last couple of years, however, has seen a growth of interest in the field, with the addition of several people from this area. The A.P.R.T. publishes a newsletter and conducts both workshops for the interested public as well as training sessions directed toward professionals. Their address is:

The Association for Past-Life Research and Therapy
P.O. Box 20151
Riverside, CA 92516

Of most recent origin is my own organization, the Atlantic Guild for Past-Life Awareness (A.G.P.L.A.). The purposes of the Guild are to provide information to the public about reincarnation, past-life therapy, and similar helpful concepts. We also train individuals in the techniques of past-life therapy. We, too, publish a newsletter for members. Our address is:

The Atlantic Guild for Past-Life Awareness
P.O. Box 27485
Towson, MD 21285-7485

There are a growing number of local centers, institutes, and groups that provide past-life regression and therapy as either their main or one of several services. Individual practitioners often give seminars and workshops. Information may be available through local metaphysical organizations, study groups, or New Age book stores. Hypnosis organizations, themselves struggling for their place in the therapeutic field, are sometimes hostile to the mention of past-life therapy. However, individual members of those groups may be able to direct the inquirer to such a therapist.

Rosicrucian and Theosophical groups, Edgar Cayce study groups, Summit Lighthouse organizations, holistic health networks or similar institutions may be sources of information about people who deal with reincarnation or regression.

Therapists or others who would like information about training in past-life therapy may contact any of the above organizations.

Naturally, no directory, list, or even personal reference will tell you whether you will have confidence in or be able to work with a particular therapist. Once you've obtained a name, it will be up to you to determine the regressionist's suitability for your needs.

There are a few questions that may help you not only get a feel for the prospective therapist but also gain a better idea of how he or she works. There's no need to be shy about asking questions. The therapist is, after all, your employee. Some therapists, myself included, provide written information about their backgrounds, approaches, and goals.

The kind of therapist you want will depend in part on your particular interest. If you're just curious or are seeking a very limited experience, almost any open-minded and competent hypnotherapist will suffice. However, if you really want to make changes or do considerable personal exploration, you may want to seek someone with a number of areas of expertise. Here are a few questions that you might ask of therapists you're considering for past-life work:

- What is their background and training?
- Are they certified by any of the above organizations?
- How large a part does past-life therapy play in their practice?

- Is it the only thing they do?
- Is it the only thing they're trained to do?
- Are they experienced in other types of hypnotherapy?
- Are they trained or certified to provide counseling services?
- How long are the individual sessions?
- Do they encourage or discourage tape recording the sessions?

And a final question for yourself: Is this someone with whom I'm comfortable, who treats me in a professional manner, and who seems to have my best interests at heart?*

Heed your own feelings. The right answers to all of these questions will not tell you the nature of the heart of the therapist.

THE COURSE OF THERAPY

The question sometimes arises about how long it will take to get relief, or why it is that some people seem to "get it" in one session while others may require several.

There are many reasons for this difference—aside from the skill of the therapist. Reasons vary according to the motivation of the client, the complexity of the problem, and the general mental health of the client.

First of all, the client's purpose for the regression may be aimed at understanding the problem rather than undertaking the sometimes necessary "working through." They're not interested in therapy but in information.

The client's motivation will determine his or her willingness to look at sometimes painful realities about past or present behavior. In a first session it sometimes occurs that

---

*These questions are adapted from my booklet "What Is Past-Life Therapy?" which answers in a condensed way most of the crucial questions people have about this practice.

the problem presented masks more than the client wants to deal with.

Problems that stem from one or two clear-cut lives can usually be resolved fairly quickly. However, if many lives are involved or if a number of difficulties contribute to the current life problems, more sessions are needed. Competent therapists seek to find the crucial or primary lives involved, rather than every one, so that the mind's own healing can gradually take care of the rest.

The client's general mental health also plays a very significant role. Anyone in reasonably good mental health withstands stress better, more accurately perceives the nature of his or her surroundings, and more easily integrates new information into effective functioning. The same is true for the experiences and information gained in past-life regressions.

Some individuals remain attached to their problems, no matter how painful, because of some other program or because of a fear of being truly responsible. After all, if you've resisted a process for lifetimes, it's unlikely that you'll accept it quickly in this one.

Making the decision to release one's programming is not enough. The unconscious attachments to that mind–set also need to be released.

One of the factors that also causes delays is clients who come into the office already convinced of what they will find or with rigid expectations of the way things are to be done. In these instances, the beginning of therapy becomes a process of unlearning the old before the new can be initiated.

Finally, it's also possible that the lesson to be learned or the karma to be fulfilled by the current problem may or may not be complete. In this instance, additional learning situations will be needed either in the office or in life in order to be ready to move on.

THE NEW FRONTIER

The course of past-life therapy can be as individual as the clients and therapists themselves. Yet, among these differences can be found reliable sources of hope, understanding and relief for present and past difficulties—if we are willing to face that paradox of our inner experience.

The paradox is that what is closest to us—our inner mind—often seems out of reach, mysterious, or too frightening to contemplate. However, if we make the commitment we can find there a new frontier for exploration and growth.

No matter how technical or complex our society becomes or how expensive its diversions, this inner world of the mind—your mind—will always remain the ever-new frontier. As close as a thought or image to some; to others it is practically untouchable. The people you've read about in these pages have begun their journey. They have been willing to go beyond established cultural limitations to consider something quite "unorthodox". They have chosen to face their inner world, and to accept the responsibility therein. The next step into your own past, and future, is yours.

BIBLIOGRAPHY

Ahsen, Akhter, *Basic Concepts in Eidetic Psychotherapy*. N.Y.: Brandon House, 1973.

Banerjee, H. N. and Oursler, Will, *Lives Unlimited*. N.Y.: Doubleday, 1974.

Cerminara, Gina, *Many Mansions*. N.Y.: Wm. Morrow and Co., 1950.

Developmental Psychology Today. Del Mar, CA: CRM Books, 1971.

Erickson, Milton, Ernest and Shiela Rossi, *Hypnotic Realities*. NY: Irvington Publishers, 1976.

Fiore, Edith, *You Have Been Here Before*. N.Y.: Ballantine, 1978.

Gendlin, Eugene, *Focusing*. NY: Everest House, 1978.

Goldberg, Bruce, *Past Lives Future Lives*. N. Hollywood, CA: Newcastle Publishing Co., 1982.

Gordon, David, *Therapeutic Metaphors*. Cupertino, CA: Meta Publications, 1978.

Grinder, John and Richard Bandler, *Trance-Formations*. Moab, Utah: Real People Press, 1981.

Grof, Stanislav, *Realms of the Human Unconscious*. N.Y.: E.P. Dutton, 1976.

Hall, Manly P., *The Phoenix*. Los Angeles: Theosophical Research Society, 1968.

Head, Joseph and S. L. Cranston, *Reincarnation: An East West Anthology*. Wheaton, Ill: Theosophical Publishing House, 1961.

Head, Joseph and S. L. Cranston, *Reincarnation in World Thought*. N.Y.: Julian Press, 1967.

Humphreys, Christmas, *Karma and Rebirth*. Wheaton, Ill: Theosophical Publishing House, 1983.

Jameison, Bryan, *Explore Your Past Lives*. Van Nuys, CA: Astro-Analysis Publications, 1967.

Jung, Carl, "Concerning Rebirth," in *Archetypes and the Collective Unconscious*. N.J.: Princeton Press, 1959.

Jung, Carl, *Memories, Dreams, Reflections*. N.Y.: Vintage Books, 1961.

Lao Tzu, *The Way of Life According to Lao Tzu*, trans. by Witter Bynner. N.Y.: Capricorn Books, 1944.

Lenz, Frederick, *Lifetimes: True Accounts of Reincarnation*. N.Y.: Bobbs-Merrill Co., Inc., 1979.

Lewis, H. Spencer, *Mansions of the Soul*. San Jose, CA: Supreme Grand Lodge of AMORC, 1954.

Netherton, Morris and Nancy Shiffrin, *Past Lives Therapy*. N.Y.: Wm. Morrow and Co., 1978.

Roberts, Jane, *The Nature of Personal Reality*. N.J.: Bantam, 1974.

Steiger, Francie and Brad Steiger, *Discover Your Own Past Lives*. N.Y.: Dell, 1981.

Stevenson, Ian, *Twenty Cases Suggestive of Reincarnation*. Charlottesville: University Press of Virginia, 1974.

Sutphen, Dick, *Past Lives, Future Loves*. N.Y.: Pocket Books, 1978.

Sutphen, Dick and Lauren Taylor, *Past-Life Therapy in Action*. Malibu, CA: Valley of the Sun Publishing, 1983.

Verny, Thomas (with John Kelly), *The Secret Life of the Unborn Child*. N.Y.: Summit Books, 1981.

Wambach, Helen, *Life Before Life*. N.Y.: Bantam, 1979.

Wright, Leoline, *Reincarnation*. Wheaton, Ill: Theosophical Publishing House, 1975.

ABOUT THE AUTHOR

KARL SCHLOTTERBECK's background includes a master's degree in school psychology, a certificate of advanced study in Counseling and Therapy, eleven years' experience as a school psychologist, and studies in clinical hypnotherapy and past-life therapy. He is the founder of the Atlantic Guild for Past-Life Awareness, an organization for providing past-life therapy services, public education regarding reincarnation and training for past-life facilitators and therapists.

He invites anyone interested in sharing their past-life experiences to write to him in care of his publisher, Ballantine Books, 201 East 50th Street, New York City, New York 10022.